The Culinary Renaissance:

CREATIVE FOOD PROCESSOR RECIPES

By
Anne Lindsay Greer

Creative recipes for both
standard and large capacity machines.

Eighth Printing, April 1982

ISBN 0-936662-01-8

SYMBOLS FOR DLC–7

In order to use this book for all machines, recipes are presented in quantities and methods designed for average size work bowls. Recipes are marked with special symbols when quantities may be doubled for the DLC-7. Whenever possible, recipe preparation is complete in the food processor bowl. However, in some recipes (i.e., large cakes) it is necessary to empty the food processor bowl when using the average size machine. Therefore, another symbol indicates which recipes may now be prepared completely in the food processor bowl if you have a DLC-7. If additional instructions are needed, they are added with a footnote, also marked with a symbol.

Here is a complete set of symbols to guide you through the book.

 Use the same quantities but prepare the recipe all in one bowl . . . when the instructions state to empty half or all of the contents from the bowl, disregard and proceed in the food processor bowl.

x2 Double the recipe and use the same instructions, applying double quantities to all ingredients and directions.

 Use the plastic dough mixing blade. This applies to all yeast bread recipes in which you will use more than 3 1/2 cups of flour. Do not confuse this blade with the plastic mixing blade which has a different design.

dlc-7 Additional instructions for the DLC-7, to further clarify recipe preparation, baking times or baking dishes.

TABLE OF CONTENTS

Introduction I
Blades IV
DLC-7 IX
Adapting Recipes XI
Tips and Techniques XIII
Basics and Adaptations 1
Family Fun 49
Flavorings 61

Breakfast 69
International Crepes and Pancakes 93
Soups 109
Luncheon, Light Supper 131
Cocktail Food 143
First Course and Salads 159
Main Dishes 181
Roasts 197
Fish, Seafood 209
Poultry 223
Vegetables 235
Desserts 253
Breads, Pain de Mie, Rolls 293
Holiday Specials 325
Demonstrations (Recipes and Outlines) .349
Recipes from Classes and Demonstrations 353
Kitchen Equipment 381

To my inspirational mother-in-law
who opened a whole new world of
food preparation fun, and
encouraged me to write
this book

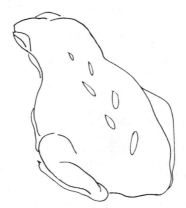

INTRODUCTION

American home cooking has been quietly moving from the dark, deep depths of Hamburger Helper and TV dinners, into a bright, refreshing era of creative cooking. This culinary renaissance is explosively evident in almost every newspaper and magazine. Jacques Pepin's illustrated classical cooking techniques are replacing "Start with a Mix" columns in the Thursday food sections of major newspapers. Americans are thirsty for more than recipes: chefs appear on talk shows, variety shows, news shows: someone's always in the Kitchen with Dinah!

Our interest in the cuisines of other cultures, our quest for knowledge about fresh foods, about kitchen equipment - our abundant cooking literature are all rapidly establishing cooking as a respected art in our country. This rebirth, this renaissance, recalls the transition from medieval to modern times - the period which saw the first emergence of fine cooking as a recognized art form. But interest in good cooking alone can be sterile - taste is but one of our senses. A cultured person harmoniously integrates pleasure in fine food with other paths to aesthetic fulfillment. Blaise Pascal, 17th century physicist, mathematician and philosopher, wrote of Renaissance and the Renaissance Man:

> *Since we cannot be universal and know all that is to be known about everything, we ought to know a little about everything. For it is better to know something about everything than to know all about one thing. This universality is best. If we can have both, still better; but if we must choose, we ought to choose the former. And the world feels this and does so; for the world is often a good judge.*

Technological progress keeps altering the techniques of our arts: new and revolutionary kitchen appliances which eliminate so much tedious preparatory work, and increase in affluence and leisure time, are creating an American cuisine. Just as French cuisine learned from the Italian chefs of Catherine de Medici, we Americans now learn from the European chefs who travel to our country where their skills are admired, prized and highly marketable. Their methods are adapted, adopted and applied to our native foods, and are producing a new "American Cooking".

What has American cooking been? Meatloaf? Hot dogs? Apple pie? Boston Cream Pie? Apple pie originated in Normandy and

Boston Cream Pie is the result of recipe adaptations ranging from Italian "Drunken Cake" and "Tipsy Cake" to English "Trifle." American cooking has had many roots. Now, for the first time, America is producing great chefs, respected in Europe, whose cookbooks are becoming classics and who have made the kitchen a theatre and the preparation of food more than a culinary performance. Julia Child is a household word. James Beard, patron and master of cookery and other arts, is the most influential culinary force in America and the only American authority highly respected in Europe as well. His books are classics in their time, and he has influenced American cooking as significantly as the chefs of Europe's royal families influenced classic cuisine.

Startling as it seems, in a fast food culture where families have an increasingly difficult time sharing a meal together, the art of gracious dining in America is enjoying a renaissance. Entire magazines are devoted to beautiful table settings and the artistic presentation of food. This is even more startling when one considers the demands on the American mother and housewife. Who can make fresh baby food between the lunchbox rush, lost shoes and forgotten homework? Who can poach quenelles between the carpool and Cub Scouts? Homard a l'Americaine after football practice and before the PTA? . . . when the fish market is clear across town and it's rush hour? Brioche for breakfast before the 8:15 bus? Gracious dining between dancing lessons and 12 dozen cookies by 9:00 AM? Only the new time and effort saving machines make it possible.

"You are what you eat" appears on everything from aprons to the cover of Time Magazine. Cooking schools and gourmet specialty shops are turning up on every corner. The American housewife reads labels, knows nutritive values and wants to learn the **whys** of food preparation as well as the **hows**. The rich and famous, the talented, creative people of the theatre, symphony and the arts are expressing their artistic ability in the kitchen. Danny Kaye, extraordinary man, pilot, musician, a great performer and a dedicated human being is as daringly skilled in his kitchen as on the stage.

During the gay nineties, Fannie Farmer made cooking schools fashionable. Women were taught to sift and measure (as opposed to experiment, taste and enjoy!) and convenience foods flooded the market. Now, an array of kitchen equipment is revolutionizing the way America cooks.

We have machines to make yogurt, pasta, ice cream and bread; machines to wash dishes, keep food warm, to steam, stir-fry, poach and reheat ... but at the top of the list is the food processor which has made extraordinary cooking possible for the ordinary cook. The phenomenal food processor is embraced by cooks and non-cooks alike. It brings the non-cook into the kitchen with armloads of fresh fruits and vegetables. It introduces him or her to a world of cooking he or she didn't have the time or opportunity to learn before. It fascinates men ... now that the kitchen is becoming efficient and fun they're interested again. This innovative appliance allows a busy mother to make pastry in minutes, grind fresh meat, grate fresh cheeses, produce homemade bread in 90 seconds (brioche for breakfast?), knead pasta and process fresh, nutritious peanut butter. (If you are what you eat, who wants to be sodium propionate, diglycerides, xantha gum and triethyl citrate?) American cooking habits change ... mature ... after grinding your own meat, homemade stock is inevitable; the quest for better cooking techniques begins. Convenience is finally possible without sacrificing quality.

> Gourmandism is an act of judgment by which we prefer things which have a pleasant taste to those that lack quality ... it deserves nothing but praise ... (and) is one of the main links uniting society.

> Brillat-Savarin

The preparation and presentation of fresh, seasonal food is a perfect marriage of form and function. Now that technology has eliminated the drudgery of the kitchen you may have a little time to study the masters ... Italian, French, Chinese or American. Enjoy the wealth of revolutionary kitchen equipment and information at your fingertips. Join in the "Culinary Renaissance" around you and gather together with your family and friends to create culinary masterpieces.

> If misery loves company then
> Triumph deserves an audience.
> Brian Moore

BLADES

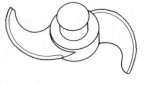

Steel Blade CFP 5, 9, 5A
All purpose processing, mincing, chopping, pureeing, pastry, bread.

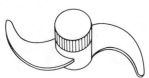

Plastic Knife CFP 5, 9, 5A
Mixing without mincing, cakes.

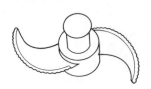

Steel Blade DLC-7
All purpose processing, mincing, chopping, pureeing, pastry, bread with 3 cups of flour.

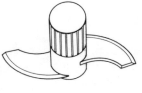

Plastic Dough Blade DLC-7
Bread with over 3 cups of flour, heavy cookie doughs with over 2 1/2 cups flour.

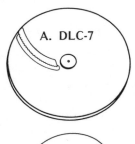

A. DLC-7

B. CFP 9, 5, 5A

Medium Slicing Disk CFP 5, 9, 5A, DLC-7
This comes with the machine . . . for slicing tomatoes, strawberries, grapes, any vegetables, meat or cheese. (See A and B)

Fine Serrated Slicing Disk CFP 5, 9, 5A
This makes an extremely thin slice . . . for meat, cheeses, pepperoni, or any vegetables. The blade looks like the Medium Slicing Disk but has a more narrow opening.

IV

Fine Vegetable Slicing Disk CFP 5, 9, 5A
For vegetables (not meat and cheese) . . . this blade has a smooth edge, makes a thicker slice than the fine serrated (thinner than the medium serrated) . . . especially good for mushrooms, carrots, cucumbers, zucchini, onions.

CFP 5, 9, 5A

French Fry Blade CFP 5, 9, 5A (French Fryer)
To make slightly curved strips of vegetables . . . also for all-purpose dicing of any vegetable, chopping nuts, dicing hard boiled eggs.

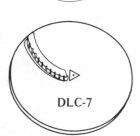

DLC-7

French Fry Blade, DLC-7 (French Fryer)

Shredding or Grating Disk CFP 5, 9, 5A
For grating cheeses, vegetables, coconut or finely grated nuts, chocolate.

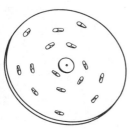

Shredding or Grating Disk DLC-7
For all purpose grating of cheeses, vegetables; this produces a "squared-off" "shred."

Fine Shredding Disk 5, 9, 5A
This makes a product like the shredding disk that comes with the machine, only finer.

V

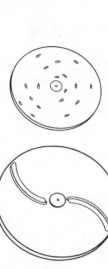

Julienne Blade 5, 9, 5A
This makes a finer, more "squared-off" product than the shredding or grating disk. Vegetables are less "moist".

Slicing Disks for the DLC-7:

Dual-Ultra Thin Slicing Disk: translucent, 1/20 of an inch thick slices.

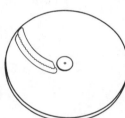

Thick Slicing Disk: Thicker slices than the one that comes with the machine produces.

Thin Slicing Disk: Thinner slices than the one that comes with the machine.
(No Illustration)

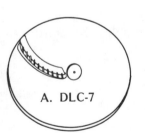

A. DLC-7

Square Julienne Blade 5, 9, 5A, DLC-7
For long, square shredded vegetables like carrots, zucchini, potato. (See A and B)

B. CFP 5, 9, 5A

Ripple Cutter CFP 5, 9, 5A
Makes decorative slices of vegetables. You can make your own "Ruffles with Ridges."

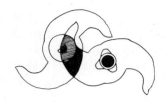

A word about Blades . . .

The first time I demonstrated a processor, people asked me so many questions about blades I had to go home and start experimenting all over again . . . and I really do think that's the best advice I can give about what to do with different blades.

First, read the instruction booklet carefully (the one that comes with the machine) so you know what NOT to do. One of the greatest features of the machine is the versatility you have in the chopping, slicing and mincing. We are all geared to a push button appliance world, and it does take a little getting used to. When demonstrating the slicing disk at one store, I invited a skeptical gentleman to come try it out . . . he hesitated at first but I could hardly get another turn myself before he had sliced all my vegetables!

Steel Blade:
This is the one you'll use the most. You will read over and over "do not over-process" . . . this means, do not turn the machine on and let it run. Use an on/off method to process and check, check, check. You can dump everything into the bowl, or drop things through the feeder tube (good way to mince small quantities). To avoid tough cakes or muffins add flour last and process just several times on/off. Remember, when adding liquids first, 2 cups is around capacity. If your mixture is quite thick you may be able to add more. **Do** try anything you usually do in a mixing bowl.

Plastic Knife:
Many claim the steel blade does everything the plastic knife does only better . . . however I find it indispensable in the preparation of meat and poultry salads. First use the slicing disk (or French fryer) to cut up or dice the vegetables, then put the meat through the serrated slicer and change to the plastic knife to mix it all together . . . add salad dressing directly into the bowl and process with an on/off method. Use it also to get a coarse chop with nuts . . . it has a "beating action" and is therefore good for whipping cream and beating eggs with sugar. The steel blade also whips cream with less "splashing" but some students tell me they get more air with the plastic knife.

Slicing Disks:
There are three. One has a smooth cutting blade and is the perfect blade for mushrooms. You do not get as thin a slice as with the thin serrated slicing blade. It is not to be used for meats or cheese. It is a vegetable slicing blade only and does not tear the edges of carrots or mushrooms. The medium serrated slicing disk comes with the machine and is an all purpose slicer that slices soft strawberries, bananas or firm meats. The thin serrated slicing blade is for all purpose slicing also and does a particularly nice job with raw and cooked meats (for stroganoff). There is an additional slicing blade, the ripple slicer, which makes the most marvelous ruffled potato chips. There is quite a lot of variety available in slicing and you'll find some of the accessory blades very useful.

French Fryer:
This is really the most fantastic blade . . . it makes lovely little "sticks" out of any vegetable when you pack the feeder tube with the vegetable laying sideways. Amazingly, it will also dice vegetables when you toss them in the tube cut into chunks . . . great for chunky Gazpacho, Vegetable Soup or any recipe that calls for diced vegetables . . . and that's a lot of recipes!

Julienne Blade:
Try zucchini or spaghetti squash (packed in the feeder tube horizontally) . . . it looks like Fettucine. Vegetables are "drier" than when shredded with the shredding disks. Great for coconut and cheese. Use it also for grating nuts or chocolate into other mixtures . . . you'll have a marvelous light texture.

Shredding Disk:
Also two . . . one fine and one medium. Pack the feeder tube horizontally for longer shreds. The fine shredding disk is especially nice for coconut. Both are good for grating cheese, however, reserve Parmesan for the steel blade. When shredding, use a "bounce" action with the pusher when objects argue. Forcing or pushing harder just gums or bends the disk . . . bounce lightly with the pusher. Try shredding carrots, squash, root vegetables and broccoli stems. If you like fine coleslaw you can pack the feeder tube with green pepper, carrots and cabbage all at once, then change to the plastic knife to mix with dressing.

The bottom of the feeder tube in many machines is slightly larger than the top. This allows firmer pack (load from the bottom), easier loading, and whole onion and pepper rings . . . particularly if you shop selectively.

DLC-7

The DLC-7 is one of the new additions to the Cuisinart line of food processors. This larger capacity machine, a result of consumer demand, will allow you to process double (sometimes triple) quantities. In addition, it has many features everyone has been asking for. Read your instruction booklet carefully so you are familiar with all the safety features and re-read them from time to time as you and your machine get acquainted.

The feeder tube has a slightly different shape . . . easier to load and holds a slightly larger vegetable.

There is both an "on" control and an "on/off"—"pulse" control. This does not operate automatically . . . **you** control the length of processing. The blades will stop rotating quickly, both an added safety feature as well as controlling "over-processing".

The slicing disk (that comes with the machine) slices extremely well . . . smooth, even and efficient. If you enjoy slicing Pain de Mie loaves, you will be delighted.

The shredding disk looks like the julienne blade (of previous models) and has many of its good features. The shreds are larger, "drier" and nicely squared off.

The steel blade is very much the same, only larger as the new work bowl is wider as well as deeper. Several important things. The liquid capacity of the bowl is significantly greater . . . 6-7 cups as opposed to 2—2-1/2. The amount of meat that can be ground (at one time) is 1-1/2—2 pounds rather than 3/4—1 pound. Bread crumbs using 8 slices of bread may be processed at one time . . . that means you can prepare the stuffing for an 18 pound turkey all in one bowl.

You may mix and knead bread for recipes that require up to 6 cups of flour. To do this big job there is an innovative blade specifically designed to prepare bread. This plastic dough mixing blade is also more efficient in preparing the heavy doughs like Brioche and Kugelhopf batters that are rich with butter and eggs. The first two weeks I used this machine I filled a freezer with breads, cakes, "double batch" cookies, fruitcakes and all of the things I formerly prepared with the "dice and dump" method. In addition, if attention is paid to the order of ingredients when processing (as presented in the recipes in this book) you can prepare chicken salad, coleslaw, crepe fillings and a variety of other recipes for a **crowd**, all in the food processor bowl. This is truly the ultimate answer for anyone who entertains.

I would like to emphasize, strongly, that this machine does not out-date the previous two Cuisinart direct drive machines. Rather, it amplifies the total line in an endeavor to give the serious, amateur or "sometime" cook what she (or he) needs and wants for food prepara-tion. The DLC-7, like the many new blades and accessories available for all machines, adds a new dimension to efficient food processing and allows the person who prepares food in quantity or entertains frequently, to have her cake and eat it too.

In order to use this book for all machines, recipes are presented in quantities and methods designed for average size work bowls. Recipes are marked with special symbols when quantities may be doubled for the DLC-7. Whenever possible, recipe preparation is com-plete in the food processor bowl. However, in some recipes (i.e.: large cakes) it is necessary to empty the food processor bowl and complete the recipe in another mixing bowl. Therefore, another sym-bol indicates which recipes may now be prepared completely in the food processor bowl. If additional instructions are needed, they are added with a footnote, also marked with a symbol.

Here is a complete set of symbols to guide you through the book.

Use the same quantities but prepare the recipe all in one bowl . . . when the instructions state to empty half or all of the contents from the bowl, disregard and proceed in the food processor bowl.

x2
Double the recipe and use the same instructions, applying double quantities to all ingredients and directions.

Use the plastic dough mixing blade. This applies to all yeast bread recipes in which you will use more than 3 1/2 cups of flour. Do not confuse this blade with the plastic mixing blade which has a different design.

dlc-7
Additional instructions for the DLC-7, to further clarify recipe preparation, baking times or baking dishes.

HOW TO ADAPT YOUR RECIPES

All your favorite recipes are easily adapted to the processor, although it does take a little while to change your favorite habits. I'll never forget visiting a friend who had a new processor and watching her dice and slice most of her salad ingredients by hand . . . then make the dressing in the machine. Any recipe that calls for something sliced, diced, ground or chopped is a candidate. The problem is in figuring which blade, how long, and in what order. In most instances the ingredient amount will remain the same. One exception is in pastry where you may need less liquid . . . just add it gradually, processing with the pulse or an on/off method and STOP as soon as it begins to hold together . . . then chill 30 minutes (minimum). If using shortening or lard chill very firm first. Another exception is in meat or chicken salads where you'll need slightly less mayonnaise or dressing. The biggest problem is in over-processing . . . go slowly at first, starting with an on/off method.

Which Blade:

Refer to the Blades Section (VII). The important things here are:
Pack the feeder tube with thought and care in the beginning. Things can go in horizontally, vertically, or in chunks. If you're aiming for uniform slicing, be sure the things are packed firmly . . . loading from the bottom helps as does "uniform" loading.

Vary the pressure with which you push things through the feeder tube. If you're doing lettuce for a tossed salad, push through very rapidly and load from the bottom of the tube. For thin slices, let things almost "self-feed". Choosing the right size vegetable helps too. Try packing a small carrot or celery on either side of a whole cucumber to hold it firm.

How Long:

For pastry . . . until it begins to form a dough ball. For bread . . . until it LOOKS as it should (smooth and elastic but still fairly soft). To avoid over-processing always begin with on/off's and check often. There are not many instances where the machine needs to run very long or continuously. Important: Read the instructions carefully as you get acquainted with your machine. When using the pusher, begin pushing things through the moment you engage the spring (by turning the lid). Otherwise the vegetable will often self-feed before you have a chance to catch it and you'll be unhappy with the texture (as well as not having a chance to do anything)!

XI

What Order:

Generally work from dry to wet or wet to dry. Also think about washing the bowl. (See p. 133, Chicken Chalupas and Brownies, p. 360.) If you're doing a cream sauce with cheese, process the cheese (cut in chunks) with the steel blade, add butter and flour, processing to a paste, then add some of the hot liquid and finish off on the stove.

The problem comes in making pastes when you WANT paste rather than the other way around. Experience, experimenting, trial and error and attending a few classes and demonstrations will help you master the machine . . . and you'll love the ease and speed with which you'll turn out lovely, nutritious, beautifully textured dishes.

Measuring:

The hollow plastic pusher measures 1 cup . . . therefore, the feeder tube is also 1 cup . . . handy!

A vaincre sans peril,
on triomphe sans gloire.

"Nothing ventured, nothing gained"

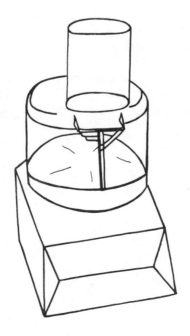

TIPS AND TECHNIQUES FOR BETTER PROCESSING

ON/OFFS
Use a quick on/off method of processing to 1) "chop" and control texture and 2) to prevent over-processing.

SIFTING FLOUR FIRST
When adding flour, baking powder and baking soda to quick breads, cakes or muffins that require very brief mixing, be sure to blend them together when measuring. A few on/off's with the steel blade will accomplish this.

CHOPPING NUTS
To chop nuts coarsely, process with the plastic knife or steel blade using the on/off method until reaching the texture you want . . . or use either the slicing disk or French fry blade.

GRATING PEELINGS
When grating citrus peelings (steel blade) do more than you need and either sun dry or freeze the rest . . . adding a little sugar helps the processing.

DICING DATES
To dice dates, combine with nuts or about 1/3 cup sugar and start processing (steel blade) with an on/off method to get things started . . . then run the machine 5 seconds, check and repeat until the right size.

LOADING THE FEEDER TUBE
Load the feeder tube carefully, from the **bottom**, using the pusher to hold the food in . . . firm packing = more uniform processing . . . loading vegetables horizontally produces longer "shreds" . . . slicing the ends off round vegetables = more uniform slicing and less slipping in the slicing.

To slice uniformly (carrots, celery, apples, tomatoes, squash, cucumbers, oranges) pack firmly in the bottom of the feeder tube.

Strawberries, grapes, radishes, mushrooms are loaded through the top.

SLICING MEAT AND CHEESE
To slice meats and cheeses use the serrated slicing disk.

To slice raw meats, chill the meat first until firm, but not frozen, and slice with the serrated slicing disk.

SALAD SPREADS
To mix chunky meat, tuna or egg salad, dice vegetables (quick on/off's with the steel blade . . . or cut in chunks and push through using the French fryer) then slice in(medium serrated slicing disk) the chicken or eggs and change to the plastic knife to mix it all together with mayonnaise . . . use several quick on/off turns.

GRINDING MEAT
To grind raw meat for hamburger or sausage cut up to 3/4 pound in medium size chunks and process using the steel blade on/off 5-6 times. The DLC-7 will process 1-1/2 pounds at one time. Check consistency often. Addition of chilled fat will help you control texture. You will find it helpful to save (freeze) all trimmings from steak to use when grinding lean meats for hamburger or sausage.

PASTRY
When adapting your own pastry recipes, chill shortening first and if using ice water, add gradually.

THIN SLICING
For thick slicing use more pressure and push the food through the feeder tube more rapidly. For thinner slicing let the food almost "self-feed" through the tube. Several slicing blades soon become a necessity.

MATCHSTICK SLICING
For matchstick slices of vegetables use the medium serrated slicer (the one that comes with the machine) and run the vegetable through horizontally first . . . put it back together again and run through horizontally the opposite way . . . tricky . . . pack the feeder tube carefully. Better yet, get a French fry or julienne blade.

BREADCRUMBS
For breadcrumbs (or crumb crusts) tear the bread or crackers in pieces and drop down the feeder tube with the machine running. Stop to add the cold butter directly into the bowl processing on/off to combine. For coarse crumbs use quick on/offs with the steel blade.

XIV

MASHED POTATOES

To mash potatoes, cut the hot, cooked, dry potatoes into chunks. Shred through the shredding disk (fill the feeder tube twice). Remove disk and put butter, seasonings and milk on the hot potatoes. Replace the shredding disk and shred in the remaining potatoes. Put in the plastic knife, twisting to secure in place, and mix with a couple on/off's. A dash of baking soda will also help keep them light.

CHEESES

To grate soft cheeses, cut cheese into chunks and process with the on/off method several times, using the steel blade, then run the machine a couple of seconds, checking often . . . (cheese paste happens all too quickly). Or use the shredding disk (or julienne blade) with steady but not hard pressure. Pushing too hard gums up the blade. A "bounce" action with the pusher is helpful with soft cheeses . . . this "jars" the cheese loose (if sticking), and it will process more efficiently.

To grate hard cheeses, cut into medium size pieces and place directly into the bowl using the steel blade. Start the machine and use the on/off method to break up, then process to the desired texture. You may also drop the pieces through the feeder tube with the machine running.

DICING VEGETABLES

To dice vegetables, cut them in chunks and push through the feeder tube using the French fryer . . . for a fine dice use the steel blade.

COLESLAW

To make coleslaw, finely shredded, alternate cabbage, onions, green pepper and carrots in the feeder tube . . . use the shredding disk. When the bowl is half full change to the plastic knife, adding dressing and seasonings, processing on/off a couple of times. For long slender shreds use a fine slicing disk.

To make coleslaw with longer, larger shreds try the slicing disk (medium). If you are still not happy, try a thin slicer or julienne blade. You **can** get what you want.

PROCESSING A GREEN PEPPER

For rings, first choose a pepper that will fit the bottom of the feeder tube. Cut out the stem, cut the round bottom off so you have a flat surface against the cutting blade, then load the pepper through the bottom of the tube compressing it so it fits tightly. Push through with firm pressure. For short slices, wedge chunks tightly in the feeder tube and push through. For long strips, remove core and cut open one side of the pepper. Compress pepper together overlapping ends so it fits (vertically) in the feeder tube and push through.

PROCESSING AN ONION
To slice, cut the onion to fit the feeder tube, using lemon juice on both the blade and onion. This cuts the bitterness as well as the odor. Have a flat edge against the cutting blade. To dice, without watery results, either use quick on/off's with the steel blade or cut the onion in quarters and process through the French fry blade. A bit of lemon juice is a help here also.

TOMATOES
To slice tomatoes, use the medium serrated slicing disk. Core the tomato, cut in half, cut off the round end and fit vertically in the feeder tube. Push through with firm pressure.

BREAD
To make bread use the steel blade with the first two "pioneer" Cuisinart machines. The new Cuisinart, the DLC-7, has a special plastic dough mixing blade specially designed for bread. It is extremely efficient for mixing and kneading bread in recipes using over 3 1/2 cups flour.

PERFECT APPLE SLICES
Cut the apple in half, vertically, and remove core. Cut off the round end and lay the apple horizontally in the feeder tube (cut side against the cutting blade). Load from the bottom of the feeder tube so you do not have to trim the apple.

DIPS AND SPREADS
When preparing dips or spreads process the "firmer" ingredients first (cold butter, cream cheese, cheese) using the steel blade to process smooth ... then add the "softer" ingredients (mayonnaise, sour cream) processing with a few on/off's to combine.

CHOPPING ICE
To chop ice, use the steel blade, start with a dry bowl, and with the machine running, drop the ice down the feeder tube.

Basics
and
Adaptations

*. . . even old standbys can be transformed
and made fresh with creative innovations*

Albert Stockli

And they . . . ran faster and faster and faster, 'til they all just melted away, and there was nothing left but a great big pool of melted butter (or "ghi" as it is called in India) . . .

Little Black Sambo

CLARIFIED BUTTER

While it is not made from hungry tigers, it is a lovely golden brown "residue" which will be referred to again and again, and often used instead of oil or margarine because of its lovely flavor.

The procedure is simple:

> Melt the butter slowly, and skim off the frothy milk solids, discarding the foam.

> The Clarified Butter remains, and will not burn as easily as butter, but retains the delicious flavor.

2

Use as a cereal by itself or with dates or raisins, or sprinkle on other cereals, ice cream or yogurt.

Pre-heat oven to 250°

6	cups dry oatmeal (any kind)
1 1/2	cups nuts (any kind)
1 1/2	cups coconut
1	cup untoasted wheat germ
1	cup powdered milk
3/4	cup salad oil
3/4	cup honey melted in 1/4 cup water
1	T. vanilla
1	tsp. cinnamon and nutmeg
1/2	tsp. salt

Dates, raisins or dried fruits (optional)

Steel Blade, Shredding Disk

Put the nuts, coconut and seasonings in the processor bowl and process on-off (to break up the fresh coconut chunks) and run the machine to combine. If using packaged coconut, just "chop" with the nuts. If you wish to "grate" the coconut, use the shredding disk first, loading the feeder tube with the coconut in chunks, pushing through the feeder tube and remove. Add nuts and seasonings and use the steel blade to combine. Dates, raisins or dried fruits are "diced" along with nuts using the steel blade. Remove to a mixing bowl, adding oatmeal, wheat germ and milk.

Melt the honey in hot water, combine with vanilla and oil and stir into ground nuts and oatmeal mixture. Spread on oiled baking sheets (jelly-roll pans are perfect) and roast about one hour. Check every 15-20 minutes and "stir" so the cereal browns evenly. Let cool and store in a tight container.

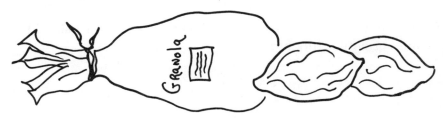

x2 FRUIT-GRANOLA BARS

In somebody's cupboard
There's everything nice.
Cake, cheese, jam, biscuits. . . .

Beatrix Potter

Pre-heat oven to 300°

1 1/2	cups Natural Cereal or
	(I cup oatmeal and 1/2 cup nuts)
1/2	cup whole figs
1/2	cup dates
1/2	cup dried apples
1/2	cup raisins or butterscotch morsels
1	jar of marmalade, jam, jelly (8 oz.)
1/2	tsp. salt
1/3	cup flour
1	egg
1	tsp. vanilla

Cinnamon sugar

Steel Blade

Butter a 9 by 13 pyrex dish.

Put the fruits (and nuts) in the processor bowl and process until chopped and minced. Add the egg, flour, spices and jam, process again. Then add the cereal (or oatmeal) and vanilla, and process a few more seconds. The bowl will be very full.

Remove the blade and stir in the raisins or butterscotch morsels.

Spread in the pan, sprinkle with cinnamon sugar and bake 20-25 minutes or until lightly browned.

x2 NUTRITION CRUST

1	cup dates
1	cup figs
1/2	cup raisins
1 1/2	cups Natural Cereal (p. 3)

Steel Blade

Put everything in the processor bowl using the steel blade and process until minced and combined. If dry, add 2-3 T. butter, in chunks, and process with on/off's. Press into a pie pan or flat dish.

Variation: Melt some butter and marshmallows in a double boiler and fold into the mixture, then into a buttered dish. . . .great snack.

x2   COCONUT CRUST

Pre-heat oven to 300°

2	cups shredded coconut (If you use fresh, shred in the processor using the shredding disk or julienne blade.)
1	cup almonds
1/2	stick butter
1	T. sugar

Steel Blade, Plastic Knife

Put the almonds in the bowl and grind. If using a fresh coconut, change to the shredding disk and shred in. Add sugar and butter (plastic knife) and process together with on/off's.

Bake at 300° for 20-30 minutes or until golden in color.

x2   GINGER-SPICE CRUST

Pre-heat oven to 350°

1	cup gingersnaps
2	cups natural type cereal
1	tsp. each cardamon, cinnamon, nutmeg
1/2	stick of butter

Steel Blade

Put the gingersnaps, spices and the cereal in the processor bowl with the steel blade and process. Add the butter through the feeder tube and bake about 8-10 minutes before filling.

x2   MACAROON CRUST

Excellent crust.

Pre-heat oven to 350°

	8 large or 16 small macaroons (broken in pieces)
1	cup almonds
1/2	stick butter
3	T. sherry (sweet or dry)
2	egg whites
1/8	tsp. cream of tartar

Steel Blade

Put the macaroons in the processor bowl with the almonds and process until minced and combined. Add the sherry and the butter through the feeder tube, with the machine running.

Beat the egg whites until very stiff with 1/8 tsp. cream of tartar. Fold quickly into the macaroon mixture and bake in a 9 or 10 inch pie plate for 15-20 minutes or until lightly browned. Leave in an additional hour with the oven off and the door ajar.

Fill with fresh fruit folded into "imbibied" whipping cream or ice cream.

x2 BASIC BREAD CRUMB TOPPING

Pre-heat oven to 350°

3-4	pieces of bread (any leftover rolls or bread)
1	T. sesame seeds
1	tsp. seasoned salt (p. 68)

Dash pepper
Several sprigs parsley

2	ounces Parmesan cheese (optional)

Steel Blade

Tear bread in half or fourths and put in the processor bowl with the other ingredients. Process until coarsely ground. Add 1/2 stick of butter cut in 3-4 pieces, and process until blended in. If you are using fresh Parmesan, process the cheese with the steel blade to a powder first.

x2 PROCESS AND BAKE

Use with chicken, pork, or fish, and freely add or delete seasonings.

Basic Bread Crumbs

3	T. flour
2	T. corn meal
1	tsp. each seasoned salt, chervil and parsley
1	T. lemon juice

Steel Blade

After preparing the crumbs, dry them out in a warm oven, but do not brown.

Put the crumbs into the processor bowl and process until finely ground. Add the flour, corn meal and seasonings, processing to combine.

Dip the meat or fish in some beaten egg, then in the crumbs and bake for 35-50 minutes, depending on the kind of meat.

Note: 2 ounces grated Parmesan is a nice addition after browning crumbs.

This is a **guide** *. . . substitutions, experiments and variations to be the rule rather than the exception. Bake muffins in greased tins.*

2	cups flour (1 cup may be cornmeal, bran flakes, oatmeal or cereal products)
1	cup milk (sour cream, buttermilk or yogurt)
3	T. sugar (molasses, honey or substitute sugars)
1	T. baking powder (increase 1 tsp. for bran muffins)
1/2	tsp. salt
1	egg
3	T. butter, oil, or shortening
1	tsp. soda (if using raw fruits)

Additions or variations:
1	cup pureed vegetables
3/4	cup dried fruits or nuts
1	cup loosely packed fresh fruit
1	cup grated cheese

Herbs, spices, flavorings

Steel Blade, Shredding Disk (for fruits and vegetables)

When using your own recipes work from dry to wet or wet to dry . . . you need not change ingredients or amounts . . . just be careful not to overprocess. Add nuts or raisins last if you prefer them quite coarse or whole . . . process them by the on/off method once or twice. If using whole raw fruits process them first and work from wet (eggs, shortening, milk) to dry, processing the dry ingredients in with the on/off method once or twice. If using dried fruits you may "cut" them into the dry ingredients first, adding liquids last . . . you can make a larger recipe this way as it's too much liquid *alone* that causes problems with liquids running through the center. Bake muffins at 425° 15-25 minutes . . . bran muffins tend to brown more quickly so watch them.

Note: See Muffin Mix on page 95.

One of the things so often demonstrated is pastry. The Cuisinart makes lovely pastry but the secret is not to run the machine too long.

1 1/2	cups all purpose flour
1	stick, less 1 T. very cold butter
1	T. Crisco
1/2	tsp. salt
4-6	T. ice water
1-1 1/2 tsp. vinegar or lemon juice	

Steel Blade

Use the steel blade and put flour, salt, Crisco and butter (in chunks) in the bowl. Process with on/off's until mixture resembles a coarse meal. Add the ice water and vinegar or lemon juice in 1-2 T. amounts, running machine a couple seconds between additions. Stop processing as you see it <u>begin</u> to form a dough ball. Remove and chill 1-2 hours before using.

VARIATIONS:

For a sweet crust add 2 T. sugar to the dry ingredients. For flavored crust add flavoring to either liquid or dry ingredients (i.e. add almond extract with the water).

For a richer pastry add an egg yolk or whole egg, replacing some of the water.

For a sour cream pastry use 1/2 cup sour cream and an egg yolk for the water. You may need a small amount of ice water to get pastry to hold together.

Pre-bake pastry crusts at 375° until lightly browned (10-15 minutes) . . . line with wax paper and dried beans or rice and chill formed crust 30 minutes before baking for best results.

Save and freeze all little bits of pastry . . . they make great little canapes (the kids can do this) for spreads and other mixtures.

x2 CREAM CHEESE PASTRY

If you are having trouble with pastry try this one . . . almost fool-proof.

1	cup flour
1/2	tsp. salt
1	stick butter
4	ounces cream cheese

Steel Blade

Process flour and salt together with an on/off (pulse). Add butter and cream cheese in chunks, processing in with on/off's. Pat together and chill before using.

(Alternate method: cream butter and cheese, working in flour with on/off's.)

dlc-7 You may triple this recipe in the DLC-7. It may be necessary to add a couple teaspoons of ice water to get pastry to hold together.

x2 BASIC PASTA

This is a contribution from Creative Cookery in Oklahoma City. I've enjoyed many good times (and good food) in their kitchen.

2	cups flour
3	eggs
1-2	ounces each oil and water
1/2	tsp. salt

Optional: 2 T. spinach (cooked and drained)

Steel Blade

Combine flour and salt with an on/off (pulse).

Add eggs and process to combine. Run machine between additions of oil and water and knead (by running machine) until smooth and elastic. Let the dough rest at least 30 minutes. If adding spinach, add with the eggs. Roll and cut (by hand) in thin strips or process with a pasta machine.

MOCK PUFF PASTRY

Bake cold pastry in a hot (450°) oven.

1   recipe Basic Pastry, prepared and chilled (p. 9)
1   stick very, very cold unsalted butter
"Enough" flour and a sifter

Steel Blade, Slicing Disk

Put the slicing disk in the processor. Cut the stick of butter in half and fit both halves in the feeder tube (from the bottom). Push through to slice.

Remove the chilled dough and roll out in an oblong rectangular shape about 1/4" thick.

Dot the dough all over with the butter, then dredge with flour, using the sifter. Better to use too little than too much flour. Flour the rolling pin, and roll over the butter and flour a couple of times, gently:

1. Fold the pastry by folding the top third down and the bottom third up (like a business letter) to encase the butter.

2. Turn the pastry "package" so the folded edge is to the right. Chill, wrapped in wax paper.

Remove after it rests 30-45 minutes and

1. Roll it out again in an oblong rectangular shape (on a floured surface . . . don't bother cleaning the board until you're through).

2. Fold it up the same way and turn again. Chill, wrapped in wax paper.

Repeat this process at least 3 more times. Handle briefly during rolling and folding being sure the pastry is COLD. Brief handling and cold pastry produce lighter, flakier results. Use the pastry in several days (or freeze) but roll and turn one time before using. Some recipes call for addition of 1 tsp. baking powder to the initial pastry recipe. If you have trouble with unbaked center portions when you use in a recipe, try this addition.

This is a cream puff pastry as well as a base for donuts, fritters, and all sorts of interesting combinations

Pre-heat oven to 400°

1	cup water
1	stick butter
1/8	tsp. salt
1	cup flour
4	eggs
1	T. sugar

dlc-7 *Omit 1 T. sugar if using for savory appetizers. If doing a double recipe in the DLC-7, omit 1 egg.*

Steel Blade

In a saucepan, melt the butter in the water with the salt and bring to a boil. Add the flour all at once and stir vigorously until it forms a ball around the spoon. Cool a few minutes, then transfer to the processor bowl with the steel blade, and add the eggs one at a time, processing until smooth and shiny.

For dessert size shells, using a tablespoon, drop onto a cookie sheet. Dash some water drops on the cookie sheet and bake at 400° for 15 minutes. Reduce heat to 350° for 15 to 20 minutes.

Smaller puff shells require shorter baking time . . . have a look after 20 minutes or take one out to test. Spear with a knife or needle at the end of the baking time and return to the oven 5 minutes or so. (Or turn oven off and leave in an additional 20 minutes . . . you'll have less unbaked dough in the center.) If you make these ahead, re-crisp in a hot oven a few minutes before filling.

Choux Pastry keeps well in the refrigerator and, I'm told, even freezes.

Choux Pastry may be used as a base for many dishes from Quenelles to Potatoes Dauphine. Try the 3 recipes in your Cuisinart instruction booklet on page 31. In addition, try combining equal amounts of Choux Pastry and pureed vegetables (great for leftovers) using the steel blade. Shape into balls and deep fat fry. Tasty puffed appetizers can be created with Choux Pastry, minced ham, nuts and cheese.

Following are some ideas for transforming Choux Pastry into White Sauce, Crepes, and Popovers. All use the steel blade.

Rich White Sauce: Scald **1 1/2 cups milk** in a saucepan. Process **1 cup Choux Pastry** with **1/4 cup powdered milk** to combine. With the machine running, add hot milk through the feeder tube. Transfer back to the saucepan, stirring to thicken. Do not boil . . . if you have any problems with lumps, the steel blade will eliminate them very quickly. If you wish a cheese sauce, grate the cheese first (steel blade), then add Choux Pastry and follow the same directions.

Crepe Batter: Process **1 cup Choux Pastry** a few seconds. Add **1 cup milk, 1/2 cup flour, 1 T. brandy** (machine running). The batter should be the consistency of heavy cream. Let the batter rest at room temperature 15 minutes, then prepare as you would crepes (p. 25).

Yorkshire Pudding or Popovers: Prepare the batter the same as crepes only omit brandy. Let the batter rest at room temperature 30 minutes to an hour. Proceed as in Popovers (p. 86) with or without the sausage. Or, use as Yorkshire Pudding (p. 26). The popover tins should be well greased and hot. Bake in a pre-heated oven (450°) for 20 minutes. Turn the oven down to 375° for an additional 10-15 minutes or until puffed and brown.

Breakfast Puffs: These are much like Popovers, only thicker. They fall rapidly and should be served at once . . . moist and excellent flavor. Process **1 cup of Choux Pastry** with **1/2 cup milk, 1/2 tsp. vanilla** and **1/3 cup pecans.** Add **1 tsp. baking powder, 1 cup flour** and **1 egg white** beaten very stiff. Process in with on/off's (pulse) to combine. Put in greased muffin tins and sprinkle with a combination of **2 tsp. cinnamon, 1 T. pecans** and **2 T. sugar.** (Process together first with the steel blade.) Bake at 400° 15-20 minutes, turn oven down, and bake an additional 5-10 minutes at 350°.

dlc-7 You may triple these recipes in the DLC-7, except with the White Sauce. Add only 2 cups of the scalded milk to the bowl (leaving the remaining milk in the saucepan), then proceed as directed. Then, larger quantities may be prepared without adding too much liquid to the bowl.

Let eggs sit at room temperature an hour before using. . . .they'll reward you with a better performance.

x2　　SHORTCAKE PASTRY

Be careful not to overprocess! Take very little.

Pre-heat oven to 450°

2 1/2	cups biscuit mix
3	T. butter + 1 T. melted butter
3/4	cup milk
2	T. sugar
1	tsp. almond or vanilla extract
1/2	tsp. salt

Steel Blade

Put the biscuit mix, salt, sugar and 3 T. butter in the processor bowl and "cut-in" by rapidly turning the machine on and off. Add the extract to the milk and pour it in, blending the same way. Handle as little as possible . . . turn out on a floured board and roll out 2 circles (to fit a cake pan). Butter the pan and put one circle in . . . brush with melted butter and repeat with the other circle in the same pan. Bake 10-12 minutes. Cool before splitting in half.

x2　　PIZZA CRUST

1	package dry active yeast
3/4	cups warm water
1	tsp. sugar
2	tsp. salt
3	T. oil
2-2 1/2	cups flour

Steel Blade

Dissolve the yeast in the water and add 1 tsp. sugar. Let it sit until it gets bubbly.

Put oil, yeast mixture and half the flour (all the seasonings) in the bowl and process 5-10 seconds to a smooth batter. Add the remaining flour 1/3 at a time processing on/off until it begins to hold a dough shape . . . if the machine slows down, add more flour. Stop when smooth and elastic . . . let machine run 30 seconds or so to knead. Place in a greased bowl, cover and let rise until doubled. Punch down on a floured board and let it sit 10 minutes. Grease your pizza pan, sprinkle with cornmeal and roll out the dough in a circle. Chill until ready to load up with sauce and cheese. Bake at 400° 20-25 minutes.

x2   BASIC YEAST DOUGH I

Pre-heat oven to 350°

This dough is easy to mix and requires very little kneading. Perfect for rolls . . . after it has risen once you may chill or freeze.

1	package dry active yeast
1	T. sugar
1/2	tsp. salt
1	cup milk (120-130°)
1/2	stick butter
1	egg (for rolls)

2 3/4-3 cups unbleached flour (more or less)

Steel Blade

Heat the milk and sugar to 130° . . . stir in butter to melt. Check temperature to be sure it is above 120°.

Put the dry yeast and flour in the processor bowl and use the on/off method to process once. Add egg and warm milk with the machine running. Process with on/off (or pulse), adding more flour if necessary. What you want is a smooth, elastic ball of dough. Do not run the machine to knead but be sure the "dough ball" has formed. Remove and place in a bowl with 1 tsp. oil, turn over, cover and let rise in a warm place until doubled. It will rise fairly quickly (30 minutes).

Punch the dough down on a floured surface. Prepare to make bread, rolls or Pain de Mie loaves. The second rising is also short (20-25 minutes) and the bread should not be allowed to over-rise or it will collapse when baking. Glaze with melted butter, egg wash (beaten egg and milk) or water plus a dash of salt and cornstarch (crispier crust). Do not glaze if using the Pain de Mie pans.

Baking Times:

Bread (1 loaf):	35-40 minutes at 375°
Rolls:	20-25 minutes at 350°
Pain de Mie:	30-35 minutes at 350°

BASIC YEAST DOUGH II

Pre-heat oven to 350°

1	package dry active yeast
1	tsp. sugar
1/4	cup warm water (105-115°)
2	T. butter
1	cup warm milk (beer, water or other combinations of liquids)
1/2	tsp. salt
3	cups flour (about)
	May be whole wheat, rye, or any combination

Steel Blade

Dissolve the yeast in warm water and sugar letting it sit until it becomes foamy. This is proofing the yeast.

Put 2 cups of the flour (4 cups for the DLC-7) plus salt and butter (in chunks) in the bowl and process with on/off's (or pulse) until combined. Add yeast mixture and milk, processing smooth. You may need to scrape down the sides of the bowl.

Add remaining flour in 1/3 cup amounts, processing in between additions until you have a ball of dough that will form around the top of the blades. Knead by running the machine continuously about 30-40 seconds. The dough should be smooth and elastic.

Remove and place in an oiled bowl, cover and let rise until doubled. Punch down and place on a floured board and use for a loaf of bread, rolls, or Pain de Mie. See "Breads" for variations and additional bread and roll recipes.

The second rising will take about 30-40 minutes. Bake according to directions:

Bread (1 loaf):	35-40 minutes at 375°
Rolls:	20-25 minutes at 350°
Pain de Mie:	30-35 minutes at 350°

PROCESSING AN ALMOND

One of the great pleasures of owning a Cuisinart is the ease with which you can process nuts. Ground nuts are not only a marvelous flavor and texture enhancement to many foods but may be used to replace an equal amount of flour in many recipes. Ground almonds are marvelous in cookies, cakes or pastry shells. Almond paste has a variety of uses from Marzipan candies to cake fillings and pastry cream. You will find making your own not only tastes better but is less expensive. Add almonds to bread crumb toppings, crumb crusts, meringue and nut fillings for rolls and coffee cakes.

One has to break the stone
to find the (almond) seed

French Proverb

x2   ALMOND PASTE

There are many formulas for Almond Paste, or you can buy it in the gourmet food section of most grocery stores. It is not only a base for making macaroons, but used in cake fillings, custards, candies and fruit tarts.

1/2	pound shelled almonds (2 cups)
1	cup powdered sugar
1/2	stick of butter (do not use margarine)
2	egg whites

Steel Blade

Put the almonds in the processor bowl with steel blade, and process until ground. Add the sugar, the butter cut in several pieces, and process 10-20 seconds. Beat the egg whites very stiff in a separate bowl. Add to the processor bowl and process by turning the machine on and off several times. You should have a smooth paste. Store in a tightly covered jar and keep in the refrigerator (keeps well for a month).

x2   MACAROONS

Pre-heat oven to 350°

1	cup Almond Paste
1	T. flour
1	tsp. baking powder
2	egg whites, beaten very stiff with 1/2 tsp. salt and 1/2 cup sugar
1/2	tsp. vanilla and almond extract

Steel Blade

Break up the paste, if it has hardened, and put it in the processor bowl and process until smooth. Add the flour sifted with baking powder, and flavors. After beating the egg whites very stiff, add the mixture to them. If it does not seem to hold its shape, add more stiffly beaten egg white and sugar. Bake on greased cookie sheets about 25 minutes. Turn the oven off as soon as they are a delicate brown. Leave them in the oven with the door ajar another 30 minutes, or until they are dry.

x2   MARZIPAN

Decorate your beautiful desserts!

1	recipe Almond Paste
1/2	tsp. vanilla
1/2 to 2 cups powdered sugar	

Steel Blade

Put the Almond Paste into the processor bowl with the vanilla and add the powdered sugar in small amounts, processing with a steel blade, until it is stiff. Add more powdered sugar until very stiff and will hold its shape. Chill. Press into rubber candy-type molds in different shapes, or shape by hand. Coat with chocolate or melted mints or paint with food coloring. It can also be baked in a 325° oven 15-20 minutes.

ALMOND TEA CAKES

This is like an almond "brownie". . . .introduced to me by a very good Dutch friend. Its only drawback was the tedious mixing of all those stiff ingredients.

Now, happily, the processor does the work.

Pre-heat oven to 350°

2	sticks butter
2	cups sugar
2	cups all purpose flour
3	eggs
1/2	cup Almond Paste (p. 17)
2	tsp. baking powder
1	egg white
2	T. apple jelly
2	tsp. water

Steel Blade

Put the butter and sugar in the processor bowl using the steel blade, and process 10-20 seconds until creamed. Add the eggs and the almond paste and process until smooth. Add the flour 1 cup at a time with the baking powder and process until mixed together.

Spread in a greased baking pan (9 by 13).

Melt the apple jelly in the water. Beat the egg white until foamy, then mix with the jelly. Brush over the top.

Bake 30-35 minutes.

The bowl will be quite full but the Cuisinart handles the load without any problem. You may need to scrape down the sides of the bowl a couple times when creaming butter and sugar.

dlc-7 You may increase this by 1/2 with the DLC-7. Use a jelly roll pan with sides at least one inch high. The baking time will be about 5 minutes less.

x2   ALMOND COOKIE DOUGH

2	cups unbleached flour
1/2	cup Almond Paste (p. 17)
1 1/2	sticks butter (unsalted)
1/2	cup powdered sugar
1	egg
1	egg yolk
1/2	tsp. almond flavoring

Dash of salt

Steel Blade

Start machine running and drop butter through the feeder tube to "cream". Add Almond Paste and sugar, processing in well. Add eggs, salt and vanilla, processing in. Add flour all at once and process in with on/off's (or pulse). Chill the dough before using. If it is too stiff to put through a cookie press, let it sit out until pliable. If cookies are too runny, work in some additional flour when rolling out.

This is a basic dough . . . decorate with diced fruit or cherries, or cover with shredded chocolate and nuts. Fill with dabs of jelly or try different icings.

x2   QUICK ALMOND PASTRY CREAM

1	recipe Choux Pastry (p. 12)
2 1/2	cups cream or half and half
1/2	cup Almond Paste (p. 17)
1/2	tsp. almond flavoring
1/2	tsp. rum or vanilla flavoring
1/4	cup sugar

Steel Blade

Heat the milk or cream very hot. Process sugar, Almond Paste and flavorings together until smooth. Add Choux Pastry, processing in. With machine running add 1 cup liquid (hot) through the feeder tube. Transfer to the remaining hot liquid and stir to thicken. Since the flour is already cooked, this is almost instant.

Note: If you do not have Almond Paste made up, simply process 1/3 cup almonds, 2 T. butter and an additional 3 T. sugar first (steel blade).

ITALIAN PASTRY CREME

It is said that an Italian named Frangipane who lived in Paris in the 17th Century invented a perfume for gloves which had a sweet smell. The name was apparently transferred to an almond pastry cream much later, because of its lovely fragrance. You'll find the taste as marvelous as its fragrance.

1	cup sugar
5	eggs
1	cup flour
1/2	tsp. salt
3	cups milk
1	tsp. vanilla
2	T. rum
1 1/2	cup almonds
3	macaroons
1	stick unsalted butter

Steel Blade

Heat the milk and the vanilla to a boiling point. Cool slightly. Put the almonds and macaroons in the processor bowl using the steel blade and process until crushed and finely ground. Remove. Put the eggs, sugar and flour in the processor bowl and process 10-20 seconds or until combined. Add half of the milk through the feeder tube with the machine running. Transfer to the rest of the milk over medium heat, stirring constantly, until thickened. Do not worry if it seems lumpy when it thickens . . . it will be all right when you're finished.

Add the almonds, macaroons and butter to the hot mixture, stirring them in. Add rum, continue to cook over medium heat a few more minutes. Use in cake fillings, cream puffs, crepes or the Almond Cake on page 90.

Variation: Try substituting 3 T. praline powder (caramelized almonds) for the macaroons.

Keep some sugar in a container with a vanilla bean. . . . .great flavor.

PROCESSING A COCONUT

Fresh coconuts have such marvelous delicate flavor even though they are securely housed in a very tough shell. However, once the shell is cracked they are quite simple to grate with the processor. (I have some not so fond memories of tackling little pieces of coconut with a hand grater and grating my fingers while trying to hold on to the coconut.) As for cracking the shell, there will certainly be someone in your house who will enjoy beating it with a hammer. You can simplify the job by putting it into a 350° oven for about 20-25 minutes (or until the shell is hot . . . pierce the eyes first, draining the liquid), then crack with a hammer on each end. The inner brown skin peels off or you can use a vegetable peeler. It will come away from the hard shell easily. Grate with the shredder (for long shreds) by placing fairly large pieces sideways in the feeder tube, or cut into chunks and place directly into the bowl and use the steel blade.

The meat can be grated and frozen, or you can make coconut milk to use in soups, sauces, and a variety of creations. Opinions vary, but I always save the watery liquid and keep it with the grated coconut if I freeze it, or add it to the coconut milk. One coconut yields about 2-3 cups grated meat for 30 to 40 cents. One pays 3 times that amount for it in a can or package.

COCONUT MILK

To obtain a clear coconut milk without the shreds of the meat, boil together equal amounts of whole milk and freshly grated coconut (in its liquid). Boil about 2-3 minutes, and cool. Place a clean dishcloth over a bowl, pouring the mixture into it and squeezing it to extract all the liquid. This is the "milk". . .discard the meat. Add whole milk to complete the amount called for in a recipe, if needed.

x2   SWEET COCONUT CREAM CUSTARD

This is a sweet, rum flavored custard that is delicious either warm or chilled over fruit and cakes (or by itself).

1	cup Coconut Milk (p. 22)
1	cup milk
4	eggs
2	T. cornstarch
1/4	tsp. salt
1/2	cup sugar
1	tsp. vanilla (or vanilla bean)
1	tsp. rum flavoring

Steel Blade

Heat the milk and the vanilla and rum flavoring slightly in a saucepan . . .if you have a vanilla bean, add it to the milk. Put the eggs, salt, cornstarch, and sugar in the processor bowl and process until combined. With the machine running, add half of the milk through the feeder tube, then transfer the mixture to the saucepan. (Remove the vanilla bean at this time) Stir constantly, do not let it boil, over medium heat until thick. Cool over a bowl of cold water.

Thin with cream or liqueurs, if using as a sauce.

x2   RICH COCONUT CREAM FILLING

1/2	cup freshly grated coconut
The coconut liquid, and milk to make 2 cups	
1/4	tsp. salt
2	T. cornstarch
1/2	cup sugar
5	eggs
1	tsp. vanilla

Steel Blade

Heat the milk, coconut, and coconut liquid in a saucepan, boil 5 minutes. Cool. Put the eggs, sugar, vanilla, salt and cornstarch in the processor bowl, and process until combined. Add one cup of the warm milk with the machine running, then transfer to a saucepan and thicken over medium heat. Do not let it boil, stir constantly.

Cool over a bowl of cold water.

x2   COCONUT MACAROONS

Pre-heat oven to 350°

1/2	of a fresh coconut (1 1/2-2 cups)
1 1/2	cups sugar
2	T. cake flour
1	tsp. vanilla
3	large egg whites

Shredding Disk, Plastic Knife

Prepare baking sheets with parchment paper, waxed paper or rice paper. Lightly spray pans first with non-stick coating spray.

Use the grating blade and grate the coconut . . . you should have almost 3 cups from a large coconut. Use about 3/4 of a small coconut. If you have heated coconut (350°) for 30-40 minutes before opening, the peeling comes off very easily. Add vanilla, half the sugar, cake flour and one egg white . . . use plastic knife to combine well.

Beat egg whites very stiff in another bowl (but <u>not dry</u>), then add remaining sugar. Add mixture from the processor bowl, beating together well. Drop by rounds on the paper and bake at 350° about 20 minutes.

Yield: 18-20 macaroons

COCONUT FROSTING

1/2	of a fresh coconut	2	T. corn syrup
1 1/2	cups sugar	2-3	egg whites
3-5	T. water	1	tsp. vanilla
Dash salt		Dash Cream of Tartar	

Julienne Blade

Grate the coconut by loading the feeder tube with the chunks laying horizontally. Combine egg whites, water and sugar in the top of a double boiler (over boiling water) and beat with an electric mixer 5-7 minutes or until spreading consistency.

Cool slightly and add vanilla. Fold in some of the coconut reserving some to scatter over the top. This amount will frost a 2-layer cake.

The first is for Peter
The second for Paul,
And the third for the One
Who rules us all

An ancient rhyme

A word about Pancakes. . . .

The "pancake" is a historical and an International food appearing in various forms in nearly every country.

The following are all "pancake"type batters.

x2   CREPE BATTER
a French pancake

Makes 14-16 crepes

1 1/2	cups all purpose flour
3/4	cups milk
3/4	cup water
3	large eggs
2	T. butter
1/4	tsp. salt

Steel Blade

Put the flour, salt and butter in the work bowl with the steel blade. Process to thoroughly cut in butter. Break in the eggs and with the machine running add the water and milk through the tube. Process until smooth.

Let rest 3-4 hours in the refrigerator. Heat the crepe pan with a bit of lard. When water sizzles . . . it's ready. (Expect to throw away the first crepe.) Pour enough batter to cover the bottom of the pan, picking up the pan and tilting it. Return to flame; when the liquid "look" goes away, turn and brown on opposite side. Stack between wax paper. Take the phone off the hook . . . this is a tough time to be interrupted until you finish the batter. Go ahead and use when cooled or freeze.

Note: Add different flavorings or liqueurs to the batter.

x2 "SKINNIER" CREPE BATTER

1 1/2	cups flour
1/2	tsp. salt
3/4	cups water
3/4	cups skim milk
3	eggs
1/4	tsp. imitation butter flavoring

Steel Blade

Proceed as in directions for crepe batters or egg roll batter.

Note: For sweet crepes add some liqueur to batter, herbs for savory crepes.

x2 YORKSHIRE PUDDING
a baked pancake

Pre-heat oven to 450°

1 3/4	cups flour
4	eggs
1/2	tsp. salt
1 1/2	cups milk

Fat drippings from a roast of beef

Steel Blade

Put all ingredients in the work bowl and process until well-combined (you may have to scrape down the flour on the bowl once.) Let sit in bowl at room temperature at least 1 hour. . . .don't worry -- it will not spoil. Put about 1/4 tsp. of the drippings in muffin tins and heat in a 450° oven 10 minutes. Fill the tins a little over half full and bake in the following manner: 15 minutes at 450°; 15-20 minutes at 350°. Serve at once — traditionally with Roast Beef. Makes 12-14.

x2   EGG ROLL BATTER
an Oriental pancake

2   cups flour + 2 T. cornstarch
1   tsp. salt
5   eggs
2 1/2 cups water
1   T. melted butter

Steel Blade

Put the flour, salt, and eggs in the processor bowl and process about 5-10 seconds. With the machine running, add the water and butter through the feeder tube; the batter should be smooth.

Using a crepe pan, heated with a bit of lard, pour a small amount of batter in the pan, tilting the pan quickly to cover the bottom thinly. Be careful not to get it too thick or it will be impossible to deal with when rolling up. Cook about one minute, turn it gently, cooking about half as long on the other side. Stack between wax paper, and plan to add a little more lard to the pan from time to time. Use that day, or freeze.

x2   FRENCH TOAST BATTER
a dunked pancake

1/2   cup milk
1   T. flour
3   eggs
1/4   tsp. cinnamon
1   tsp. orange juice concentrate
1   tsp. rum flavoring, almond or vanilla
1   T. melted butter

Steel Blade

Put everything in the processor bowl and process until smooth. Let rest 5-10 minutes. Dip bread into batter and saute in Clarified Butter (p. 2).

My youngest son, who would gladly bathe in chocolate, told me I should add cocoa to the batter -- so we tried 1 T. cocoa -- try it! You'll like it!

27

x2 FRITTER BATTER
a fried pancake coating

1	cup flour
1/4	tsp. salt
1	cup stale beer
2	egg yolks
1	T. butter
2	egg whites
1/8	tsp. cream of tartar

Steel Blade

Put the flour, salt and egg yolks in the bowl and with the machine running add the beer and butter in a slow, steady stream. Let it stand several hours. When ready to use, beat the egg whites very stiffly. Stir the batter by hand and fold into the whites.

x2 BUÑUELOS
a Mexican pancake

2	cups flour
1/2	tsp. salt
1	tsp. baking powder
1/4	tsp. each anise, cardamon
1/8	tsp. cinnamon
1/4	cup milk
1/4	cup water
2	eggs
2	T. melted butter
1	T. sugar

Hot oil for frying

Steel Blade

Put the dry ingredients in the processor bowl and process a few seconds. Add the liquid ingredients and process until smooth, then the melted butter through the feeder tube. Let it stand, covered, 30 minutes or refrigerate overnight.

Roll into little balls, flatten with your hand, and deep fat fry until crisp (not brown) on both sides. Drain on a paper towel and coat with cinnamon sugar or powdered sugar.

28

x2 FLOUR TORTILLAS

2   cups flour
1/2   tsp. baking powder
2   T. Crisco
1   tsp. salt
2/3   cups warm water

Steel Blade

Put the flour, baking powder, salt and Crisco in the processor bowl and process to a "meal". Add the water through the feeder tube, and with the machine running, process until a ball of dough just forms. Chill 20 minutes. Roll into little balls and let stand 10 minutes. Then pat or roll to thin circles and fry on both sides in an ungreased, well-seasoned crepe pan.

Note: You may prefer to use 1 tsp. baking powder and/or lard instead of Crisco . . . more shortening makes a softer tortilla. Try using half whole wheat flour . . . a tortilla press is a great aid.

Try warming in foil, buttering and use as bread, or spread with cheese dip.

x2 CANNOLI BATTER
a fried pancake

May be filled with various sweet or savory fillings. Cannoli forms may be bought in nearly any kitchen supply store.

Makes 12-14

2	cups all purpose flour
1/4	tsp. salt
1	egg
2	T. butter
2	T. white vinegar
2	T. sugar (omit for savory shells. . .try an herb or spice to blend with your filling)
1	egg white, beaten a little bit

Vegetable oil

Steel Blade

Put the flour, salt and sugar in the processor bowl with the steel blade. Cut the butter in two pieces and process with the flour until in coarse crumbs. Do this by turning the machine on and off several times. Add the vinegar and the egg and process until it just forms a dough-like pie pastry. Let chill in the refrigerator at least 1 hour.

Divide in half and roll on a floured surface as thin as you can. Then cut into six circles. Keep dough you are not working with covered with wax paper.

Wrap each circle around a cannoli form, sealing the edge with egg white. Fry in hot vegetable oil (400°) until golden -- about 2 minutes -- holding with some tongs. Set on a cake rack to cool. Remove pastry from shells after they have cooled a minute or so. Fill when completely cool. You may freeze, and crisp in hot oven when ready to use.

Note: See fillings (International Pancakes and Crepes)

*"Parents can set an example for their children. . .
especially . . ., a willingness to try new things."*

Albert Stockli

A word about Sandwich Spreads . . .

This is where the whole family will have fun experimenting with the processor (even the kids will have fun searching for ingredients) . . . use tuna, crab, shrimp, chicken, turkey, leftover luncheon meats, cheese, nuts, meat.

Process crunchy ingredients first, mayonnaise last. You may need slightly less mayonnaise than usual as dicing with the steel blade will make finely diced peppers, onions and celery a little watery.

x2   SUPERMAN SANDWICH SPREAD

My son Don's invention.

Serves 4

Pre-heat oven to 450°

4	hot dogs (boiled and cooled)
1/4	onion
2	sweet pickles
2	tsp. mustard
1	T. chili sauce
4	slices American cheese
1	T. mayonnaise
3	T. chili (no beans)

Steel Blade

Cut the hot dogs in chunks and put everything but the cheese in the work bowl, and process by turning on and off -- do not process smooth. Put on half a hamburger bun and top with cheese. Bake at 450° for 10-15 minutes. Or spread between slices of bread, with the cheese, butter both sides and grill like a sandwich.

Note: The cheese may be processed with the rest of the ingredients and used in canapes.

31

x2 EGG SALAD

This particular combination evolved at the end of a demonstration when I was left with bits of "this and that" plus some round ends of cucumbers left from showing how to prepare vegetables for the feeder tube.

6   hard boiled eggs
Several sprigs parsley
2   chunks of cream cheese
3-4   chunks of celery
Several chunks of cucumber (seeded)
1-2   tsp. capers
2-3   T. mayonnaise
Several green onions
Salt and pepper to taste

Steel Blade, Medium Serrated Slicing Disk, Plastic Knife

Process the cream cheese and parsley first with the steel blade. Add celery, onion and cucumber processing with a few quick on/off's. (If you have the French fryer you may wish to use it to get a larger dice.)

Change to the slicing disk and slice in the eggs. Remove and insert the plastic knife (it does not need to lock into place). Add mayonnaise, capers and process in with several on/off's.

x2 SHRIMP SALAD

1/2   pound (more or less)
         cooked shrimp
1/2 of a green pepper
1   T. capers
1   stalk celery
2   tsp. horseradish

2-3   T. mayonnaise
Dash of lemon juice
1   T. medium hot
         piquant sauce
Salt and pepper to taste

Steel Blade, Plastic Knife

Put chunks of green pepper and celery in the bowl with a little lemon juice. Process with a few rapid on/off's to dice. Change to the plastic knife and add the rest of the ingredients. Process with on/off's to combine.

x2 CHUNKY CHICKEN SALAD

After several months of pureed vegetables, creamy soups, pates of infinite variety and steak tartar, your family will appreciate something with a few chunks.

About 2 cups (or fill the feeder tube twice) cooked chicken or:
      Meat from one chicken
1   ounce cream cheese
Several sprigs parsley
1/2   of a summer squash
3   green onions
1   stalk celery
Several small pieces of apple
2   T. mayonnaise (about)
Some pecans or walnuts
Salt and pepper to taste

Steel Blade, Slicing Disk, French Fryer, Plastic Knife

Put the cream cheese and parsley in the bowl (steel blade) and run the machine to mince. Remove the steel blade.

Use the French fryer and load the feeder tube with pepper, onions, celery, apple and squash (all in chunks) and push through. Alternate method: Put all vegetables in the bowl (in chunks) and process with on/off's (or pulse). By processing items of different textures together you obtain a larger "dice".

Change to the slicing disk (medium serrated) and load the feeder tube with chicken and nuts. Push through . . . the chicken will come out in chunks.

Insert the plastic knife . . . you'll have to twist a bit to get the food out of the way, just be careful not to push any down the center. Add mayonnaise and seasonings and process with the on/off method a couple of times. By using a variety of blades you can get a chunky textured salad without changing, washing or removing the bowl.

dlc-7 Since the plastic blade is for bread doughs rather than mixing, use the steel blade (pulse) for final mixing.

x2 TURKEY SALAD

2	stalks celery, cut in chunks
2	cups turkey meat
1/2	green pepper, in chunks
3	T. almonds
1	bunch green grapes
1	3 oz. package cream cheese
2	T. mayonnaise
1	tsp. A-1 steak sauce
2	tsp. fresh minced parsley

Steel Blade, Slicing Disk, Plastic Knife

Using the steel blade, process the parsley. Add the cream cheese, cut in chunks, processing with the on/off method to combine. Change to the serrated slicing disk and push the vegetables, grapes and meat through using moderate pressure. Change to the plastic knife, adding the mayonnaise and steak sauce directly to the bowl and process on/off rapidly to combine.

If you want a meat salad that's crunchy, try slicing some of the ingredients with the slicing disk. Remove, and process the meat (steel blade) very briefly by turning the machine on and off rapidly, then change to the plastic knife to mix it all together. Check often so you do not over-process.

. . . sauces are an indispensable part of good cooking. The more one knows about their preparation, the greater the variety in one's cooking. This does not mean the sauces need be complicated or expensive.

Tante Marie

A word about Sauces . . .

I have included several basic sauces I find I use a great deal (usually adding to them one way or another). If I have some broth to use up, I'll prepare sauces and freeze them. Any separation damage the freezer does, the steel blade takes care of nicely.

Marie Moser, a "processing" friend of mine from the Pampered Pantry in St. Louis shares her innovative White Sauce Mix. Her marvelous kitchen, creative chefs, delightful Shop and Cooking School are the fringe benefits of being a traveling cook.

x2 PROCESSOR WHITE SAUCE MIX

1	cup flour
4	cups non-fat dry milk
4	tsp. salt
1	cup butter

Steel Blade

Process together and store in refrigerator.

Thin Sauce: 1/3 cup mix plus 1 cup milk or stock (or wine)
Medium Sauce: 1/2 cup mix plus 1 cup milk or stock (or wine)
Thick Sauce: 1 cup mix plus 1 cup milk or stock (or wine)

Combine mix and liquid (steel blade). Transfer to a saucepan to heat and thicken.

See pages 12 and 13 for another White Sauce Mix using Choux Pastry.

x2 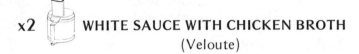 **BASIC WHITE SAUCE**

2	cups milk
4	T. flour
4	T. butter
1	tsp. salt
1/2	tsp. pepper

Steel Blade

Put the flour, butter, spices in the bowl. Bring the milk to a boil. Run the machine to combine flour and butter adding 1 cup hot milk through the feeder tube. Return to remaining milk, stirring to thicken.

x2 **WHITE SAUCE WITH CHICKEN BROTH**
(Veloute)

2	cups chicken stock
4	T. flour
4	T. butter
1	tsp. salt
1/2	tsp. pepper
1	tsp. parsley (3-4 sprigs fresh)

Steel Blade

Put the flour, spices, and butter in the work bowl with the steel blade. Warm the chicken broth. Process the flour and butter until smooth and add the broth through the feeder tube with the machine running. Transfer to a saucepan and thicken on the stove.

x2   CHEESE SAUCE

4	ounces cheese
3	T. flour
2	cups liquid (chicken broth, milk, wine or combination)
3	T. butter
1/4	tsp. salt

Coarsely ground black pepper
Dash cayenne pepper, Tabasco or

1/4	tsp. nutmeg

Steel Blade

Put the cheese, in chunks, in the bowl and process with on/off's to grate. Add flour, butter and seasoning choices. Bring the liquid to a boil. Process in the flour and butter to make a paste then add 1 cup of the liquid through the feeder tube (machine running). Transfer to the remaining liquid to thicken further. If you want a thicker sauce increase the flour.

x2   WHITE SAUCE FOR FISH

1	cup white wine
1	cup fish broth (or clam juice)
4	T. flour (or 2 T. flour and 1/2 cup pureed fish)
4	T. butter
1/2	T. lemon juice
3-4	sprigs fresh parsley
1/2	tsp. salt

Steel Blade

Heat the wine and broth. Using the steel blade process the flour, butter, parsley and lemon juice until smooth (5-10 seconds). Add half the warm broth through the feeder tube, with the machine running. Transfer to a saucepan and thicken over medium heat.

Variations: Add herbs, fresh tomatoes, cream, seasoning; Swiss, Cheddar, Gruyere. . .almost any cheese can be added. It's fun to use your imagination here — just be careful not to add too much cheese for the amount of sauce and to add some liquid with it.

x2   CREOLE SAUCE

Hearty sauce for baked fish, seafood, or vegetables.

1	green pepper
1	onion
2	sticks celery
1	clove garlic
5	T. Clarified Butter (p. 2)
4	large tomatoes
2	tsp. chili powder
1	T. brown sugar
2	bay leaves
1	tsp. thyme and salt
1/2	tsp. red pepper flakes

Steel Blade, French Fryer

Start the machine (steel blade) and drop garlic through the feeder tube. Add onion, peppers and celery processing with on/off's to dice. Remove and saute in butter. Add seasonings. Use the French fryer. Cut the tomatoes in quarters and process through. Add to vegetables and simmer 40 minutes.

x2   OYSTER SAUCE

Delightfully low in calories

1	10 oz. jar fresh oysters
3	leek tops, cut in chunks
2	T. soy sauce
1	can beef consomme, warmed
2	tsp. cornstarch

Dash salt and pepper

Steel Blade

In a saucepan bring leeks, oysters and their liquid to a boil and cook one minute. Cool 5 minutes and transfer oysters and leeks to the processor bowl with the steel blade. Process until well minced. Mix cornstarch and pepper with soy sauce and consomme, and add to oyster liquid. With the machine running, pour the liquid through the feeder tube. Transfer to a saucepan and thicken 5-8 minutes. Keeps well a week in refrigerator or freeze.

Note: Try on different fish and chicken or roast beef.

x2 MAYONNAISE

2   egg yolks plus 1 whole egg
1 1/2 T. lemon juice
1   T. vinegar
Dash salt and white pepper
1   tsp. dry mustard
2   cups salad oil

Steel Blade

Put everything but the salad oil in the processor bowl and process 5-10 seconds, or until combined and light in color. With the machine running, slowly add the oil. Process until thickened.

Let imagination and taste be your guide and try different herbs and flavors.

x2 HERBED MAYONNAISE

1 Recipe Mayonnaise (above)
3-4   green onion tops
Dash of lemon juice
1/4   cup cooked spinach,
      all moisture removed
1   anchovy filet

1   shallot
Several sprigs fresh parsley
Salt to taste
1   T. capers

Steel Blade

Put the shallot and onions in the bowl (steel blade) along with a dash of lemon juice and run the machine to mince. Add parsley, anchovy, capers and spinach processing in with on/off's. Add several tablespoons of the Mayonnaise, process in with on/off's. Stir into remaining Mayonnaise and adjust salt to taste.

Use with cold fish, chicken or tuna salad mixtures or stuffed avocados.

x2 HOLLANDAISE SAUCE

The processor will allow you to make this in double quantities if needed.

1   stick unsalted butter, in pieces
3   egg yolks
1/2   tsp. salt
Dash cayenne
Juice of one lemon
1   tsp. hot water

Steel Blade

Put the butter, egg yolks, lemon juice and seasonings in the processor bowl and process about 20 seconds, or until well combined. Add the hot water with the machine running (if it is quite stiff, add a little more hot water.) This keeps 2 weeks in the refrigerator. Heat and thicken over medium heat, stirring constantly.

Note: If you wish to make this and use it immediately, heat the butter until it bubbles, adding it to the eggs, lemon juice and seasonings through the feeder tube, gradually, with machine running.

x2   BEARNAISE SAUCE

Use the same ingredients and procedure as for Hollandaise, but add to the seasonings:

1   tsp. freeze-dried shallots (or)
2   green onion tops, minced
1   tsp. tarragon
3   T. red wine or red wine vinegar

Steel Blade

Boil the seasonings in the red wine or red wine vinegar until the liquid has evaporated, and add to the processor bowl with the rest of the seasonings.

Note: Either may be used cold as a "butter".

BROWN BUTTER SAUCE

Use on broiled fish or chicken.

1/2	cup Clarified Butter (p. 2)
1	T. fresh parsley (minced)
3	T. lemon juice
1	tsp. capers

Salt and pepper

Steel Blade

Heat the butter in small heavy saucepan and let it turn light (very light) brown. Remove from heat. Stir in lemon juice. Using the steel blade, put the parsley, capers, and spices in the bowl and process until well minced. Add to the butter and lemon.

You may use one whole lemon, peeled and seeded, adding the sections and juice to the bowl with parsley and capers. The sauce will have some lemon pulp and a very fresh flavor.

x2 LOUISIANA REMOULADE

Lots of fresh parsley

2	cups salad oil
1	cup red wine vinegar
1/2	cup water (more may be necessary)
10	ounces Dijon or Zataran's mustard
1	large bunch green onions, tops and stems
1/2	cup lemon juice
1	ounce Hungarian paprika
1	tsp. celery salt

Salt and pepper to taste

1	T. capers

Steel Blade

Put green onions, in chunks, into the bowl with lemon juice and process with on/off's to mince. Add paprika and celery salt. Process, then remove.

Put about 1 1/2 cups fresh parsley in the bowl and process to mince. Add mustard, vinegar, capers, water and process to combine. With machine running, add oil slowly . . . empty machine as soon as you stop processing and combine with onions and lemon juice. Adjust seasonings (salt and pepper) to taste and store in glass jar. Use on seafood, stuffed avocados, oysters . . . anything!

It isn't so much what's on the table that matters, as what's on the chairs.

W. S. Gilbert

A word about Low Calorie Sauces. . .

The processor introduced me to the great variety and uses of fresh fruits and vegetables. Being interested in saving calories as well as good nutrition, these sauce substitutes evolved.

Save all those fibrous roots you cut away from the vegetables (broccoli stems, cauliflower cores, cabbage cores) -- boil them until they are very tender and use them in white sauces -- or save them to slice thinly in salads or with other vegetables.

Find some prepared salad dressing you like (preferably low calorie) and freshen it with a processed tomato, shallot, avocado, or soak a garlic clove in one overnight. . . . .or add some vegetable juice and cut the calories even further.

x2 SKINNY WHITE SAUCE

2   cups heated skim milk
2   tsp. dried chicken bouillon
Eggstra egg substitute (1/2 package)
1   cup any loosely packed cooked vegetable
        cauliflower, squash or carrot
1/2   tsp. dry mustard
Several sprigs parsley
1/2   tsp. pepper
2   tsp. arrowroot
1/4   tsp. imitation butter flavoring

Steel Blade

Put the cooled vegetable, the spices, flavorings and egg substitute in the bowl with the steel blade. Process smooth. Add the milk. Transfer to a saucepan, cooking until well thickened. (Or, refrigerate and thicken when using.) Use in any recipe that calls for white sauce . . . especially good with fish and chicken dishes.

Variation: Add one fresh, diced tomato.

Experiment drying your own herbs. . . . .celery tops, parsley, bits of carrot. . . .minced parsley will keep a week or so, then dry it in the oven and store in a spice jar.

x2 SKINNY HOLLANDAISE

It's very hard to duplicate that luscious buttery, lemon sauce, but in many dishes this is quite acceptable.

3   egg yolks
1   tsp. chicken bouillon powder
1   T. unsalted butter
Juice of one lemon
1/2   tsp. arrowroot
Dash cayenne
1/3   cup water

Steel Blade

Put the egg yolks, chicken bouillon powder, butter, lemon juice, cayenne, and arrowroot in the processor bowl. Process 10-15 seconds, until combined. Add 1/3 cup very hot water with the machine running. Heat and thicken over direct heat when ready to use, stirring constantly.

Note: Makes about 1 cup -- 300 calories (regular Hollandaise sauce – 950)

x2 SKINNY BEARNAISE

1   recipe Skinny Hollandaise
1   tsp. tarragon
1/2   tsp. freeze-dried shallots
2   T. red wine

Steel Blade

Follow the directions for Skinny Hollandaise, only boil shallot and tarragon in red wine until liquid is nearly gone and add hot water. Heat and thicken over direct heat, stirring constantly.

x2 SKINNY LEMON SAUCE

Juice from one large lemon
Some of the zest
1/4   tsp. dry mustard
2   egg yolks
1   tsp. chicken flavoring or cube
Dash salt and white pepper
1   tsp. arrowroot
Dash cayenne
1   cup water (very hot)

Steel Blade

Process the zest with salt and pepper. Process in egg yolks, lemon juice, seasonings and arrowroot. Add the chicken flavoring (if using a cube, process with the zest) and the hot water through the feeder tube. Transfer to a saucepan to stir and thicken.

Use as is or beat the egg whites very stiff and mix together (more volume, no more calories). Try combining with yogurt or other seasonings and herbs.

x2 SUGARLESS RED SAUCE

For shrimp, oysters, crab or combine with low calorie salad dressings to "pep" up.

1   shallot
Juice from one lemon
1   green pepper
3   ripe tomatoes (quartered)
1-2   T. horseradish

1   6 ounce can tomato paste
Several drops artificial sweetener
Several sprigs fresh parsley
A little fresh basil (no substitute)
1/2 of a sweet onion

Steel Blade

Put all the vegetables (in chunks) and seasonings in the bowl and squeeze a little of the lemon juice over them. Process by running the machine and checking often . . . you want things finely minced. Add tomato paste and horseradish, processing in. Adjust seasonings and store in a glass jar. It improves with age.

Note: If you have the French fry blade, quarter the tomatoes and use the blade to "dice". Use the plastic knife for final mixing.

*Soft sweet things with a lot of fancy dressing — that's what
a little boy loves to eat and a grown man prefers to marry.*

Helen Rowland

x2 STREUSEL TOPPING

1	cup flour
1/4	cup white sugar
1/3	cup brown sugar
1/2	tsp. cinnamon (optional)
1/2	cup ground nuts
1	stick butter, cut in pieces

Steel Blade

Put all in the processor. Process until a crumbly mixture. Use on
cakes, coffee cakes or rolls.

x2 BROILED STREUSEL TOPPING

1/2	cup pecans
2/3	cups shredded coconut (about) or 1/3 of a fresh coconut
1/2	stick butter
2/3	cups brown sugar (packed)
3	T. heavy cream

Steel Blade

Combine pecans, sugar and coconut with the steel blade. Process in
butter and cream with on/off's (pulse). Spread on coffee cakes, quick
breads, or sheet cakes and place 6-8 inches away from the broiling
unit for about 5-8 minutes.

x2   SWEET SHERRY SAUCE

This was served traditionally in my family with a divine semi-sweet chocolate steamed cake, however, never seeming able to get enough of the sauce, I have devised many ways to use it.

3	egg yolks
1/4	cup sweet sherry
1/4	tsp. salt
1/2	cup sugar
3	egg whites
1/8	tsp. cream of tartar
1/4	cup sugar

Steel Blade

Combine egg yolks, salt, sherry and sugar in the processor and process until well combined and very light. Put over simmering water in a double boiler and let it cook for about 2-5 minutes, stirring. Then beat over the water with an electric mixer until very thick. Let sit until ready to combine with whites (if you let it sit over an hour, you may have to beat it again). Beat the whites with the cream of tartar until foamy and gradually beat in sugar until very stiff. Fold egg yolk mixture into this.

Serve on plum pudding, cakes or fruit.

Try this: Chill the sauce, and fold it into 1 cup whipping cream for fruit shortcake — fabulous!

x2   GLAZE TOPPING

1	egg white
1/8	tsp. cream of tartar
1	cup confectioners sugar
"Enough"	boiling water or juice

Steel Blade

Beat the egg white and cream of tartar until foamy using the steel blade. Add the sugar, then the hot water a little at a time, processing until the proper consistency for a light glaze. You may prepare a triple recipe all in one processor bowl.

SKINNY PANCAKE SAUCE

2 servings

1	apple
5	T. diet maple syrup
1/2	tsp. cinnamon
1	T. apple jelly (dietetic)
1/4	tsp. imitation butter flavor

Slicing Disk

Cut the apple in half, remove the core but do not bother to peel. Use one of the slicing disks and slice. Heat the rest of the ingredients in a saute pan, add apple slices and simmer a few minutes. 54 calories per serving and the apple helps the diet maple syrup taste better.

Varieties: Blueberries and blackberry jelly
Peaches and peach marmalade

SKINNY SWEET SAUCE

Great for crepes, pancakes, ice cream. . .

1	jar low-calorie apricot jam
1	pint strawberries
1	T. undiluted orange juice concentrate
1-2	T. brandy (orange flavored)
1/4	tsp. imitation butter flavor

Slicing Disk

Wash and hull berries, then fit into feeder tube, and slice using the pusher. Heat together jam, orange juice, and brandy. Let simmer a few minutes, then add berries.

Fresh fruit is the best low calorie dessert. . . .liven it up with a low calorie custard sauce or fruit and liqueur flavorings.

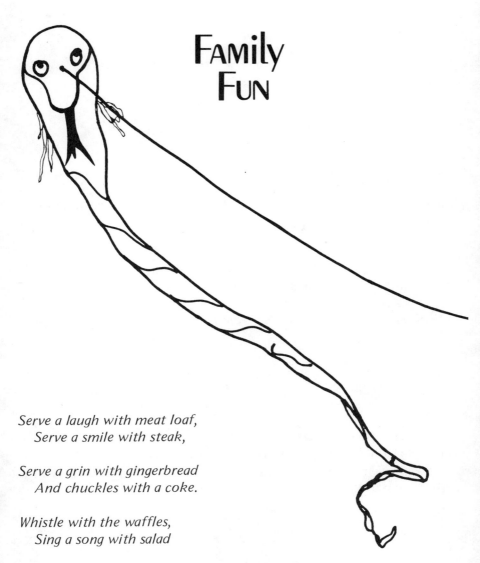

Family Fun

Serve a laugh with meat loaf,
  Serve a smile with steak,

Serve a grin with gingerbread
  And chuckles with a coke.

Whistle with the waffles,
  Sing a song with salad

Hum a tune while kneading dough,
  Don't you know a ballad?

Beat time with a rolling pin,
  Tap dance while you fry,

There's kitchen fun for everyone
  Who'll make it -- Why not try?

Morrison Wood

FAMILY FUN

There's nothing like a stomach full
To make the world seem brighter;
To banish worry, drive out fear,
And make the heart feel lighter.

The Adventures of
Bobby Coon

The current "family room" evolved from the traditional family kitchen — where the family gathered not only to prepare and eat food but to talk, to read, to plan, to share — to cry and to laugh — to live and enjoy.

That's what the kitchen is all about. . .

"Food and a delight in cooking seem to be of International interest."
Alex D. Hawkes
Gourmet
Magazine
1976

Let your husband chop and slice with the processor. . .your only problem will be when you may have your turn. Set out some fresh fruits . . . some liqueurs . . . some ice cream . . . and be prepared for a taste sensation.

Popcorn Tree (see p. 59)

A few "delights" from our family kitchen:

x2   CHOCOLATE-BANANA MILKSHAKE

The first day I received my processor we had processed everything but the childrens' toys, and my husband was just getting started. The only thing left he could find to process was a very ripe banana half someone had left in their lunchbox and a handful of chocolate chips. Into the processor with a little ice cream, an ice cube, and here it is:

For 2

2	ripe bananas
3	T. chocolate syrup
1	pint vanilla ice cream
1	cup milk

Steel Blade

Start the machine running and drop the ice cream, in spoonfuls, through the feeder tube. When smooth, add bananas in the same way. Pour in liquids with machine running and empty liquid right away.

x2   AMARETTO FREEZE

I can only say it's very hard to have just one.

Serves 4

1	quart vanilla ice cream
1/3	cup Amaretto liqueur
1/8	cup Triple-Sec
1/4	cup Creme de Cocao

Steel Blade

Start the machine running and drop the ice cream, in spoonfuls, through the feeder tube. Add liqueurs and chill. If too thick (or too strong) add heavy cream.

x2 MINT CHOCOLATE FREEZE

Serves 8

1	quart peppermint ice cream
1	quart chocolate ice cream
1/2	cup Creme de Menthe
1/2	cup Kahlua
2	T. chocolate fudge topping

Steel Blade

Start the machine running and drop ice cream, in spoonfuls, through the feeder tube. When smooth add liqueurs and chocolate. Chill.

x2 SUPER COCONUT FREEZE

If ice cream is more your thing than liqueur . . .

Serves 4-6

1/2	cup coconut ice cream
1	pint vanilla ice cream
1	pint pistachio ice cream
1/3	cup chocolate-coconut liqueur
1/3	cup Amaretto liqueur
1/2	cup heavy cream

Chocolate curls

Steel Blade

If you don't have coconut ice cream substitute coconut milk or heavy cream plus 1 tsp. coconut flavoring. Start the machine running and drop ice cream through the feeder tube in spoonfuls. Add liqueurs and heavy cream. Chill and serve with a few chocolate curls, or chocolate cigarettes.

"The more one has, the more one wants"

French Proverb

x2 ORANGE JULIUS

For the Kids!

Serves 2

1/2	tsp. vanilla
1/2	cup powdered milk
Peelings from half an orange	
3	T. sugar
3	T. orange juice concentrate
3-4	scoops vanilla ice cream
Juice and sections from an orange	
2	cups soda water

Steel Blade

Process peelings with sugar to mince. Add powdered milk, orange sections, orange juice concentrate, vanilla and process smooth. With machine running, add scoops of ice cream through the feeder tube. Combine with soda water (use more or less depending on thickness desired) and serve. Just as good using lime concentrate, fresh limes.

x2 FROG-NOGGER

For the Adults!

Serves 4-6

1/2	cup Creme de Menthe
1/2	cup apple brandy
1	quart vanilla ice cream
1	cup rich egg nog
1/3	cup apple cider

Steel Blade

This is a dynamite after dinner drink in more ways than one! You may wish to thin with more cider or cream. Use the steel blade and drop ice cream through the feeder tube, processing smooth. Add egg nog, cider and brandy . . . remove bowl from base as soon as the blades stop whirling and transfer to a pitcher or individual glasses.

Garnish with mint sprig and maraschino cherry.

PROCESSING A PUMPKIN

Carving the Halloween pumpkin is a great family project that can be enhanced by processing the inside of the pumpkin as well as carving the skin.

While some of the family creates scary faces on one pumpkin, make some pumpkin treats for trick or treaters.

1. Pumpkin Bars, cookies, or candy.
2. Create a pumpkin soup.
3. Cook the meat, process it smooth and freeze it for Thanksgiving pies.
4. Salt and roast the seeds.
5. Ask the grandparents what they did!

I'll never forget when my 5 year old burst home from kindergarten wanting to make and eat a new discovery—pumpkin pie. He advised me that his teacher had the recipe; however, in my motherly superiority I was confident nothing could surpass "my way". So amidst protestations that "this wasn't the way they did it at school," I prepared my magnificent pie. My heart warmed in motherly anticipation for great praise, as he prepared to dig in — only to sink as I was informed it wasn't pumpkin pie. After retrieving the can from the garbage to prove it was, I finally realized they had made a real pie at school from a real pumpkin. So we began again, this time the real way.

To process a pumpkin:

1. Remove the seeds and discard the stringy portion (the seeds really are good seasoned, buttered, and roasted).

2. Cut the pumpkin in several pieces, removing seeds and strings, and place skin side up in a pan of simmering water. Bake at 350° 25-30 minutes, or until tender. Drain and cool. Scoop out meat and process (steel blade) to puree. You'll have 2 1/2-4 cups. It freezes well.

3. Explore the possibilities — pudding, bread, cookies, ice cream, pie. Here are a few ideas:

PUMPKIN SEEDS

To roast PUMPKIN SEEDS sun dry the seeds or place in a slow oven an hour (200°). They'll look wrinkled when dry. Melt together 1/2 stick butter, 1 tsp. liquid smoke, 1 tsp. seasoned or barbeque salt and saute the seeds. Sprinkle with Parmesan cheese and bake at 350° 10-15 minutes . . . they'll snap and krackle some . . . watch them closely.

ROCKY ROAD PUMPKIN ICE CREAM

1/2	gallon vanilla ice cream
12-14	miniature marshmallows
1/2	cup cooked, processed smooth, pumpkin meat
1	cup sugared pecans
1/2	tsp. ginger
1	T. cinnamon sugar
1/2	tsp. rum flavoring added to:
1/3	cup cream

Steel Blade

Set out the ice cream to soften. Dice the pecans with quick on/off's with the steel blade. If you don't have sugared pecans, combine 3 T. water, 1 egg white and 4 T. sugar in a saucepan and bring to a boil. Stir in pecans and place on a lightly greased jelly roll pan and broil 6-8 inches away from the broiler until they bubble. Cool. Put the marshmallows and cream over medium heat and stir to soften. Fold pecans, marshmallow mixture and seasonings into ice cream and re-freeze.

Serve with toasted coconut topping, caramel sauce or chocolate sauce.

When you make cones, sprinkle them with peanut brittle, which you have crushed by processing with the steel blade.

PUMPKIN SOUP

1/2	stick butter	6-8	cups chicken broth
3-4	chunks of fresh pumpkin meat	1	cup cream
3	assorted winter squashes	1/4	tsp. each thyme,
	(butternut, acorn or		marjoram
	hubbard . . . peeled)	1	tsp. salt
3	large tomatoes		Dash of sugar
1	clove garlic		Fresh parsley
1	onion		Fresh basil (if available)
1/2	of a green pepper		

Garnish:
Roasted pumpkin seeds (or)
Croutons

French Fryer, Steel Blade

Start the machine running and drop garlic through the feeder tube to mince. Remove blade and use the French fryer to dice the pumpkin, squashes and onion. Load the feeder tube with the vegetables in chunks. Remove and saute in hot butter. Dice the tomatoes the same way, cutting into quarters first. Bring stock to a boil and add tomatoes (including juices) and all the seasonings. With the steel blade mince several sprigs of fresh parsley and basil.

Add vegetables after 15 minutes of simmering and continue to simmer an additional 15 minutes (or until it tastes great!). Stir in the cream, basil and parsley.

FRENCH FRIED PUMPKIN RINGS

When removing the meat from the pumpkin, use a melon baller or butter curler to scoop out some strips. Dip in a Fritter Batter (p. 28), roll in cornmeal and deep fat fry. Lovely!

PUMPKIN COOKIES

Use the recipe for Nutrition Cookies (p. 262) substituting 1/2 cup processed pumpkin meat for the banana. Glaze with white icing and decorate with some candy corn.

MORE PUMPKIN FUN

Good conversation piece, good eating, good centerpiece.

Serves 10-12

Pre-heat oven to 375°

8	ounces cheddar cheese
1/2-1	stick butter
Meat from the pumpkin . . . 3-4 feeder tube size chunks	
3-4	zucchini
3-4	small white squash or crook-neck squash
1	onion
1	green pepper
2	large fresh tomatoes
2	T. tomato paste
1	tsp. salt
1/2	tsp. ground pepper
1	T. medium-hot piquant sauce (or Tabasco)
Basic Bread Crumb Topping (p. 7)	

Thin Serrated Slicing Disk, Medium Serrated Slicing Disk, Steel Blade, French Fryer

Remove the top and meat from the pumpkin.

Wash, but do not peel the squashes. Slice the zucchini with the medium serrated slicing disk, the crook-neck with the same disk and the pumpkin with the French fryer (cutting into chunks first). Use the thin serrated slicing disk for the onion and green pepper. Saute onion and pepper in butter, removing when onions are translucent. Saute the squash in batches very briefly.

Use the steel blade and grate the cheese with on/off's and remove. Use the French fryer again and cut the tomatoes in quarters to dice.

Rub the pumpkin shell with butter and layer squash, diced tomatoes, peppers, onions and grated cheese, in the pumpkin. Sprinkle layers with salt and ground pepper. Shake piquant sauce over the last layer and top with the Bread Crumb Mixture (p. 7).

Bake at 375° for about 15 minutes. Serve with great fanfare!

x2   PUMPKIN BARS

Orange, and pumpkin combine with a sugary-nut crust.

Pre-heat oven to 350°

1 1/2	sticks butter or margarine
1 3/4	cups flour, measure before sifting
1/2	cup powdered sugar
1/2	tsp. salt and cinnamon

Steel Blade

Combine the dry ingredients in the processor bowl and process with on/off's. Add butter or margarine, processing in.

Press into an 8 x 10 greased pan and bake about 20 minutes. Cool.

Filling:

1/2	cup cooked, processed pumpkin meat
1	3 ounce package cream cheese
1	cup sugar
1	T. molasses
3	T. orange juice concentrate
3	T. water
4	eggs
1/2	tsp. salt, nutmeg, and baking powder
1	tsp. vanilla
2	T. flour
2/3	cup dates, diced
1/2	cup sugar
1	cup pecans
1/2	tsp. cinnamon

Steel Blade

Put the dates in the processor bowl with 3 T. of the sugar and "dice" by processing with rapid on/off's. Remove. Add cream cheese, sugar and molasses, processing to cream. Add pumpkin, eggs, orange juice, water, and spices. Process to combine. Add dates and flour and process just enough to incorporate flour. Spread on top of baked crust.

Put the nuts, sugar and cinnamon in the bowl and process until chopped and combined. Sprinkle over the top of the batter and bake about 30 minutes, or until "set". Cut into bars.

More Family Fun . . .

> *". . . the history of civilization will always include*
> *. . . .man's efforts to beautify and otherwise en-*
> *hance the food he eats."*

Albert Stockli

There are millions of fun "finishing touches" the whole family can do . . . even pre-schoolers are a whiz at frosting grapes. Beat **1 T. white wine** with **1 egg white,** dip the **grapes,** and roll in **sugar.**

Get out the fancy cookie cutters and pastry shells. . .put the little people to work and you'll have lots of interesting shapes for sesame toast rounds or pastry tart shells.

Marzipan is another great project (p. 18).

Fill up several pastry tubes and cake decorators, set out an assortment of decorative tips and let some budding artist decorate pates, and cakes. Fish molds are great fun. . .all those scales to enhance. Olive eyes.

Give someone a presto glue stick, a twig, some clay, and some popcorn and you'll have dogwood trees for a centerpiece. Or try gumdrops. . .or frost the popcorn with food coloring and melted marshmallows. Pile after dinner mints around the base to hide the clay.

Let someone fix the lemons for the fish the way the fancy restaurants do it. Tie a half lemon in cheese cloth (to strain for the seeds) and tie with some string.

Place cards are always a challenge to an eager young artist. Get out the cookie cutters, process some play clay and you'll have some unique placecards.

Make up some sculpture dough. . .someone can make little baskets for nuts or mints or a large basket for the rolls. Bake until browned as with the play clay, then varnish or paint.

x2 PLAY CLAY

2 1/4	cups flour
1/2	cup salt
1	cup water
1	T. oil (warm)

Steel Blade

Put everything but the water into the processor bowl using the steel blade. Process 5-10 seconds. With the machine running, add the water gradually through the feeder tube. Chill the clay 30 minutes before rolling out. You may bake the creations in a 300° oven, removing when they are lightly browned.

x2 SCULPTURE DOUGH

2	cups flour
1/2	cup salt
3/4	cups water
1	T. sugar

Shortening for the molds

Steel Blade

Put everything but the water in the processor bowl using the steel blade, process 5-10 seconds. With the machine running add the water through the feeder tube gradually. Chill before using.

Note: Use an oiled bowl to form a large basket.

Be sure to invite your helpers to share all the kitchen efforts or you might hear them exclaim as they vanish from sight;

> *Hey Mom — it was fun*
> *decorating the cakes and the fishes*
> *But now that we're done*
> *—you do the dishes!*

Flavorings

Greet each day as a new adventure . . . and be

adventuresome with herbs, spices and new flavors.

STOCKS

The preparation of homemade stocks is a natural result of being a food processor owner. First, you'll be grinding all your own hamburger . . . for economy as well as taste, and you'll be using far more fresh foods. The result; lots of bones, trimmings, celery tops . . . even some round ends you cut off of vegetables to get a neater slice. Homemade stocks are the key ingredient to fine sauces . . . acquire a large stockpot and develop a habit of tossing the bones in. Remember to skim off the fat from time to time. When you have time, reduce the stock to make Meat Extract or Demi-Glace (p. 63). Stocks freeze well and will add so much to all your cooking. The following is just a guide to get you started. If you really get into making stock, there are excellent chapters in many books that will elaborate on the subject.

Bones, meat scraps (chicken, beef, veal)
Bouquet Garni (bay leaf, thyme and parsley)
Turnips
Onion pieces
Leeks
Carrots
Celery tops
Mushrooms
A few whole cloves (stick in the onions)
Peppercorns
Salt
Water

Steel Blade

Brown the meat scraps, meat and bones in hot fat. Cover with plenty of water (adjust to the amount of meat and bones). Add vegetables, seasonings and bring to a boil. If you are using whole vegetables, rather than leftovers, dice them first with the steel blade.

Simmer 2-3 hours, skimming fat. Strain and chill. If you used a considerable amount of meat, take it off the bone and use for stew or barbeque beef. Remove hard fat after chilling and store in the refrigerator or freeze.

Note: Water, leftover from cooking shrimp, (providing you don't drowned them) makes excellent fish stock. Reduce it by boiling 5-10 minutes. After cleaning the shrimp, return the shells to the stock while it boils. Use fish stock to make White Sauce or as a fish soup base.

MARINADE FOR BEEF

Marinating meat has two purposes:
1. to tenderize the meat 2. to inject flavor

1	onion
3	celery stalks (including tops)
1	carrot
1	tsp. thyme and sage
1	cup beef stock
2	bay leaves
1 1/2	tsp. allspice
1/4	cup brandy
1/4	cup vermouth
1/2	cup Clarified Butter (p. 2)
1	tsp. peppercorns

Steel Blade

Put the onion (cut in quarters), the carrot, celery (cut in chunks) and seasonings in the processor bowl and process 5-10 seconds. Add to the brandy, vermouth and beef stock. Transfer to a shallow pan, combine with the Clarified Butter and cover the meat.

Since meat marinates a minimum of 24 hours, some of the juices seep into the Marinade, so rather than discard the Marinade, I use it as a base for "Brown Sauce" . . . the recipe follows the marinating instructions. This is the reason for using Clarified Butter rather than salad oil. (See page 64.)

To make a beef stock: brown beef, veal, a few onions and carrots, fat, bones, etc. in a roaster pan, adding some parsley, thyme and bay leaf, and 2-3 quarts water. Cover with foil and bake or simmer at low heat 3-4 hours. Strain, keeping fat as a base in brown sauce. Use the broth as liquid for sauces, gravies or "au jus" . . . it may be frozen . . . it will be a jelly consistency. To make a "demi-glace" heat together 1 T. each fat, tomato paste, and flour adding 4 cups of the beef stock, stirring until to a boil, then simmering about 2 hours. Skim off the fat. Keep refrigerated. Use to flavor Bearnaise or other sauces.

Note: If you're counting calories use 1/4 the amount of butter and more beef stock.

MARINADE BROWN SAUCE

The Marinade

1	T. meat flavoring*
1	cup beef broth
1	cup red wine (or Madeira)
2	T. arrowroot
3	T. currant jelly

Steel Blade

After removing the meat, add 1 cup beef broth to the Marinade and bring to a boil simmering 15-20 minutes. Skim fat. Strain, adding 1 T. meat flavoring, red wine or Madeira and 3 T. currant jelly. Bring to a boil again. Remove 1/2 cup adding 1 T. arrowroot, returning to sauce, stirring until thickened. If you prefer a thinner sauce add more stock, or if thicker, add 1/2 T. more arrowroot.

*Use Demi-Glace (p. 63) or 1/2 T. Meat Extract (below).

MEAT EXTRACT

**Meat Bones, meat scraps from preparing beef broth,
or any other scraps from beef or poultry**

2	carrots
1/2	onion
2-3	sprigs parsley
1/2	tsp. thyme
1/2	tsp. salt and pepper

Steel Blade

Whenever you cut the meat from any bone, or have bones, fat and meat leftover from a roast or a doggie bag, simmer, covered with plenty of water along with any remnants of what you may have already used for a beef stock (p. 63, see comment). Add seasonings, vegetables, with enough water to cover. When most of the water has simmered away trim the meat away from the bone, discard the bone and strain the remaining liquid into another saucepan. Reduce until thick and dark. Keep refrigerated and use whenever beef or meat extract is called for. Good project for a cold rainy day.

x2   LIVER PATE

I have found so many uses for this "basic" pate I almost always have it around. Make this when you have livers and keep in the freezer or refrigerator for use in gravies, canapes, and other pates.

1	lb. chicken, pork, or turkey livers
2	shallots
1	stick butter
2	T. bacon drippings
1/4	cup brandy
1/2	tsp. salt
1/8	tsp. allspice
1/3	cup heavy cream

Steel Blade

Saute the livers in bacon drippings. Put in the processor with shallots, seasonings and cream. Process until smooth. Melt butter and add with brandy through the feeder tube. Pack into a storage container or into nice mold to serve with crackers as an appetizer.

x2   DUXELLES

Whenever mushrooms are plentiful, make up several batches. Great flavor ingredient.

1/2	lb. mushrooms
1	shallot
1	T. butter
2	tsp. oil
1/4	tsp. salt and pepper

Steel Blade

Clean mushrooms with a damp towel and place in the work bowl. Process until finely minced. This will be better if you do not wash the mushrooms--takes a little more time but a better flavor will be your reward. Just wipe dirt off with a damp cloth.

Put them in a towel and squeeze out all the moisture. Heat butter and oil and saute the mixture with the shallots until all the liquid has evaporated. Freeze until using.

A pound is a small thing
When elephants are weighed
A quart is a mere drop
When oceans are surveyed,
But may lightening strike
And very soon
The cook who measures herbs
By tablespoon

Hemlock Hill Herbel

A word about Herbs and Spices . . .

With discretion, this is one area of imaginative fun. Appetizers come alive with herb butters and spices, and can be highly seasoned. If you are unsure what to season with what, check out the labels on the spice bottles and then experiment.

Spices, herbs and seasonings without doubt provide
the best single way to attain distinctiveness and variety
in taste appeal.

Jean N. Lesparre

HERB BUTTERS

If you use fresh herbs and spices double the amount in a recipe calling for dried. Freshness does enhance the flavor -- just remember the idea is to enhance the food, not obliterate it. If you plan to spread canapes ahead use unsalted butter, this will prevent the bread from getting soggy.

In herb butters process the flavor ingredient first, using the steel blade and then add the butter, cut in several pieces.

x2   STEAK BUTTER

1   stick butter
1   T. fresh minced parsley
1   fresh shallot
Dash Worcestershire

Steel Blade

Process the flavorings, then add the butter, cut in pieces.

x2   BEARNAISE BUTTER

1   stick unsalted butter
1   tsp. tarragon
1   shallot (minced)
1   T. red wine
1   egg yolk
1/2   tsp. salt

Steel Blade

Process butter smooth. Boil tarragon and minced shallot 1 minute. Add to butter with salt and egg yolk, processing smooth.

x2   HORSERADISH BUTTER

1   T. bottled horseradish
1/2   tsp. lemon juice
1/2   tsp. dried mustard
1   stick unsalted butter

Steel Blade

Process the flavorings, then add the butter, cut in pieces.

x2   MINT BUTTER

1   T. mint jelly
1   tsp. vinegar
1   stick butter
Several fresh mint sprigs (if available)

Steel Blade

Melt the jelly with the vinegar and process 5-10 seconds with mint sprigs and butter, cut in pieces.

Use on vegetables.

SEASONINGS

Here are some seasoning combinations that are useful to have prepared ahead. You'll save time by having them at your fingertips and money by avoiding the expensive mixes at the store.

SEASONING SALT

6	T. sea salt
1	tsp. dried parsley
1	tsp. onion and garlic powder
2	tsp. paprika (Hungarian sweet)
1	tsp. dry mustard
1/4	tsp. marjoram
1	tsp. celery salt

Steel Blade

Put them all in the work bowl using the steel blade and process until combined. The processor will handle triple amounts.

SAUSAGE SPICES

2	tsp. allspice
1/2	tsp. red pepper flakes
1	tsp. freeze dried shallot
1/2	tsp. marjoram and cloves
2	tsp. tarragon
1	tsp. nutmeg and corriander
1/2	tsp. freshly ground pepper

Steel Blade

Put them all in the work bowl, using the steel blade and process until combined. This amount will season 2-3 pounds meat. I would suggest making this in larger quantities, then using 2-3 T. to season 2 pounds of meat. Increase or decrease spices to your personal preference.

Recipes

*Sharing meals. . . .is. . . .one of the most beauti-
ful and loving aspects of family life. . . There
are few childhood pleasures more glowing and
more lasting than the memories of family,
festive dinners: . . .the tantalizing, never to be
forgotten smells and delicious sounds coming
from the kitchen; the laughter and happiness
of a family gathering; . . . the sheer enjoyment
of favorite, long awaited foods.*

Albert Stockli

Breakfast

x2   CORNED BEEF HASH

Serves 4

Pre-heat oven to 350°

(About) 2 cups corned beef
2   potatoes
1/2   onion
1/8   tsp. salt
Cream
Additional seasoning to taste

Steel Blade, French Fryer, Plastic Knife

Put the corned beef in the processor bowl and process to mince by running machine. Use the pulse or on/off's to keep coarse texture control.

Change to the French fryer and cut the potatoes into chunks. Process in. Repeat, processing the onion in the same way. Use the plastic knife (it does not need to lock into place) to combine mixture with seasonings, adding enough cream to hold it together. Transfer to an 8 inch square pan.

Bake at 350° 1 hour. Serve with poached eggs and a chili-style sauce. Or, top with a bread crumb and cheese topping and brown under the broiler for a few minutes.

x2   CREATING HASH WITH LEFTOVERS

Serves 6-8

Pre-heat oven to 350°

2-3   cups leftover chunks of beef, sausage, turkey or veal
2-3   potatoes, cooked
1   carrot
1/2   of an onion
1/2   of a green pepper
Leftover chunks of squash, cabbage or other firm vegetable
1   apple
1   garlic clove
Butter
Salt, pepper to taste
1/2   tsp. nutmeg

Steel Blade, French Fryer, Plastic Knife

Mince garlic (steel blade).

Use the French fryer to dice the onion and pepper. Cut in chunks and process through. Remove and saute in butter.

Use the steel blade to dice leftover meats, carrot and apple using on/off's (or pulse). Depending on how much meat you have, you will need to do this in at least two batches, removing to a larger bowl for final mixing. After the last batch, change to the French fryer (leaving the meat and vegetables in the bowl) and dice in the leftover vegetables. Combine everything together (adding onions and peppers) in a large bowl. Season to taste and bake 25 minutes at 350°. Serve with poached eggs and a chili-style sauce.

dlc-7 When using the DLC-7 you may complete this in one bowl. The meat may be ground at one time and left in the bowl. Dice in the vegetables, then change to the plastic knife to mix everything together.

Breakfast, encouraged by educators, promoted by nutritionists, has been called everything from the "supreme good-humorer," to a "cause celebre" to the most important meal of your day.

x2 CHERRY-ORANGE COFFEE CAKE

Use this method to apply to all your favorite yeast breads.

Peelings from an orange
1	T. sugar
1	package dry active yeast
1	tsp. sugar
1/4	cup warm water

Juice from an orange plus enough milk to make 1 cup
1	egg
4	T. butter
1/2	tsp. salt
3	cups (about) all purpose flour
8	maraschino cherries
10	pitted dates
1/4	cup white raisins

Steel Blade

"Plump" raisins in a fruit liqueur or hot water reserving drained liqueur to add to glaze. Drain cherries.

Combine the yeast, 1 tsp. sugar and 1/4 cup water . . . let sit about 10 minutes to "foam".

Put the pitted dates, cherries and 1 T. sugar in the processor bowl and process with on/off's to dice. Remove and dust with flour (to prevent sinking to the bottom when baking).

Put 2 1/2 cups flour in the processor bowl (steel blade) and process with on/off's to cut in the butter. Add yeast mixture, egg, plus juice and milk combination (which should be lukewarm or at 110°), processing to make a batter. Add the remaining flour in small amounts until you have a soft dough that gathers up in a ball around the blades. Run the machine to knead about 20-30 seconds. Leave in the bowl, cover with a damp cloth and let rise in a warm place (80° is ideal) until doubled. (1-1 1/2 hours)

Place the bowl back on the base (hold the blade down as you put it on the machine, and add fruits and raisins, drained well). Process in with on/off's . . . remove dough from the bowl and onto a lightly floured board. Punch down and shape into an oval. Put in a loaf pan (or in a round pan) let rise until almost doubled.

Bake at 400° about 35-40 minutes. Cool slightly and drizzle with powdered sugar processed with the warm, drained liqueur until a glaze consistency. Decorate with slivered almonds, cherries or candied fruit.

Try using this as a guide, adding fresh seasonal fruits and inventing a sauce.

Serves 8

8 slices thick French bread
French Toast Batter (p. 27)
1 chunk leftover ham or firm sausage
Clarified Butter (p. 2)

Sauce:

1	3 ounce package cream cheese
1	cantaloupe melon, seeds removed
1	peach or apple
1	cup milk
1	T. lemon juice
2	T. flour
1/2	tsp. salt

Cinnamon sugar

Steel Blade, Thin Serrated Slicing Disk

Prepare the French toast batter in the processor and set aside.

Put the ham in the feeder tube (slicing disk) and push through. Dip the bread into the batter and saute in Clarified Butter on both sides. Divide thinly sliced ham on top.

Warm the milk. Put the melon (removing the meat from the skin and cutting in several chunks) cream cheese, flour, lemon juice, salt and a dash of pepper in the processor bowl and process until smooth. Add the milk slowly with the machine running, and transfer to a saucepan to thicken.

Core the apple or peach, and using the slicing disk, slice it thinly. Add to the sauce. Pour over the toast, and sprinkle with cinnamon sugar.

x2   FRUIT QUICHE

Pre-heat oven to 375°

1	recipe Basic Pastry (p. 9)
1	3 ounce package cream cheese
1	apple
1/2	cup pineapple chunks (canned)
1/4	cup coconut milk (optional)
2	cups milk
1/4	cup apple brandy
4	eggs
4	ounces cheddar cheese (cut in chunks)
1/2	tsp. salt and pepper
1/4	tsp. nutmeg
1/2	stick butter, flaked

Steel Blade

Roll out the pastry and line a 10" pie pan or quiche pan. Prick the bottom. Pre-bake 10-15 minutes (nicely browned) at 375°.

Grate the cheese with the steel blade. Remove. Put the pineapple and cream cheese in the processor bowl and process until smoothly combined, about 20 seconds. Put on the bottom of the pie shell. Cover with half of the cheddar cheese.

Core the apple, cut it in chunks and put it in the processor bowl, and process until chopped. Put on top of the cheese, then add the rest of the cheese.

Put the eggs, milks, brandy, and seasonings in the processor bowl and combine. Pour over the fruit and cheese, dot with the flaked butter and bake 35-40 minutes, or until the pie is set.

dlc-7 When doubling this recipe you will have enough pastry and filling for 2 pies.

ALMOND FRENCH TOAST

Serves 4-6

Batter:

4	eggs
1/2	cup milk
1/2	tsp. vanilla extract
1	T. Amaretto liqueur

White bread sliced very thin (or) oval Pain de Mie toasts,
     sliced very thin

4	ounces cream cheese
2	T. Almond Paste (p. 17)
1	stick butter plus oil
	(or Clarified Butter, p. 2)

Fresh strawberries, kiwifruit, peaches, raspberries or blueberries

Brandy Sauce:

6	ounces peach or orange marmalade
3	T. unsalted butter
2	T. fruit flavored liqueur or brandy
1/8	tsp. vanilla

Steel Blade, Medium Serrated Slicing Disk

Combine cream cheese and Almond Paste (see p. 17) using the steel blade and spread on one piece of thin bread. Use another piece to make a "sandwich" adjusting amount of filling and batter to the amount of toast you plan to make. Dip the sandwiches into the batter and saute in hot butter and oil (or Clarified Butter). Remove and keep warm.

Prepare sauce by processing marmalade with butter, liqueur and vanilla, then bringing to a boil. Slice the kiwifruit or strawberries with the medium serrated slicer and arrange decoratively with the toast. Serve with warm Brandy Sauce. Makes a dynamite brunch.

*All happiness depends on a
leisurely breakfast.*

John Gunther

x2   BREAKFAST SOUFFLE

There are endless varieties and possible combinations — and the great advantage of advance preparation.

Pre-heat oven to 350°

Serves 8

12	slices of firm bread
6	ounces Gruyere or Swiss cheese
1	pound Canadian bacon
Hollandaise Butter (p. 40)	
4	eggs
3	cups milk
1	tsp. salt
1/2	tsp. pepper
1/4	tsp. nutmeg
6-8	thin butter slices

Steel Blade, Slicing Disk

Cut the Canadian bacon so it will fit into the feeder tube and slice thinly. Repeat with the cheese. Butter a 9 by 13 pyrex dish.

Soften the Hollandaise Butter and butter 6 slices of the bread, removing the crusts, and line the bottom of the dish. Layer half the Canadian bacon on top, then half the cheese. Repeat, ending with the second layer of buttered bread on top. Increase eggs and/or cheese for a firmer souffle.

Put the eggs and seasonings in the processor bowl, using the steel blade, and process to combine. Add 1 cup milk through the feeder tube and process to combine, then add the contents of the bowl to the rest of the milk in another container and pour over the bread. You need to be flexible in liquid amounts depending on the size of the dish you use. Let it rest overnight or at least 3-4 hours. Bake in pre-heated oven 45 minutes or until browned. Serve with fresh fruit.

Variations: Try topping with thinly sliced tomatoes. Add different meats (great for leftovers), vegetables or fruits . . . serve for lunch or dinner.

dlc-7 When using the DLC-7, the eggs and milk may be combined in one bowl without spilling down the center.

FIESTA EGG SCRAMBLE

A variation on an omelet . . . Southwest style. You may omit the hot peppers or double them, depending on your palate.

"One man's food is another man's poison."

French Proverb

Serves 6

1	bag tortilla chips (or) corn tortillas cut into quarters and fried crisp
8-10	eggs
2	large tomatoes
1	green tomato (if available, a tomatillo)
3	green onions
1/2	of a green pepper
1	small hot pepper (optional)
1/4	cup green chilies
4	ounces Monterey Jack or enchilada style cheese
3	T. butter plus 2 T. very cold butter
1	cup sour cream

Steel Blade, French Fryer, Shredding Disk (or Julienne Blade)

Use individual au gratin dishes or one large oven proof platter. Layer the chips in buttered platter or dishes. Reserve about 8 for the topping.

Use the steel blade with on/off's to dice chilies and hot peppers . . . add a dash of lemon juice. Use the French fryer and put onions and green pepper through the feeder tube. Remove and saute in 1 T. butter until limp.

Beat the eggs (steel blade) and scramble in 3 T. butter until almost done . . . remove and divide on top of tortilla chips. They should be soft and a bit runny.

Put the cheese in the bowl (dry) with reserved chips and 2 T. very cold butter and combine with on/off's until a coarse crumbly texture.

Mound diced vegetable mixture on top of the eggs. Cut the tomatoes in quarters and dice using the French fryer. Spoon on top of vegetables. Put a generous scoop of sour cream on top of the tomatoes and sprinkle with cheese gratin mixture. Bake in a 475° oven 5-8 minutes, then brown under the broiler briefly.

If you have some jalapeno jelly, serve a little on the side.

HAPPY EASTER BREAKFAST

The egg has been an ancient symbol of re-birth in the spring; and as Christianity grew it became the symbol of "new life". Hence, the origin of the custom of giving Easter eggs .

For 4

Pre-heat oven to 350°

1	can Chow Mein noodles
8	hard boiled eggs
1	cup ham (or any smoked meat)
1	tsp. prepared mustard
1	T. mayonnaise
1/2	green pepper
1	honeydew melon
1	cup Basic White Sauce (p. 36)
4	ounces Swiss cheese, cut in chunks

Several sprigs parsley (mince . . . steel blade)
Salt and pepper
1/4   tsp. nutmeg

Steel Blade

Cut the eggs in half, and with the melon ball tool, scoop out a couple of "eggs" from the whites. Then scoop melon balls out of the melon. Put the yolks in the processor bowl with the ham, mustard, green pepper, and mayonnaise and process until combined. Remove from the bowl and form into little egg shaped balls. Put in a buttered casserole with the whites and cover.

Heat 10 minutes, while you make the sauce.

Put the cheese, butter, flour, and seasonings (for the White Sauce) in the processor bowl while you warm the milk. Process until smooth and with machine running, add the warm milk through the feeder tube. Transfer to a saucepan on the stove and thicken over medium heat.

Make "nests" with the noodles, put the egg and ham "eggs" in the nest with the melon balls, and pass the sauce.

CREAMED EGGS

This is something you can make after the Easter Egg Hunt.

Serves 6

Pre-heat oven to 350°

3	English muffins, split
Butter for the muffins	
6	hard boiled eggs
1	T. cream
1	7 ounce can shrimp or salmon, drained
1	tsp. freeze dried chives
1/4	cup Duxelles (p. 65)
1	cup Basic White Sauce (p. 36)
2	T. sherry wine
1/4	tsp. each parsley and dill
6	slices fresh tomato

Steel Blade

Cut the eggs in half. Put the seafood, boned and drained, in the processor bowl with the steel blade and process with the cream, chives, Duxelles, and the yolks of the eggs.

Pack this mixture into the whites. Butter and toast the muffins. Put a tomato slice on each one, then 2 egg halves, cover, and heat for 10 minutes in a 350° oven.

Make the White Sauce, adding the seasonings to the flour and butter, and stirring the sherry in last.

Pour over the top of the eggs when serving.

> *"Life. . .has few pleasanter prospects than a neatly arranged and well-provisioned breakfast table."*
>
> Nathaniel Hawthorne

SAUSAGE

This is a guide rather than an exact recipe. . .you will find your own happy medium with the spices adding or deleting some. Or try the mixture on p. 68. Try different combinations of meats . . . the joy of making your own sausage is in doing it your way . . . adjusting the fat content and seasoning to your taste.

Serves 6-8

2	pounds of raw meat

Turkey, pork, veal, beef, smoked meats

1/2	pound of pork fat or bacon
1	clove garlic
2	shallots
1	T. freshly minced parsley
1-2	tsp. allspice
1	tsp. pepper
1/2	tsp. red pepper flakes
1/2	tsp. salt
1/2	tsp. cloves, corriander, chili powder, thyme
1	tsp. tarragon

Steel Blade

Be sure to remove all the gristle or sinew from the meat. Cut into chunks and do half at a time. You may add all the seasonings with one batch, then just combine in another bowl. Process with the on/off method until the consistency you like.

Shape into patties and either fry in a little hot oil or bake at 400° for 20 minutes. You may need to bake pork 10 minutes longer.

dlc-7 The DLC-7 will grind approximately 1 1/4 pounds of meat at a time.

When processing sausage . . . or grinding any meat . . . use an on/off method or the pulse if you have a machine with a pulse. It takes about 4-6 "on/off's" or "pulse" cycles. Many of the processors on the market do not grind raw meats . . . this is one of the jobs that will stress a less powerful motor.

x2 BREAKFAST SAUSAGE

1/2   pound each pork and beef
1/2   tsp. each allspice, cloves, salt, pepper, and cinnamon
1   apple, cored
1/2   cup dry oatmeal (cook in the reserved meat broth)

Steel Blade

Simmer the meats in enough water to cover them. Remove, cool and discard the bones. Put them in the processor bowl and process with the spices and apple until ground.

Measure the broth, using 1 cup, and cook the oatmeal in the beef broth. Add water if needed to make one cup. Add by spoonfuls to the mixture in the processor bowl, processing a few seconds at a time, checking the consistency . . . it should be just stiffened.

Butter and roll the mixture in wax paper and refrigerate overnight. Slice and fry in clarified butter for breakfast.

I always say a half-breakfasted man is no good

Galsworthy

x2 BREAKFAST IN A GLASS

1   orange
1   banana
1   tsp. vanilla
1   cup yogurt
2   tsp. sugar
1/8   tsp. cinnamon

Steel Blade

Peel the orange and remove as much membrane as you can easily. Put it in the processor bowl and process to a pulp using the steel blade. Add the banana, cut in several pieces, vanilla, sugar, cinnamon, and yogurt. Process until smooth.

Nutritious!

FRESH PINEAPPLE BREAKFAST PARFAIT

Breakfast makes a good memory

Rabelais

For 6

1	whole fresh pineapple (pieces to fit the feeder tube)
1	fresh orange
1	T. orange juice concentrate
Some of the peelings from the orange	
1	quart ice cream (vanilla or fresh coconut)
3	gingersnaps or macaroon cookies
1 1/2	cups Natural Cereal (p. 3)

Steel Blade, Medium Serrated Slicing Disk

Peel and core the pineapple. If you feel "fancy", save the hollowed out halves and serve the parfait from them.

Slice the pineapple using the medium serrated slicing disk and drain off juice. Dry out the bowl and process the orange peelings with a couple tablespoons of sugar and run the machine to mince. Add sections from the orange and orange juice concentrate. Run machine to puree. Add ice cream (in scoops) through the feeder tube. Remove.

Put the cookies, in pieces, in the bowl and process with on/off's to crush. Add cereal and combine with on/off's. Alternate ice cream, pineapple slices and crunchy mixture in parfait glasses or in the hollowed out shell. Top with fresh grated coconut . . . great way to wake up!

x2 ABC COFFEE CAKE

Pre-heat oven to 375°

Buttermilk, cherries and almonds combine with hot cereal for a moist and tender coffee cake.

1	cup cake flour	1/4	cup each white and
1/2	cup Malt o' Meal (dry)		brown sugar
3	tsp. baking powder	2/3	cups almonds
1	egg	1	tsp. cinnamon
2/3	cups buttermilk	3	T. butter
1	tsp. vanilla	8-10	maraschino cherries
1/2	cup sugar	Optional: 1 ounce semi-sweet
1/2	stick margarine		chocolate

Steel Blade, Julienne Blade

Butter an 8 inch square dish. Combine the flour, cereal, baking powder with the steel blade and process once . . . remove. Put the butter and sugar in the bowl and run the machine to cream. Add egg and buttermilk, processing in, then vanilla and dry ingredients. Process once or twice, on/off's, just enough to incorporate flour. Pour half into the greased dish.

In a dry bowl combine sugars, almonds, cinnamon and butter chunks. Process with on/off's to a crumbly texture. Remove half for the topping. Add drained cherries and process in with on/off's. Sprinkle over batter and pour remaining batter on top. Sprinkle the rest of the nut-sugar mixture on top. Grate chocolate with julienne blade and sprinkle over the top of the nuts and sugar. Bake at 375° about 25 minutes.

dlc-7 If using the DLC-7, bake in a round, tube pan.

A good beginning makes a good ending

14th Century

x2 FRUITS AND DATES AND NUTS
COFFEE CAKE

Pre-heat oven to 350°

1	stick plus 2 T. butter	1	large apple
2	cups all purpose flour	10	pitted dates
1/4	cup untoasted wheat germ	1/2	cup raisins
2	tsp. baking powder	1/2	cup nuts (whole)
1	tsp. baking soda		
1/4	tsp. each cinnamon and nutmeg	Lemon juice from one
1/3	cup each white and firmly		small lemon
	packed brown sugar	1/2	cup powdered sugar
1	T. molasses or honey		
1	egg		
1	cup buttermilk		

Steel Blade, Shredding Disk

Put the flour, spices, baking powder, baking soda, sugars, wheat germ and butter (in chunks) in the processor bowl and process on/off until in coarse crumbs. Remove 3/4 cup for topping.

Add honey or molasses to the bowl plus egg, buttermilk and process with a few on/off's. Butter a 9 by 12 pan and pour the batter in.

Put the dates and nuts in the bowl (be sure to wipe the bowl dry first) and "dice" using on/off's, then running machine a few seconds until desired consistency. Add apple, cored and cut in several pieces, and raisins. Process with on/off's to chop. Put on top of the batter with reserved crumb mixture on top.

Bake at 350° for 35-40 minutes or until toothpick comes out clean. Cool 5 minutes.

Put lemon juice and powdered sugar in the bowl (steel blade) and process smooth. Drizzle on top of warm cake.

Alternate Method: If you wish the dates and nuts very fine, use either the julienne or shredding disk and load the feeder tube alternately with dates and nuts. Push through with light pressure using a "bounce" with the pusher to free up any sticky dates.

dlc-7 If using the DLC-7, bake in a large sheet cake pan, deep sided jelly roll pan, or 2 9x12 pans.

x2 OLD FASHIONED BUTTERMILK BISCUITS

Pre-heat oven to 450°

2	cups all purpose flour
1	T. baking powder (heaping)
1	tsp. sugar
1	tsp. salt
1/3	cup Crisco

About 2/3 cups warm buttermilk

Steel Blade

Put the flour, salt and baking powder in the bowl with the steel blade. Add Crisco in spoonfuls and process with quick on/off's to combine . . . do not just run machine . . . you want a "crumbly" mixture. Let buttermilk come to room temperature or warm just enough to remove the chill. Add in 1/3 cupfuls, processing with an on/off after each addition. You want enough for a soft, puffy dough. Remove dough to a floured surface and let sit 10-15 minutes. Roll out 1/2 inch thick and cut into rounds with a biscuit cutter. Place on an ungreased baking sheet and bake at 450° for 12 minutes.

Makes about 18-20.

We may live without friends;
we may live without books;
But civilized man cannot live without cooks

Edward G. Bulwelytoon

x2 SAUSAGE POPOVERS

Not an original inspiration as it was suggested to me by an English friend who told me this was the custom in England during the war.

Pre-heat oven to 450°

2	cups flour
1/2	tsp. salt
2	tsp. sugar
2	T. melted butter
2	cups milk
3	eggs

A small amount of leftover sausage

Steel Blade

Put all the ingredients except the sausage in the work bowl and using the steel blade process until well-combined. Let the batter rest.

Grease muffin tins generously with clarified butter and pre-heat in the oven about 5 minutes. Fill them half full, with a little piece of sausage in the bottom.

Bake at 450° for 20 minutes. Turn the oven down to 375° and bake 15 minutes longer.

Note: Fill all those little holes with jams and jellies.

All batters of this type perform beautifully if let rest at room temperature at least one hour.

TOMATOES HOLLANDAISE

For 4

4	tomatoes
1	bunch fresh asparagus (or)
1	package frozen asparagus (tough ends removed)
1/2	Basic White Sauce (p. 36)
2	green onions
1	cup ham
4	eggs
1	recipe Hollandaise Sauce (p. 40)

Steel Blade

Core the tomatoes and scoop out the pulp. Turn them upside down to drain out all the juice. Cut the tips off the asparagus, boiling them until they are just tender. Continue to boil the stems, they will take longer.

Using the steel blade, process the ham by turning the machine on and off rapidly until coarsely chopped. Remove.

Prepare the White Sauce. Remove 1/2 cup to a saucepan. Put the stems of the asparagus in the processor bowl with the onions and process until pureed. Add to the White Sauce, stirring over a medium heat until thick. (This may be done the night before.) Season to taste.

Put the warmed cream mixture in the bottom of the tomato. Next divide the ham among the 4 tomatoes, on top of the creamed mixture. Break an egg into the top (have it at room temperature) and bake at 400° about 15 minutes or until egg is done.

Prepare the Hollandaise and pour over the top of the tomato to serve. Garnish with warmed asparagus tips.

Note: Try with a cheese-bread crumb topping (p. 7).

Serve with some fresh yeast rolls (prepared the night before) and you'll have a great start for the day.

x2   PEANUT BUTTER AND JELLY MUFFINS

Pre-heat oven to 400°

1 1/2	cups flour
1	tsp. baking powder
3	tsp. baking soda
2	eggs
3/4	cups buttermilk
2	T. oil
2/3	cup peanuts
2	T. sugar
1/2	tsp. salt
1/2	of an apple (or 1/2 cup canned pineapple)

Assorted jellies

Steel Blade

Put the fruit and peanuts in the processor bowl and process to chop (a few seconds). Add the eggs, sugar and oil processing until light and fluffy. Add the buttermilk, process to incorporate.

Add the dry ingredients directly into the bowl and process on/off several times just enough so that the flour disappears.

Butter muffin tins (or use the paper baking cups) and fill them 1/3 full. Spoon a teaspoon of jelly on top (vary the kind. . .some grape jelly, some marmalades) and then more muffin batter.

Bake 12-15 minutes at 400°.

No man in the world has more courage than the man who can stop eating after one peanut.

C. Pollock

x2 QUICK DOUGHNUTS

Re-discover doughnuts!   These are quick and easy, needing only a short resting period before frying. . .try cutting the doughnuts out with deep sided cookie cutters and experiment with different toppings.

1	T. shortening
1/3	cup sugar
2	eggs
1/2	tsp. salt
1 2/3	cup flour
3	tsp. baking powder
1	tsp. vanilla
1/3	cup buttermilk

Steel Blade

Put everything but the buttermilk in the processor bowl and combine by turning the machine on and off several times. Pour the buttermilk in the bowl and process just enough to incorporate. Be careful not to over-process. Let rest 30 minutes at room temperature.

Heat the oil. Pat the dough out gently on a floured surface about 5/8" thick and cut out shapes, frying them in hot oil (30-40 seconds each side). Dunk in glaze or sprinkle with a favorite topping.

Topping Suggestions:

1. Powdered sugar
2. Cinnamon sugar
3. Glaze (p. 47)

This is a soft dough . . . better to work in additional flour (just enough so you can work with it) by hand when it is on a floured surface.

A giraffe must get up at 6 in the morning if it wants to have breakfast in its stomach by nine.

Samuel Butler

DUTCH ALMOND CAKE

For a very special occasion.

Pre-heat oven to 425°

1	recipe Mock Puff Pastry (p. 11)

Italian Creme (p. 21)

Streusel Topping:

1/3	cup flour
1/2	cup sugar
1	stick butter (in chunks)
1/2	cup almonds

Steel Blade

Roll out the pastry on a floured board and fit into a 9 by 13 pyrex dish.

Spread with the Italian Creme (using half the basic recipe).

Put the ingredients for the streusel mixture in the processor bowl and process until in coarse crumbs. Spread on top of the creme.

Bake in a 425° oven, for 20-24 minutes. The top tends to brown rapidly; plan to cover it with foil when it is lightly browned.

Cool before cutting as it needs a little time to set.

He who works with butter gets sticky fingers.

French Proverb

Make your own sweet butter . . . process whipping cream with the plastic knife until it separates and starts looking like butter pieces. Add 1 tablespoon crushed ice, process again, then drain off the liquid and pack into ceramic container (or crock) and chill.

x2 SOUR CREAM COFFEE CAKE

Pre-heat oven to 350°

2	cups all purpose flour
1 1/2	tsp. baking powder
1/2	tsp. salt
2	sticks unsalted butter
1 1/2	cups sugar
2	eggs
1	cup sour cream
1	tsp. vanilla

Topping:

1	tsp. cinnamon
4	T. brown sugar
1 1/2	cups whole pecans

Steel Blade

Butter an angel food tube pan and dust with flour.

Use the steel blade to combine topping ingredients, processing until very fine. Remove. Use the steel blade again to sift flour, baking powder and salt (on/off's). Remove.

Run the machine adding butter through the feeder tube in chunks. When all the butter is creamed pour in sugar. You may need to scrape down the sides of the bowl or use some on/off's to break things up a bit. Add eggs, processing in well, then vanilla and sour cream combining with a few on/off's. Add flour mixture and process with a few quick on/off's . . . just enough to let flour disappear. Pour half the mixture into a tube pan and sprinkle with half the topping mixture. Pour in the rest of the batter, and add remaining topping.

Bake at 350° about 60 minutes. Cool before cutting.

Definition of unsalted butter: "Over-processed whipping cream"

x2 QUICK BREAKFAST ROLLS

2 1/2   cups flour (all purpose)
1/2   tsp. salt
2   tsp. sugar
1   envelope dry active yeast
4   T. butter
1/2-1   cup milk (120°)

Steel Blade

Use a yeast thermometer to be sure the liquid is not too hot (result . . . dead yeast) or too cold (result . . . inactive yeast). Put the dry ingredients in the processor bowl and add butter, in chunks, processing with on/off's to combine well. Add the milk through the feeder tube (machine running) and stop when you have a soft ball of dough forming around the blades. If you add too much milk, sift in a little additional flour. Run the machine just a few seconds so the dough is smooth and elastic. It requires very little kneading.

Place the dough in an oiled bowl and cover with a towel. For quick rising place in the oven (turned off) and put a bowl of hot water under it (on the lower rack). It will rise quickly (15-20 minutes). Punch down and roll out on a floured surface.

Make cinnamon rolls by rolling in a rectangle, folding in thirds, rolling out again and spreading with a little soft butter, cinnamon sugar and plumped raisins. Then roll up and slice into rolls. Try any shape or variation that strikes your fancy. The rolls do need to rise again before baking. If you put them in a warm place (85°) they'll be ready in 15 minutes. Bake most rolls at 425° for 12-15 minutes. Try filling with ground nuts, diced fruits, or the following:

1   cup firm cottage cheese
1/3   cup white raisins
Candied fruit or 8 drained cherries
2   T. sugar
1   tsp. vanilla

Put the cottage cheese (steel blade) in the bowl with sugar and vanilla, processing smooth. Add cherries and raisins and process in with on/off's until cherries are diced. Spread on dough that has risen once and been rolled out and folded once. Roll up. Cut into 1 1/2 inch rolls and place in a baking dish. Let rise again (15-20 minutes), brush with melted butter and bake at 425° for 12-15 minutes. Sprinkle with cinnamon sugar or coat with the glaze on page 47.

> *Until the nature of man is completely altered, cooking is the most important thing for a woman.*
>
> Arnold Bennett

The International Pancakes and Crepes

"Now" said she, "we'll all have

pancakes for supper!"

Little Black Sambo

From tortillas to egg rolls, the overwhelming popularity of the pancake is indisputable.

Everybody is having lots of fun with crepes and the varieties of fillings and sauces are endless. Some Sunday. . .make up several batches of batter, get a couple crepe pans going—give everyone a place to "create" and set out plenty of fresh fruits and vegetables for inspiration. Or check the refrigerator. . . .you might see some possibilities there. Have a glass of wine and dream up some sauces. Invite the neighbors over and have a crepe party!

Included are some recipes for breakfast, lunch, dinner, dessert, and appetizers.

GOOD MORNING AMERICA CREPES

Pre-heat oven to 350°

8 crepes (Basic Crepe Batter, p. 25)

1/2 to 1	cup ham or crumbled bacon
1	T. peanuts
1	3 ounce package cream cheese
2	T. apricot marmalade
2	T. butter

Sauce:

| 1 | cup Cheese Sauce (p. 37) |

Steel Blade

Put the ham (or crisp bacon), cream cheese, butter, marmalade, and peanuts in the processor bowl and process until combined (10-15 seconds). Spread on the crepes and roll up, putting in the oven to keep warm.

Make the Cheese Sauce and pour over the crepes when serving.

Nothing helps scenery like ham and eggs.

Mark Twain

94

x2   INSTANT PANCAKE MIX

4	cups all purpose flour
5	tsp. baking powder
4	T. powdered milk
1 1/2	tsp. salt
1 1/2	tsp. baking soda
1	T. sugar
6	T. chilled Crisco or margarine

Steel Blade

Put the flour, salt, milk, baking soda, baking powder and sugar in the bowl and process on/off (pulse) to combine. Add Crisco, in 1 T. chunks, and process in first with a couple on/off's, then by running the machine. Store in the refrigerator.

For Pancakes:

Makes about 8-10

1	cup mix
1	egg
1/4	tsp. vanilla
3/4	cup milk or buttermilk
1/2	cup drained blueberries or pitted cherries, chopped (drained)

For Muffins:

Makes about 8

1	cup mix
1	egg
1	T. butter
1	T. sugar (honey)
1/2	cup milk or buttermilk
1/2	cup raisins, chopped nuts or:
1/2	cup drained blueberries

Steel Blade

Use the same method for either pancakes or muffins. Put the mix in the bowl. If using nuts, add with mix and cut in with a couple on/off's (pulse). Put the rest of the ingredients on top of the mix (**except** blueberries) and process in with on/off's (pulse) until combined. Stir in blueberries by hand. Bake muffins (filling greased muffin tins 3/4 full) at 350° about 20 minutes. Fry pancakes on a hot, lightly greased griddle.

Note: Coat muffins (before baking) with 2 tsp. cinnamon, 2 T. sugar and 1 T. nuts (processed very fine with the steel blade).

dlc-7 You may make up to 4 times the Muffin or Pancake recipes in the new DLC-7.

x2 FRUIT PANCAKES

So she got flour and eggs and milk and sugar and butter, and she made a huge big plate of most lovely pancakes.

Batter:

2	cups flour
1	T. sugar
2	tsp. baking powder
1/2	tsp. salt
2	tsp. baking soda
2	cups milk
2	egg yolks
2	T. melted butter
2	egg whites, beaten very stiff

Clarified Butter for frying

Filling I

1	T. finely minced orange rind
1	T. orange juice concentrate
1	ripe banana (process until mashed)

Filling II

2	apples, cored
1/2	cup raisins
1	tsp. rum flavoring
1/2	tsp. cinnamon

Steel Blade

If using Filling I process the rind and sugar together first. Then the banana, egg yolks, butter, juice and half the milk. Combine the dry ingredients and add all at once. Process once on/off . . . then add the rest of the milk and process on/off several times to combine.

For Filling II do the apples first following the same general procedure as in Filling I except if you prefer the raisins whole, add last with the remaining milk.

Let the batter rest at room temperature at least 30 minutes. When you are ready to use it beat the egg whites very stiff and fold into the batter. Makes about 16 medium size pancakes.

And she fried them in the melted butter
(clarified butter) which the Tigers had made. . . .

And Black Mumbo ate Twenty-seven pancakes
and Black Jumbo ate Fifty-five, but little Black
Sambo ate a hundred and Sixty nine because
he was so hungry!

Little Black Sambo

x2 PONNUKOKUR

A pancake from Iceland.

The batter:

1 1/2 cups flour
4   eggs
1 1/3 cups milk
3   T. melted butter
2   tsp. vanilla

The filling:

1   cup heavy cream, whipped
Assorted jams and jellies
Powdered sugar

Steel Blade

Put everything but the melted butter in the processor bowl and process until smooth. Add the melted butter through the feeder tube with the machine running. Let the batter rest at room temperature for at least 30 minutes, or chill 2-3 hours.

Using a crepe pan, and the crepe method (p. 25) fry the pancakes in Clarified Butter (p. 2), browning on both sides.

Spread when fresh and warm, with 1 teaspoon of jam and a tablespoon of whipped cream. Sprinkle with powdered sugar and enjoy!

An English friend of mine tells me it was customary to eat crepes this way in England, only with sugar and orange butter.

x2 TINY FRIED CREPE APPETIZERS

Well worth the last minute effort.

12-18 tiny crepes (see p. 25 Crepe Batter)
6　　ounces Monterey Jack cheese
1　　fresh shallot
Hot oil

Steel Blade

Prepare the crepes using a 5 inch pan. Heat the oil in a deep fat fryer.

Put the cheese, cut in chunks and the fresh shallot in the work bowl and process until grated. Put a small spoonful in each crepe, roll it up folding the edges inward so it is sealed. Lay on the sealed edge and fry one at a time holding the sealed edge together. Drain on paper towels and serve immediately.

The outside will be crisp and the cheese melted on the inside.

x2 PEPPERS AND CHEESE CREPES

12-18 tiny crepes (see p. 25 Crepe Batter)
4　　ounces processed American cheese
8　　ounces cream cheese
1　　jalapeno pepper or several small hot peppers
1/4　of a bell pepper
2　　green onions

Hot oil

Steel Blade

Prepare the crepes using a 5 inch crepe pan.

Put the processed cheese, in chunks, in the bowl with the steel blade. Add onions, peppers, in chunks (removing some of the seeds from the hot peppers) and process with a couple on/off's.

Add cream cheese, (cold) in chunks, and process in by running the machine a few seconds. If the mixture is quite runny, chill until firm but still spreadable. Fill crepes, roll up and deep fry in hot oil, holding sealed edges together.

EGG ROLL FILLINGS

These are two fillings for egg rolls that will fill about 12 medium size egg rolls (batter on p. 27). Serve as a first course or for a light luncheon. A great way to re-cycle leftover meats and vegetables. The two-stage cooking is not only a convenience but is claimed to be an old Chinese chefs' secret to the perfectly prepared egg roll.

Filling I

1/2	head cabbage
2	stalks celery
1	carrot
2	green onions
1/3	cup bamboo shoots
6	water chestnuts
1	tsp. sugar and salt
1-2	tsp. soy sauce
Several	chunks of beef, pork or chicken, cooked

1   beaten egg, to seal the wrapper

Julienne Blade, Thin Serrated Slicing Disk, Plastic Knife

Cut the cabbage to fit the feeder tube and slice into the bowl (thin slicing disk). Remove. Repeat with the beef or chicken, and water chestnuts. Change to the julienne blade and process in the carrots, celery, green onions. Load the feeder tube with vegetables in chunks. Change to the plastic knife (it does not need to lock into place) and add seasonings and bamboo shoots. Process with a couple on/off's. Combine with cabbage, fill the egg roll wrappers, seal with the beaten egg and fry in hot oil until lightly golden. You may need to hold the sealed edge together with some tongs. Drain on paper towel and complete frying to a golden brown just before serving.

For a first course serve on a bed of shredded lettuce with a choice of sweet or hot mustard sauce.

Use leftover mousse or vegetable casseroles to fill crepes. . . . .add a fresh sauce—it looks and tastes like you planned it that way.

Filling II

1/2   cup bamboo shoots
1   stalk celery
1   carrot
1/4   cup cashew nuts
1/4   cup almonds
1/2   lb. shrimp, cooked and deveined
1/2   tsp. ginger, salt, and pepper
1   tsp. sugar
1/4   tsp. red pepper flakes
A few drops lemon juice

1   beaten egg

Slicing Disk, Steel Blade

Using the steel blade process carrot, celery and nuts with on/off's to chop. Change to the slicing disk (thin serrated if you have it) and slice in the shrimp. Change to the plastic knife, adding bamboo shoots and all the seasonings and combine with several on/off's.

Fry according to directions in Filling I.

SAUCES FOR EGG ROLLS

Sweet-Sour: Hot Mustard:

1/2   cup currant jelly   3   T. dijon type mustard
1/4   cup vinegar   2   tsp. horseradish
1/4   cup beef broth   4   T. sour cream
1   T. orange juice concentrate

Melt the jelly with the rest of the ingredients. Cool slightly and serve.

Mix together the mustard, sour cream and horseradish.

*You can find an outlet for your
creative genius and accomplish a great deal*

Chinese fortune cookie

ZESTY
CHICKEN CREPES

For 12 to 18 crepes

Pre-heat oven to 350°

Filling:

2	cups cooked chicken
2	stalks celery
1	zucchini
2	green onions

Dash Tabasco
Salt and pepper

1/4	cup mayonnaise
1/4	tsp. chili powder

Sauce:

1	recipe Basic White Sauce (p. 36)
1	avocado, peeled and seeded
2	tsp. lemon juice

Steel Blade, Slicing Disk, Shredding Disk

Start with the shredding disk and cut celery, onion and zucchini in chunks and push through the feeder tube. Change to the slicing disk and slice the chicken (use the fine serrated slicer if possible). Add seasonings and mayonnaise directly into the bowl and mix with the plastic knife on/off. Fill crepes and warm in the oven, in a buttered 9 x 12 dish, for 15 minutes.

Use the steel blade to puree the avocado and lemon juice. Add the white sauce, process to combine, then heat in a saucepan. Serve with sliced lettuce and chopped tomatoes.

x2 SEAFOOD CREPES WITH
VEGETABLE SAUCE

12-18 crepes (p. 25)

Pre-heat oven to 350°

Filling:

1	package frozen crabmeat (save the liquid to use in the white sauce)
1/2	pound cleaned, cooked shrimp
1	8 ounce package cream cheese
1	T. horseradish
1	tsp. lemon juice
3	green onions

Sauce:

1	recipe Basic White Sauce for Fish (p. 37)
3	T. cream
1/2	cup frozen peas
4	ounces Swiss cheese

Steel Blade, Shredding Disk

Put the cream cheese and lemon juice in the bowl and process smooth. Add the rest of the filling ingredients, processing by turning the machine on and off several times until everything is combined. Fill the crepes, rolling them up, and putting in a buttered baking dish. Heat them in the oven while you prepare the sauce (15 minutes).

Prepare the White Sauce. Grate the cheese and stir into sauce. Thaw peas, puree with the steel blade along with 1/2 cup hot White Sauce. Return to saucepan and heat thoroughly. Garnish with almonds.

Many of the great renaissance men were gourmets.

x2 JAMBALAYA CREPES

18 crepes

Pre-heat oven to 350°

Filling:

1/2	pound shrimp, cooked and cleaned
1	chunk of ham or sausage
1	clove garlic
1/2	onion (in chunks)
1/2	green pepper (in chunks)
1	stalk celery
1/2	cup cooked rice
1	T. sherry
1/4	tsp. each cayenne pepper, bay leaves, salt
3	T. butter
2	T. mayonnaise
2	tsp. Worcestershire sauce

Sauce:

1	recipe Creole Sauce (p. 38) (which has simmered 30-40 minutes)
1	peeled eggplant
1	T. tomato paste
3	T. oil

Steel Blade, Thin Serrated Slicing Disk, Shredding Disk, Plastic Knife

Run the machine and drop garlic through the feeder tube to mince. Add onion, celery, and peppers and chop with on/off's to dice. Saute in 3 T. butter until limp. Change to the thin slicing disk and load the feeder tube with shrimp and ham. Push through. Change to the plastic knife and add seasonings, mayonnaise, rice and sherry. Process to combine and toss with vegetables. Fill the crepes and roll up. Place in a baking dish on sealed edge and warm for 10-15 minutes.

Cut the eggplant in chunks to fit the feeder tube. Sprinkle with salt and let stand 5-10 minutes. Use the shredding disk (or the julienne blade if you have it) and shred through. Place in a tea towel to wring out excess moisture (and bitterness). Saute in hot oil, add tomato paste and Creole Sauce. Heat thoroughly and serve with crepes.

x2 CANNOLI

12-14 Cannoli Shells (p. 30)

Prepare and fry the shells.

Filling:

2	cups Ricotta cheese
1	8 ounce package cream cheese
1/2	of an orange, peeled
3/4	cups powdered sugar
3	T. sweet butter
1	tsp. vanilla
1	tsp. almond extract
1/2	cup miniature chocolate chips

Pistachio nuts

Steel Blade

Use a little of the zest from the orange for added flavor. Process first (steel blade) with some granulated sugar. Add butter and cream cheese next (in chunks) and process until creamed. Add orange sections, sugar and Riccota cheese, processing smooth. Process in flavorings and add chocolate chips last . . . use a quick on/off to blend in.

Crisp the prepared shells in a hot oven and cool. Fill them just before serving. Sprinkle with powdered sugar or some ground pistachio nuts.

While Ricotta cheese is somewhat traditional, almost any creamy filling is very good.

x2 COCONUT CREAM CREPES

The versatility of crepes is demonstrated by a whimsical little Inn in mid Florida, Chalet Suzanne, which serves a tiny unfilled crepe lightly sauced in an orange liqueur to tease your palate while you select dessert. Delightful!

These are a bit more substantial and promise you will not leave the table hungry.

Pre-heat the oven to 350°

12 crepes

Filling:

Rich Coconut Cream (p. 23)

Topping:

1	cup canned, drained pineapple
1	stick butter
1/2	cup sugar
Juice of one orange	
1	ounce Triple-Sec Liqueur
2	ounces rum

Steel Blade

Fill the crepes with the Coconut Cream, roll them up, and put them in a baking dish. Warm in the oven 10 minutes while preparing the sauce.

Using the steel blade, process the pineapple. Melt the butter in a frying pan until it bubbles. Add the sugar gradually, stirring constantly. Add the juice of one orange, pineapple, Triple-Sec, and finally the rum. If you have the equipment and a volunteer . . . . do this at the table. Watch it when you add the rum . . . the sauce may ignite.

Pour over the crepes to serve.

x2 SKINNIER CREPES

Surprisingly good. Use the Skinnier Crepe Batter (p. 26) to prepare the crepes.

Pre-heat oven to 375°

Filling for 8:

1	3 ounce package low calorie cream cheese
1/4	tsp. imitation butter flavoring
1	tsp. grated orange rind
1	tsp. orange juice concentrate
1	tsp. vanilla
4	T. cottage or Ricotta cheese

Artificial sweetener to equal 2 Tablespoons sugar

Sweet Skinny Sauce (p. 48)

Steel Blade

Run the machine and drop orange peelings through the feeder tube to mince.

Put the filling ingredients in the processor bowl using the steel blade and process until combined. Fill the crepes and roll up, folding the edges inward so the filling is enclosed. Warm the crepes 10 minutes at 375°. Heat the sauce and serve over the crepes.

Vanilla comes from a tropical orchid plant. . .using the bean itself imparts the very best flavor.

ITALIAN CREME DESSERT CREPE

The filling is Rich . . . . but well worth the indulgence.

Makes 12 crepes.

Pre-heat oven to 350°

Filling:

Italian Creme (p. 21)

Sauce:

3/4	cup apricot or peach marmalade
3	T. butter
1	ounce peach or apricot brandy
2	ounces Curacao
1	tsp. vanilla

Fresh seasonal berries

Put a generous spoonful of Italian creme in each crepe and roll it up, placing it in a lightly buttered baking dish.

Combine the sauce ingredients in a saucepan and heat until the jellies melt.

This may be done ahead and refrigerated (or the crepes may be frozen).

When ready to serve, warm the crepes in the oven 15 minutes, heat the sauce, and serve with some sauce poured over each one.

Garnish with a handful of fresh seasonal berries.

Note: For something different you may deep fat fry the crepes. When filling them turn the edges inward. Hold the sealed edge together when frying. Sprinkle with powdered sugar and the berries when serving.

FROSTY ORANGE CREPES

Crepe Batter (p. 25) using almond flavoring

1/2	gallon vanilla ice cream

Peelings from 1 orange plus 4-5 sections

1	T. orange juice concentrate
1-2	T. orange marmalade (optional)
2	T. orange flavored liqueur

Instant Chocolate Sauce:

6	squares semi-sweet chocolate
1/2	cup water
1/3	cup sugar
2	T. orange liqueur
2	T. Creme de Cacao
2	T. orange juice

Prepare the crepes (p. 25) using 1 tsp. almond flavoring in the batter. Cool between sheets of wax paper.

Put the orange peelings into the bowl adding 2 T. of sugar and mince by running the machine. Add sections, marmalade and liqueurs. Process to combine, then fold into softened ice cream. Freeze until firm, then fill crepes, roll up and freeze. When ready to serve, prepare the chocolate sauce.

Place the chocolate pieces into the bowl processing (steel blade) on/off to break up, then running the machine to chop fine. Boil the water, liqueurs, juice and sugar 1-2 minutes, then add through the feeder tube with the machine running, processing smooth. Pour over the crepes and garnish with a whipped creme rosette.

Note: The ice cream mixture is also good in the Macaroon Crust (p. 6). Easy and so good.

Use a recipe as a guide . . . and give your old, borrowed, and newly discovered recipes a fresh new taste with your imagination.

Soups

Soups have seven virtues;
They satisfy hunger and
They don't make you thirsty.
They help you sleep and
Aid digestion.
They never tease and
Always please; and
Put color in its place
On each face.

Aragon Proverb

x2 CHILLED OCTOBER SOUP

2   large potatoes
3   leeks, tops only
3   zucchini squash
1   large Mexican squash (optional)
3   white squash
4   cups chicken broth
1   cup cream
6   T. butter, melted
1/2   tsp. salt and pepper

Garnish:

1/2   cup chives, chopped
2   ounces grated sharp cheddar cheese (optional)

Steel Blade

Peel and boil the potatoes until tender in the chicken stock. Remove, adding leeks and squash. It is not necessary to peel the squash unless you prefer a pale-colored soup. Boil 5 minutes or until tender.

Put the squash and leeks, in chunks, into the bowl and process smooth. Add the potatoes, in chunks, processing first on-off to break up, then running the machine a few seconds to incorporate. Add butter and 1/2 cup of the hot liquid. Transfer to the remaining stock, stirring to combine, adding seasonings, and adjusting them to suit your preference. Chill.

When ready to serve, whip the cream by running the machine (steel blade), adding the cream through the feeder tube in a steady stream. Fold into the chilled soup. Top with chives and grated cheddar cheese. (Use the shredding disk.)

Soup of the evening . . . beautiful soup.

Lewis Carroll

x2 ARTICHOKE SOUP

People who claim they don't like artichokes probably never made it to the "heart" of the matter. A delicate flavor which makes a delicious soup.

4	artichokes
2	cups chicken broth, hot
1	T. freshly minced parsley
1-2	T. lemon juice
1	cup cream
1/2	stick butter
1	T. flour
1/2	tsp. salt
1/4	tsp. pepper

Steel Blade

Clean the artichokes well. Cook them in enough water to cover them completely until the bottoms are tender (40-50 minutes). Cool and drain. Heat the chicken broth. Peel the leaves from the artichoke, scraping the edible portion from the core of the leaves and putting it into the processor bowl. Remove the choke, (that's the feathery material on top of the heart) and add the heart to the bowl. Add the butter, cut in several pieces, and flour, lemon juice, parsley and seasonings. Process until smooth.

With the machine running add the cream through the feeder tube and one cup of the hot chicken broth. Transfer the contents of the processor bowl to the saucepan with the remaining chicken broth and stir until thickened and very hot.

Serve with buttered, herbed toast rounds or croutons.

> . . . *a truly fresh vegetable, decently prepared is something to experience.*
>
> Edward Harris Hesh

x2 LORRAINE SOUP

This soup is the result of a search to treat my family to some of the native Scottish dishes my ancestors thrived on. The processor adapts so well to many of these old classic recipes, making them so easy. (Our ancestors didn't have all that stuff at the grocery store, canned and processed). It's a joyful experience for our family to dine on the fare of our heritage — like having Thanksgiving all over again. The recipe is slightly modified for the processor.

1	cup chicken meat
4-6	cups chicken stock
1/2	cup almonds
1	piece stale bread
1	tsp. each grated lemon peel and nutmeg
1	cup cream
4	T. flour
4	T. butter

Salt and pepper to taste

Steel Blade

Put the chicken, almonds, bread, and all the seasonings except the salt and pepper in the processor bowl and process until the chicken is minced. Put with the broth and heat in a soup pot.

Put the butter and flour in the processor bowl and process until creamed. Add 1 cup of the boiling hot broth through the feeder tube, with the machine running. Transfer to the soup pot, add the cream and stir until it reaches a boil again.

Season with salt and pepper to taste and serve with some toast rounds.

The BEST chicken soup ever.

When slicing or mincing onions, squeeze a little lemon juice on your hands and into the processor bowl — it reduces the odor and the tears. Onions tend to be a little bitter when chopped in the machine. This goes away in cooking but the lemon juice helps eliminate bitterness if used raw.

x2 SEAFOOD BISQUE

1	package frozen crabmeat (including liquid)
1	cup shrimp or lobster (cooked, prepared)
1	cup White Sauce for Fish (p. 37)
1/2	cup white wine
1	cup cream
1 1/2	cups fresh peas in their pods (1 package frozen if fresh are not available)
1	3 ounce package cream cheese
2	leeks
1	tsp. sugar
1/2	tsp. salt
1	tsp. horseradish
1	T. minced parsley

Steel Blade, Slicing Disk

Using the slicing disk, slice leeks (2 fit snugly in the feeder tube). Wash.

Thaw the crabmeat, and combine with the shrimp or lobster. Boil leeks and peas in sugar, salt and 1 cup water for 3 minutes. Drain. Put the leeks, peas, cream cheese and horseradish in the processor bowl with the steel blade and process until minced and combined. You may need to scrape down the sides of the bowl a few times.

Prepare the White Sauce (use the liquid from the crab to make up the liquid called for in the basic recipe) and process with the ingredients in the bowl to combine. Transfer to a saucepan, add the wine and cream, and stir and heat until thickened. Add the seafood and minced parsley last. Do not boil.

Serve with small crepes, which you fold in quarters and deep fat fry. A nice "final touch."

ONION SOUP

My husband has always adored creating in the kitchen and many a Sunday morning I would wake up to Beethoven on the stereo and the kitchen wallpapered in onions. The soup, however, was perfect.

12-14	red onions
1	stick butter (you may need a little more)
4	T. olive oil
6-7	cups beef broth
3	T. brown sugar
3	whole cardamon (seeds only)
Salt and pepper to taste	
2	whole artichokes, cleaned and trimmed
1/4	cup brandy
1/8	cup sherry
Mozzarella cheese	
Croutons	

Steel Blade, Thin Serrated Slicing Disk

Peel the onions, and cut them to fit the feeder tube. Using the slicing disk, slice all the onions. Heat the broth in a large soup pot. Melt the butter and olive oil in a large skillet. Saute all the onions (in several batches) and transfer them to the soup pot. When sauteeing the last bunch, add the brown sugar.

Bring the broth to a boil, add the artichokes, the seasonings, and simmer the soup until the artichokes are tender. (40-45 minutes) Remove them to drain. Add the brandy and sherry.

Prepare the croutons. Butter French bread generously and toast under the broiler, then broil opposite side with a slice of cheese. If you have oven proof crockery, fill the bowls with soup and toasted crouton. Shred the cheese (light pressure) with the shredding disk and mound on the toasted crouton. Put 8 inches away from the broiler about 3-5 minutes. I'm sure a Frenchman would be appalled using Italian cheese in French onion soup . . . feel free to substitute.

Preceding the soup, enjoy the artichokes with a tomato-French dressing. A green salad, a bottle of wine, and some outstanding crusty bread makes a very satisfying meal.

Onions tend to be more watery when sliced in the machine and therefore need to be browned in smaller batches.

x2 SEAFOOD SHERRY BISQUE

This is an old recipe with convenience soup that used to require messy, tedious mixing. If you have a homemade pea soup, it will add considerably to the taste.

Serves 6

1	can cream of tomato soup
1	can green pea soup or split pea soup
1/2	cup dry sherry
1	cup heavy cream
1	7 ounce package frozen crab meat (including juice)
1	cup milk

Steel Blade

Scald milk in a 2 quart saucepan.

Thaw the crab meat by running under cold water. Put the pea soup in the processor bowl and process smooth. With machine running, add tomato soup through the feeder tube, then the sherry. Transfer, adding to the scalded milk. Add crab (undrained) and cream, stirring to thicken.

Slivered toasted almonds or fresh minced basil are good additions.

A HOT, HEARTY LOW CALORIE SOUP

1	cup V-8 juice	1	leek
2	cups beef broth	1/2	tsp. pepper
2	large tomatoes	1/2	tsp. seasoning salt
1	carrot, in chunks	1	T. butter
1	stalk celery, in chunks	1	T. minced parsley

French Fryer

Bring the broth to a simmer.

Cut the carrots, celery and leek in chunks and process with the French fryer. Saute in sizzling butter a few minutes. Process the tomatoes in the same way, adding to saute pan. Add seasonings, then transfer to simmering broth. Simmer until vegetables are tender, skimming any fat or scum from the surface. There are several handy tools for this job at your local gourmet shop.

x2 BROCCOLI SOUP ALMONDINE

1	bunch of fresh broccoli
3	cups chicken broth
1	cup sour cream
1/4	cup almonds
1	large onion
4	T. butter
1	T. lemon juice
1	T. flour

Salt to taste

Sliced almonds

Steel Blade

Cook the broccoli in salted water until it is just tender . . . do not overcook. Drain, and run under cold water to retain the green color. Warm the chicken broth with the butter. Put the almonds, onion, and broccoli (cut in pieces) in the processor bowl and process until smooth and combined. Add the flour, lemon juice and sour cream and with the machine running pour one-half cup of the chicken broth through the feeder tube. Transfer to a saucepan with the remaining chicken broth and heat to the boiling point.

Saute the sliced almonds in a little butter to put on top of each bowl of soup. Or, if you have a thin slicing blade, reserve one broccoli stem and cut in pieces to fit the feeder tube. Slice . . . you'll have flower shapes to saute and float in the soup.

Home grow some chives, parsley and dill . . . mint makes a beautiful hanging basket . . . so do strawberry plants.

The fate of a nation has often depended on the good or bad digestion of a prime minister.

Voltaire

THREE CHEESE SOUP

There's a time and a place for everything and the time I make this soup is when I have accumulated some bits of different kinds of cheese. You can start fresh with any cheese.

6-8	ounces cheese (in chunks)
4	stalks celery
1	onion
4	carrots
1	cup White Sauce (p. 36)
1/2	cup white wine or vermouth
2	cups chicken or turkey stock
1	green pepper, cut in chunks
1	cup milk
1	tsp. hot minced peppers (optional)

Steel Blade

Using the steel blade, process the onion, celery, and green peppers until minced. Remove to a soup pot and simmer with the chicken stock and carrots.

Put the assorted cheeses in the work bowl, and process until grated fine. Add 1/2 cup liquid from the soup pot with the machine running.

When the carrots are tender, remove from the broth. Stir in White Sauce and milk. Put the carrots in the processor bowl and process until smooth.

Return the carrots to the soup pot . . . heat thoroughly . . . and serve.

Top with some chopped almonds or peanuts.

Never underestimate the finishing touches. . . . .having to say that it tastes great even though it doesn't look great is like saying a woman looks good. . . . . "for her age".

x2 QUICK HOT AVOCADO SOUP

Even though I feel convenience foods do not go hand and hand with the food processor, this is a delightful hot soup. Additions of either chopped leftover shrimp, salmon or ham are welcome.

1	clove garlic
2	cans cream of chicken soup
5	green onions
1/2	tsp. salt
1/2	tsp. chili powder

Juice of two lemons

1	cup cream or half and half
3	large ripe avocados
1	T. unsalted butter

Several generous sprigs of fresh parsley

Steel Blade

Put the green onions and garlic in the bowl with the steel blade. Add some zest from one of the lemons and run the machine to mince. Saute in 1 T. sizzling butter. Put peeled, seeded avocados in the bowl and run the machine to puree. Bring chicken soup and cream to a boil and add 1/2 cup to the puree. Transfer to the rest of the soup along with garlic, green onion and all the seasonings except the parsley. Stir in lemon juice and heat through. Remove from heat, adjust seasonings and serve with freshly minced parsley.

SUPERMARKET VEGETABLE SOUP

My youngest son, who has generally felt that vegetables should be seldom seen and never heard, announced one day he had a recipe for vegetable soup. To watch this child, whose favorite story is about George the Hippopotamus, who poured his wife's vegetable soup in his loafers in order to have a chocolate chip cookie, load up the grocery cart with all sorts of unfamiliar vegetables, was a revelation. When he came to the turnips and cucumbers it was difficult to refrain from directing his culinary creativity; however, the result was a wonderfully rich vegetable 'stew' which needed little or no seasoning (except salt). The texture is like a "gumbo," nutritiously delicious all by itself or as a base for adding meat or fish.

2	tsp. salt
6	medium tomatoes (or 2 cans stewed tomatoes)
6-8	cups of water (you need enough to completely cover vegetables)
6	tsp. beef bouillon powder
1	turnip
4	potatoes
3	stalks celery (tops included)
1	cucumber
1	yellow squash
1	zucchini squash
1	onion
3	carrots
2	bunches broccoli (stems included)
1/2	head of small cabbage
1/2	pound mushrooms
1	cup raw spinach
1	bunch parsley

Steel Blade, Shredding Disk

Wash all the vegetables thoroughly. Bring the water to a boil and add all the vegetables but the cucumber and squash. Add the beef bouillon powder, cover and simmer until the vegetables are tender. Remove the cabbage and celery first . . . . .cool slightly and put in the processor bowl with the steel blade and process for 15-20 seconds. Repeat with the rest of the vegetables. Put everything back in the soup pot. Cut the cucumber and the squash to fit the feeder tube, and using the shredding disc shred them and add to the soup, simmering 10 more minutes.

Note: This makes quite a lot of soup. . . . . .it freezes very well.

The pleasures of the table may be
enjoyed every day, in every climate,
at all ages, and by all conditions
of men.

Brillat-Savarin

ROMAINE SOUP

Chalet Suzanne, a most unique little inn in mid-Florida, described as architecturally "monstrous but delightful," "funky" and some-thing "inspired by a quaint, dog-eared, half-forgotten children's book," is famous for their marvelous soups, especially their Romaine Soup. The only clues I was ever able to get to the ingredients were that it didn't contain a shred of lettuce, and it did contain some of the spices in curry. You may order the soup from the Chalet . . . . . or try this adaptation.

3	cups chicken broth
1	pound fresh spinach
1/2	onion
1/2	pound mushrooms
1/2	stick butter
3	T. flour
Salt and pepper	
1/4	tsp. coriander
1/2	tsp. cardamon
1/2	tsp. nutmeg
1	tsp. lemon juice
1	cup half and half

Steel Blade, Slicing Disk (Vegetable)

Warm the chicken broth. Boil the spinach with the onion, cut in several pieces, for 3-4 minutes. Rinse under cool water and drain. Clean the mushrooms with a damp cloth, and using the slicing disk, slice them into the processor bowl. Remove, and saute in the butter. Change to the steel blade and put the spinach, onion, flour and spices in the processor bowl and process until minced and combined. Add 1 cup of the warm broth through the feeder tube, process a few seconds and transfer the mixture to the rest of the broth, adding the mushrooms. Bring to a boil, reduce the heat, and add the half and half, stirring all the time.

Note: You may puree the mushrooms if you want a smooth soup.

RED SNAPPER SOUP

3	lbs. red snapper		6	large tomatoes
1	onion			Juice of one lemon
1	celery stalk (cut in chunks)			Salt and pepper to taste
2	carrots		1/2	cup sherry
1/2	tsp. ground cloves		3-4	T. butter
3	T. flour		3-4	cups water
1	cup clam juice			

Steel Blade, French Fryer

Poach the fish (clean and remove scales but add fish heads to stock pot) in 3-4 cups water and lemon about 10 minutes (or until cooked). Strain, reserving broth. Discard bones, fish heads and separate out the meat. Cut the tomatoes in quarters and process to dice (steel blade or French fryer). Remove.

Cut the carrots, onions and celery in chunks and process with the french fryer. Saute the vegetables in 3-4 T. butter. Dissolve flour in some of the stock, add to vegetables, then transfer both to the remaining stock. Add tomatoes and their juices to clam broth and bring to a boil. Reduce fish stock by boiling freely for a few minutes, adding about 2 cups to the broth and tomatoes.

Process the fish in batches to puree. Add to the stock pot and simmer 5-10 minutes, adjusting seasonings to taste. Stir in sherry when ready to serve.

Fish should swim thrice:
> *first it should swim in the sea,*
> > *then it should swim in butter,*
> *and at last it should swim in a good claret.*

Lionel Strachey

RENAISSANCE SOUP

4	cups rich beef broth
1/4	cup Liver Pate (p. 65)
1/8	cup Duxelles (p. 65)
3	T. cream
1/2	cup port wine or dry sherry
	Fresh Parsley

Steel Blade

Heat the stock. Stir in Pate and Duxelles. Add cream, port or sherry and heat thoroughly.

Mince parsley with the steel blade and serve on top.

If you have a rosette iron, make an herbed crepe batter, fry some rosettes and float one in the soup.

Escoffier, said to be the originator of the five-course meal, has said,

> *". . . . the grand structure of gastronomy is built upon harmony and sequence of its elements"*

It has been said that the food we eat should be a "symphony of color".

x2 CREAM SOUP WITH CHIVES

This is a smooth cream soup to serve hot or cold. I compare it to the basic black dress . . . elegantly plain, ready for a few finishing touches.

1	cup cream
4	sprigs fresh parsley
1	cup fresh chives, chopped (or 1/2 cup freeze-dried)
2	cups milk
1	8 ounce package cream cheese
1	tsp. salt
1	tsp. horseradish
2	T. butter

Steel Blade

Cut the cream cheese into chunks and place in the bowl with parsley, processing smooth.

Heat the milk to a boil in a separate saucepan with the butter. Pour 1 cup through the feeder tube, with the machine running. Transfer to the saucepan, stirring to blend. Add seasonings and adjust to personal preference. Stir in cream, heat thoroughly.

Note: If you have the julienne blade, load the feeder tube with leeks, carrots and squash (horizontally). Saute briefly in hot butter and add to soup.

  CHILLED MELON SOUP

Refreshing!

2	cantaloupe melons, seeded, cut in chunks
2	cups milk
Juice of one lime	
1	3 ounce package of cream cheese, cut in chunks
3 1/2	T. flour
1	T. butter
1	tsp. salt

Garnish:

Avocado slices
Chives

Steel Blade

Put the melons and the cream cheese in the processor bowl and process until a puree.

Warm the milk. Put the butter, flour, lime juice and salt in the processor bowl and process until combined. Add one-half cup of the milk through the feeder tube, with the machine running, then transfer everything to the rest of the milk, stirring to thicken.

Chill.

Serve in chilled bowls, with thin slices of ripe avocado on top and a few chives.

x2   CHAMPAGNE AVOCADO SOUP

2   cups chicken broth
1   cup cream
1   shallot
3   medium avocados
1   cup champagne
1   tsp. salt
Dash lemon juice
1/4   tsp. white pepper
Dash of Tabasco

Steel Blade

Heat the chicken broth and champagne and bring to a boil . . . skim off any scum that rises to the surface. Start the machine running, drop shallot through the feeder tube to mince. Add lemon juice and seeded, peeled avocados. Puree. Add 1 cup of the hot broth, process to combine, then stir into remaining broth (off the heat). Add the cream. Adjust seasonings to personal preference and serve very cold garnished with chopped chives.

x2   CHUNKY GAZPACHO

1	clove garlic
	Juice of one lemon
1	tsp. coarse salt
1/4	tsp. each dill weed and red pepper flakes
1/4	tsp. oregano
1/2	onion
1	cup tomato juice
1	T. tomato paste
1/4	cup water
1/4	cup oil
1/8	cup red wine vinegar
2	tomatoes
1	green pepper
1	small cucumber

Garnish:

Croutons
Fresh basil
Additional chopped vegetables

Steel Blade, Plastic Knife, French Fryer

Use the steel blade to process together the seasonings, garlic, onion (cut in chunks) and juice from the lemon.

Measure and combine (in a large measuring cup) all of the liquid ingredients.

Using the French fryer (if you prefer smoother Gazpacho, use the steel blade) and process the cucumber, green pepper, and tomatoes by cutting them into chunks, filling the feeder tube, and pushing through. Change to the plastic knife and pour the liquid through the feeder tube processing several times to combine.

Chill, garnish and serve with additional chopped vegetables, basil and croutons.

> *A long pleasant life depended on two fluids—wine within and oil without.*
>
> A Roman Saying

x2 CHILLED SENEGALESE WITH COCONUT CREAM

3	cups chicken broth
1	bunch green onions
2	celery stalks, (in chunks)
6	T. flour
3	T. sweet butter
1/2	cup Coconut Milk (p. 22)
1	apple, cored and cut in several pieces
1/2	tsp. salt
1	tsp. curry powder
1	cup heavy cream

Garnish:

Chives

Steel Blade

Bring the broth to a boil. Process (steel blade) onion and celery to dice fine. Saute in butter, then put back in the bowl to puree with flour, spices and Coconut Milk. Add 1 cup of the warmed broth through the feeder tube with the machine running. Transfer the contents to the rest of the chicken broth. Cut the apple in several chunks, process until chopped and add to the soup along with the Coconut Milk. Cook over medium heat until thickened. Chill.

When ready to serve whip the cream until stiff. Fold it into the chilled soup and serve with chopped chives.

Note: If this is a luncheon soup, try serving it with fried cheese crepes (p. 98). All you need is a salad to make a light luncheon.

Any leftover pancake batter (crepe consistency) makes a super batter for Rosettes.

x2 QUICK VEGETABLE SOUP

3/4   pound raw chuck
2   squashes
1   onion
2   carrots
1   stalk celery
1/2   green pepper
1   cup corn kernels (do not process)
1   16 ounce can tomatoes
2-3   cups beef broth
1/2   tsp. salt
Dash   pepper
Several   minced parsley sprigs
1/4   tsp. chili powder

French Fryer, Steel Blade

Cut the beef in chunks and process on/off about 4 times to chop coarsely. Remove and saute in a little oil. Change to the French fryer and cut all the vegetables into chunks and push through the feeder tube. Add the tomatoes and broth to the sauteed beef, then add all the vegetables. Bring to a boil, then simmer about 10 minutes, seasoning to taste. Add the drained corn and heat through.

"Soup" comes from the French word "soupe" which meant a piece of bread boiled in broth. The meaning changed with time to mean boiled meat, and finally, today to mean the broth.

x2 TRIM TOMATO VEGETABLE SOUP

After I over-indulged for a week, my creative son, Don, helped me make this soup.

1/2	cucumber	2	T. tomato paste
2	tomatoes (in chunks)		Salt and pepper (dash)
2	green onions	1/2	bottle diet Italian
1/2	zucchini		Dressing
1	slice diet bread	1/2	cup ice water
1	T. lemon juice	1	bunch fresh parsley
1/2	green pepper		(4-5 sprigs)

Steel Blade

Put the parsley in the processor bowl and mince. Cut the vegetables in chunks and put in the processor with the bread and process until minced. Add the liquids and tomato paste through the feeder tube with the machine running. Process smooth.

Taste and adjust salt. Chill before serving.

Try using the French Fryer instead of the steel blade for some of the vegetables (onions, tomatoes)... just cut in chunks and force through with the pusher... now try it with Gazpacho for a chunky texture.

x2 CANADIAN CHEESE SOUP

2	potatoes
2	carrots
1	onion
1/2	green pepper
1	cup corn kernels (more or less)
2	stalks celery
1/2	stick butter
8-10	ounces cheddar cheese (or any combination of cheeses)
5-6	cups chicken stock
1	cup milk (or cream)

(Cream of corn soup plus 1 cup milk may be used in place of corn kernels and milk)

2-3	T. flour

French Fryer, Steel Blade

Cut the vegetables into chunks. Process with the French fryer, pushing through in any order until the bowl is full. Heat the butter in a saute pan and saute the vegetables. Bring milk and chicken stock to a boil in a large stock pot.

Put the cheese in the bowl (steel blade) and process with on/off's or run the machine to grate. Add flour and 1 cup hot broth, processing in well. Transfer to remaining broth and add vegetables, corn (or cream of corn soup) and heat through.

Quick, easy, nutritious. Use salt, pepper, cayenne pepper or nutmeg if you wish additional seasoning. Fresh chopped parsley or chives are good garnishes.

Cheese — milk's leap to immortality.

Clifton Fadiman

MEXICAN CORN CHOWDER

This creamy chowder, plus a salad makes a meal . . . experiment with different kinds of peppers. Most small green peppers are very hot. If you remove the seeds you will reduce the "bite". Lots of freshly chopped parsley and cilantro help to cut the sharpness of the peppers.

2	cups chicken stock
2	cans cream style corn
1	cup fresh corn kernels
1	clove garlic
1	onion
1	pepper
3-4	ounces green chilies
3	pieces of chicken (simmer in 3-4 cups water, reserving broth for soup)
1	cup sour cream or milk
3	T. butter
3-4	ounces Monterey Jack (or other yellow mild cheese)
1	T. medium hot piquant sauce
2	large tomatoes

Fresh cilantro (or parsley)

Steel Blade, French Fryer, Medium Serrated Slicing Disk

Bring the chicken broth to a boil. Use the steel blade to mince the garlic. Saute in butter. Use the French fryer to "dice" the onions (cut in quarters before loading the feeder tube) and saute with the garlic. Use the steel blade, and with on/off's chop green chilies and peppers. Add to saute pan. Use the French fryer again and cut the tomato in quarters. Dice by pushing through with steady pressure. Set aside.

Use the medium serrated slicing disk and load the feeder tube with chicken (cooled). Push through to "chunk". Wipe out the bowl and add cheese in chunks, processing with on/off's to grate. Add corn kernels, processing together to mince the corn. Add chicken, diced tomatoes (drain off the juices), cheese and corn mixture, creamed corn, sour cream and seasonings. Salt and pepper to taste and bring to a boil. Do not overcook.

In a clean, dry bowl mince parsley or cilantro and garnish the soup.

I call this the "dice and dump" method . . . any large recipe should be handled in this way as there are too many ingredients to use a one-bowl method.

Of soup and love — the first is the best.

Spanish Proverb

130

Luncheons
or
Light Supper

It has been said that Toulouse Lautrec

believed every artistic expression should

be accompanied by a culinary festivity

SPINACH AND BLUE CHEESE QUICHE

This is from Creative Cookery in Oklahoma City. I think it is a marvelous quiche and excellent for classes on the Cuisinart.

Preheat oven to 375°

Basic Pastry (p. 9)

2	ounces Swiss cheese

Dijon mustard

1	pound fresh spinach
1	bunch green onions (white part)
3	T. butter

Salt, pepper

1/4	tsp. nutmeg
3	eggs
1	cup cottage cheese or Ricotta or cream cheese
1/2	cup cream (increase to 1 cup if using cream cheese)
4	ounces blue cheese

Dash Tabasco

Steel Blade

Prepare the pastry. Before pre-baking spread with a thin layer of mustard and sprinkle with grated (steel blade) Swiss cheese.

Blanch the spinach in boiling water. Drain very well. Use the steel blade and dice onions with on/off's. Remove and saute in 3 T. butter.

Use the steel blade again to process cottage cheese smooth. Add blue cheese, processing together well. Add eggs, process to "beat" in. Remove.

Puree the spinach with the cream (steel blade). Stir into egg and cheese mixture, seasoning to taste. Pour into baked shell and bake 25-30 minutes or until set.

dlc-7 When using the DLC-7 do not remove egg and cheese mixture. Add spinach and cream to the processor bowl and complete mixing all in the food processor bowl.

x2 CHICKEN CHALUPAS

Use either the small or large size. This amount should make 8 large chalupas.

1	head iceberg lettuce
8	chalupa shells (fried tortillas)
3	cups chicken (cooked)
3	green onions
1/3	cup taco sauce
1-2	T. Mayonnaise

Dash hot sauce

2	avocados
1	cup sour cream
1	T. lemon juice
1/2	tsp. salt and pepper
1/2	tsp. chili powder
4	ounces cheddar cheese

Shredding Disk, Steel Blade, Slicing Disk

Cut the lettuce to fit the feeder tube and slice using the slicing disk. Remove, putting some on each chalupa, saving some for garnishing if using large chalupas as for a luncheon dish.

Change to the steel blade and put the onions in the processor bowl, in chunks, and mince by processing on-off. Use a little lemon juice to cut the odor. Add the pieces of chicken (or, for large chunkier texture, use the slicing disk and push through) and process with on-offs to dice and combine. Add taco sauce and mayonnaise and process on-off just to combine. (For chunky texture change to the plastic knife to mix everything together.) Remove, putting some on each chalupa.

Change to the steel blade. Put the cheese, cut in chunks, directly into the bowl and process until 'grated'. Remove.

Put the peeled avocados, lemon juice and seasonings in the processor bowl and using the steel blade, process smooth. Add the sour cream and process just a few seconds . . . taste to adjust the salt amount. Put a generous spoonful on top of the chicken.

Top with the grated cheese and a little more hot sauce for those who can manage it!

x2 STUFFED ARTICHOKES

Very nice for a first course before a light dinner.

Pre-heat oven 350°

1	pound shrimp, cooked and deveined
4	artichokes
4	slices bread
4-6	ounces Parmesan cheese
1	onion

Juice from one lemon

1	stick butter
1/2	tsp. salt and pepper
1	T. fresh minced parsley

Dressing:

1	fresh tomato
1	cup Mayonnaise (p. 39)
4	green onions
1/2	tsp. chervil

Steel Blade, French Fryer

Clean the artichokes, cut off part of the bottom stem and snip the leaves. Boil them until they are tender (test the bottom) . . . about 40 minutes. Drain.

Prepare (about) 2 cups fresh bread crumbs in the processor bowl using the steel blade. Remove. Grate the cheese by cutting it in chunks and processing with the steel blade almost to a powder. Add to the crumbs.

Put the shrimp, onion, butter, cut in pieces, and seasonings in the processor bowl with about one cup of the bread crumbs and process until coarsely chopped and combined by turning the machine on and off rapidly. Add to the rest of the cheese and crumbs.

Carefully stuff the mixture inside the leaves of the artichokes. Set them in a piece of foil, and enclose them completely. Refrigerate until you are ready to bake or bake immediately 10-15 minutes. Increase baking time 10 minutes if cold.

Dice tomato, in chunks, by processing with the French fryer. Remove. Use the steel blade to mince onions and chervil. Remove. Prepare the Mayonnaise in the processor adding the tomatoes and onions when finished. Chill and serve with the artichokes.

Note: Hollandaise is also a good sauce.

Dieters omit all but 1 T. butter and use a low-calorie Italian Dressing to which you add the tomato and onions.

BANNETON LUNCHEON TORTE

| 1 | recipe Whole Wheat Cheese Bread (p. 300) or |
| 1 | recipe Date-Nut Yeast Bread (p. 298) |

Cheese Butter:

1	stick unsalted butter
3	ounces cream cheese
Several sprigs parsley	

Olive Butter:

1	cup black olives
1	cup stuffed green olives
4	T. butter
2	tsp. Dijon mustard
1	T. mayonnaise
Dash lemon juice	

Chicken Salad:

3	chicken breasts
2	stalks celery
1/2	of an apple
1/2	of a green pepper
2	sweet pickles
3	T. mayonnaise
Handful of almonds	

Garnish:

Fresh parsley or watercress
Carrot flowers

Steel Blade, Medium Serrated Slicing Disk, Thin Vegetable Slicing Disk, Plastic Knife

Prepare the bread according to the basic recipe. Use the Banneton basket for shaping according to the directions. (If you do not have the ridged basket, you may use any round container that holds the amount for one loaf of bread.) After the bread cools completely, cut with a serrated knife into 3 or 4 layers.

Prepare the Cheese Butter by processing the ingredients together, in chunks, until smooth. Spread a thin layer on all exposed surfaces of the bread.

Use the steel blade and dice the celery, apple, pickles, green pepper and almonds with on/off's (pulse) to dice. You'll have coarser pieces by doing everything together. Use the slicing disk (medium serrated), leaving the vegetables in the bowl, and slice in the chicken. Remove slicing disk and use the plastic knife to mix everything together, adding mayonnaise. Use on/off's.

Prepare the Olive Butter by placing everything in the bowl except the mayonnaise and processing together with on/off's, then running machine a few seconds. Add mayonnaise. Process to combine. Cook the carrots until just tender. Cool.

Assemble the sandwich alternating chicken and olive spreads between the layers. Cut carrots in 1 1/2 to 2 inch pieces and make 4-5 grooves down the vertical sides. Slice with the thin slicing disk . . . they will look like flowers. Garnish the platter with carrots and parsley or watercress.

> *The discovery of a new dish does more for the happiness of man than the discovery of a star.*
>
> Brillat—Savarin

x2 CREOLE QUICHE

Everything can be prepared ahead and assembled at the last moment (or someone else can assemble it while you have a glass of sherry). Marvelous for lunch or an appetizer.

Pre-heat oven to 375°

Pastry:

8	ounces cream cheese
1	stick butter
2	cups flour

Steel Blade

Put the cream cheese and butter in the processor bowl and process until smooth. Add the flour all at once, process until it begins to form a ball. Add ice water in 1 T. amounts if it does not hold together. Chill at least an hour before rolling out on a floured board.

Line a 10 inch pie pan or individual shells.

Filling:

1	garlic clove
4-5	green onions
3-5	sprigs parsley
1/4	tsp. cayenne pepper
1/2	cup mayonnaise
1	tsp. lemon juice
1	T. A-1 Steak Sauce
1/2	pound mushrooms
1	package frozen crabmeat, drained
1	pound shrimp, cooked and deveined
1/2	cup Parmesan cheese

Steel Blade, Slicing Disk, Plastic Knife

Put the garlic and parsley in the bowl and run the machine to mince. Add green onions (in chunks) and use on-offs to dice. Change to the slicing disk and slice in the cleaned mushrooms and shrimp. Change to the plastic knife, twisting to fit down securely, and add mayonnaise, steak sauce, seasonings and crabmeat. Process on-off to combine everything (a couple of times) and fill the baked shell or shells. Use the steel blade (clean bowl) and grate the Parmesan by placing in the bowl, in chunks, processing on-off first to break up, then running the machine to grate. Top the seafood mixture and run under the broiler until hot and the cheese melts.

ENDIVES BAKED WITH HAM
AND DUXELLES

For a special luncheon or light supper.

Pre-heat oven to 375°

12	endives
1	cup chicken broth
1	T. lemon juice
12	pieces of very good boiled ham
1/2	cup Duxelles (p. 65)
1	stick butter (melted)
1	cup cream
3	eggs
1/4	tsp. nutmeg, salt and pepper
3	ounces Gruyere or Swiss cheese

Steel Blade

Wash the endive discarding any brown leaves. Place in a large skillet, covering with the broth and lemon juice and simmer 20 minutes.

Spread each piece of ham with the Duxelles. Remove the endives from the chicken broth, saving the broth, and wrap each one in a piece of ham. Put in a buttered casserole dish.

Put the eggs, half the chicken broth and seasonings, in the processor bowl and process a few seconds to combine. Add the cream through the feeder tube, then the butter in a steady slow stream. Add the rest of the broth and pour over the endives. Grate the cheese in the processor bowl with the steel blade and put on top.

Fill a larger pan with a little water and bake the casserole in it for 30-35 minutes. Cover it if it gets too brown.

Note: Try a little wine in the sauce.

x2 SALMON-STUFFED AVOCADO

Serves 6

2	cans salmon
2	T. heavy cream
1/2	tsp. each dill, parsley and chervil
1	cup sour cream
1	tsp. lemon juice
1/2	tsp. each salt and pepper

1	melon, cut in strips

Lime or lemon wedges

Fresh chives

3	whole avocados

Steel Blade

Pick over the salmon, discarding any bone. Put the salmon, cream, seasonings, lemon juice and sour cream in the processor bowl and process by turning the machine on and off rapidly to combine. Chill.

Prepare the melon and citrus wedges. Cover and Chill.

When ready to serve, cut the avocados in half, peel and put on a lettuce leaf. Divide the salmon mixture among them and garnish with the melon and fresh chives.

Serve with Herbed Mayonnaise (p. 39).

SUPREMES VERONIQUE

Pre-heat oven 350°

French Toast Batter (p. 27)

2	T. flour, in a sifter or shaker

8	chicken breasts, boned
8	thick slices of French bread

2	T. Clarified Butter (p. 2)
6	T. Clarified Butter

Salt and pepper

Sauce:

1	cup white wine
1	cup chicken broth
4	T. flour
2	T. butter (soft)
4	ounces Swiss cheese (soft)
2	cups fresh green grapes, loosely packed
2-3	sprigs fresh parsley

Steel Blade, Slicing Disk

Prepare the French toast batter, and put in shallow dish. Sprinkle the chicken with salt and pepper and saute in 2 T. Clarified Butter until browned. Put in a baking dish and bake 10-12 minutes while you prepare the toast and sauce.

Warm the chicken broth. Using the steel blade put the flour, butter, parsley, and cheese in the processor bowl, and process until smoothly combined. Add the warm broth through the feeder tube, then transfer the mixture to a saucepan and add the white wine.

139

Change to the slicing disk, and slice the grapes pushing them through the feeder tube. Add to the sauce when it has thickened. Set aside.

Dip the French bread in the batter, sprinkle with a little flour, and saute until browned and crispy.

Serve by placing a chicken breast on each piece of toast and pouring the sauce over.

SCALLOPS IN CUCUMBER SAUCE

Serves 6

2	small cucumbers
3	T. butter
1 1/2	pounds scallops
1	cup vermouth
1/2	clove garlic
5	sprigs fresh parsley
3	ounces Swiss cheese
4-5	ounces Parmesan or Gruyere cheese
1	tsp. lemon juice
1	T. flour
1/2	tsp. salt and pepper
1	recipe Choux Pastry (p. 12)

Steel Blade, French Fryer, Shredding Disk

Peel and seed cucumbers. Cut them into chunks and process with the French fryer. Salt lightly and let stand an hour.

Heat the butter in a skillet, and saute the cleaned scallops. Add the vermouth and the sliced cucumbers. If you need more liquid, add more vermouth. Simmer 2-3 minutes and remove from heat.

Put the garlic and parsley in the processor bowl and mince using the steel blade. Change to the shredding disk and shred in the Swiss cheese. Use the plastic knife (it does not need to lock into place) and add flour, salt, pepper, lemon juice plus 4-6 T. liquid from the scallops. Process with on/off's to combine. Combine with the scallops and divide between 6 medium size buttered baking shells or ramekins. Refrigerate until ready to bake.

Use the steel blade to grate Parmesan cheese.

Prepare the Choux Pastry according to the recipe on page 12, adding the Parmesan cheese with eggs. Put in a pastry tube with a decorative large tip and make ruffled edge around the edges of the scallops just before baking.

Bake at 400° for 10 minutes, then turn the oven down to 350° and bake an additional 15-20 minutes (or until the pastry is browned).

Beautiful and delicious . . . the pastry will soak up all the good sauce.

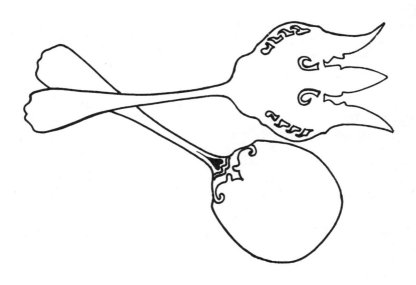

GREEK STYLE CHEESE PIE

Pre-heat oven to 350°

8 by 10 (about) deep sided dish
16   sheets of phyllo pastry
         (or use 8 and fold them to fit the pan)
16   ounces cottage cheese
1/2   cup plain yogurt (or sour cream)
4-5   ounces Parmesan cheese
5   eggs
Several sprigs parsley
1/2   stick melted butter
Coarsely ground black pepper
1/2   tsp. salt
1/4   tsp. nutmeg

Optional Addition:

1   garlic clove
1   pound cooked spinach, drained well

Steel Blade

Butter the dish . . . generously. Put the Parmesan cheese (in chunks) directly into the bowl, processing on/off several times first to break up, then running the machine to grate very fine. Add parsley, cottage cheese and seasonings, processing smooth. Add eggs . . . process by running the machine 15-20 seconds. Add yogurt (or sour cream) processing on/off just a couple of times.

Layer the pastry two sheets at a time in the bottom of the dish buttering after every other one with melted butter (use 10 sheets). Pour in the cheese mixture and use the 6 remaining sheets on top, buttering after every other one. With a very sharp knife score through the top pastry where you will be cutting it. Bake at 350° 40-50 minutes or until browned on top and "set". May be frozen after baking and re-heated successfully in a microwave.

If using spinach, mince garlic with cheese and add spinach with the yogurt.

In many Greek plays, cooks were important characters and gave out recipes in prose . . . some declared their culinary art required the skill of an architect.

Cocktail Foods

Mieux vaut bon repas que bel habit

"A good meal is worth more than a pretty suit."

SAUCEY SHRIMP COCKTAIL

Serves 6

1	pound cooked, cleaned shrimp
2	avocados
1	cantaloupe or honeydew melon
1/2	of a jicama or 1 cucumber, peeled and seeded

Boston lettuce
Louisiana Remoulade (p. 41)

Steel Blade, French Fryer, Medium Slicing Disk

Prepare 6 salad plates with Boston lettuce leaves and chill.

Use the French fryer and process chunks of melon and jicama (or cucumber) and remove.

Peel and seed the avocados and use the medium serrated slicing disk to slice. Gently combine shrimp and vegetables in a large bowl and divide among the salad plates. Cover with a generous amount of sauce.

Note: This is attractive served in a hollowed out melon half or, serve in an avocado half instead of slicing them.

The abundance of parsley in many spicy sauces (i.e.: Remoulade) stems from its powers to neutralize sharp flavors. The Mexicans use cilantro and parsley liberally to dilute hot peppers.

> *First he (Peter Rabbit) ate some lettuce and some French beans and then he ate some radishes and then feeling rather sick, he went to look for some parsley.*
>
> Beatrix Potter

SESAME TOAST ROUNDS

Pre-heat oven to 450°

Bread	Seasoning Suggestions:
1 stick butter	Paprika
Herbs and spices or	Chervil, thyme, oregano
(1/2 tsp. seasoning salt)	Onion or garlic salt
1 T. sesame seeds	Lemon pepper

Steel Blade

Using some small cutters, cut out rounds from the bread, saving the scraps to process for bread crumbs.

Children will embrace this little job . . . . especially if they can use some interesting cutters.

Put the butter, cut in several pieces, in the processor bowl with seasoning salt and sesame seed (or herbs and spices of your choice) and process until combined and smooth.

Butter the bread on both sides, put on a cookie sheet, and bake about 5 minutes on each side (golden brown)

Serve with soups, canapes, molds, or appetizers.

HAM AND ASPARAGUS ROLL-UPS

This is marvelous as an appetizer on a raw vegetable platter or to accompany brunch or luncheon dishes.

8   slices very nice boiled ham
1   package frozen asparagus
4   T. (about) Bearnaise Butter (p. 67)
Toothpicks

Steel Blade

Cut the ham slices in half.

Cook the asparagus tender but not mushy and refresh under cold water. Cut off lower stem.

Spread some Bearnaise Butter on the ham, place the asparagus on it so that the tip will be visible when rolled up, roll up and secure with a toothpick.

Cover and chill before serving.

x2 CHEESE BALL

This may be packed into a crock, or shaped into a round and coated with herbs and nuts. It makes a marvelous gift from your kitchen.

8-10	ounces cheddar cheese
1/2	stick butter
1	3 ounce package cream cheese
1	clove garlic
1 1/2	tsp. prepared mustard
1	T. brandy or cognac

Steel Blade

Put the garlic in the processor bowl and run the machine to mince. Add cheese, butter and cream cheese in chunks, processing first with on-offs to break up, then run the machine to "grate" and finally cream. Add seasonings and brandy, processing smooth.

Pack into a crock. Or shape into a round and roll in the following mixture:

1	sprig parsley
1/2	cup chopped (with the processor) nuts
1	tsp. paprika
1	tsp. freshly ground pepper

Combine the ingredients in the processor, using the steel blade. Coat the cheese. Freezes well.

Dates and nuts, loaded alternately in the feeder tube, shredded with the shredding disk make a good coating also.

SUMMER APPETIZER

An unusual combination . . . . if you use low-calorie dressing, also a thinning one.

1	pound mushrooms
2	cups watermelon balls
2	cups honeydew melon balls

Italian dressing
1	tsp. lime juice
2	tsp. chives

This recipe does not use the processor unless you wish to make an Italian dressing with it.

Clean the mushrooms with a damp cloth. Scoop out balls from half a watermelon (about) and 2 honeydew melons. Save the rest for soup, or as a fresh flavor ingredient.

Toss them gently in a glass bowl, cover with the dressing, lime juice, and chives. Toss again before serving.

Very light . . . . very nice.

x2 CLAM AND CHUTNEY
CHEESE ROUND

1	can clams
2	8 ounce packages cream cheese
1/4	of an onion

Dash of Worcestershire
Peach or Apricot chutney
1	cup fresh chopped chives

Sesame toast rounds
Sliced apples or pears

Steel Blade

Drain clams and put in the processor using the steel blade.

Add the cream cheese, cut in chunks, onion, and Worcestershire. Process until smoothly combined. Pack in an oiled mold lined with cheesecloth, or a cakepan. When ready to use, unmold on your most beautiful silver tray, spread the top with chutney, then the chives, and surround with fresh sliced apples, and Sesame Toast Rounds.

x2 CHEESE PASTRY

A food processor and a cookie gun turns these out in no time.

2	sticks butter or margarine
8	ounces cheddar cheese
2	cups flour
1/2	tsp. salt
1/4	tsp. cayenne pepper

Steel Blade, Shredding Disk

Put the cheese through the shredding disk, or cut in chunks and put directly in the bowl. Process a few seconds. Add the margarine or butter, cut in pieces and process again to combine. Add the flour . . . process until mixed together like a dough. Chill, roll out and cut into shapes or "straws". Or, use cookie gun to make different shapes.

Bake at 375° about 15 minutes.

The variations are endless. Try adding 1 cup of sausage, cooked and drained and/or ground nuts.

x2 PATRIOTIC PEANUT APPETIZER

3	ounces cream cheese
1/2	cup peanuts or smoked almonds
1	T. apricot or peach chutney
3	strips bacon, fried crisp and drained

Steel Blade

Put the peanuts, chutney, and the cream cheese in the processor bowl with the steel blade. Process until smooth.

Spread on Sesame Toast Rounds or small pieces of plain toast. Crush the bacon in the processor bowl, sprinkle on top and run in a 450° oven 3-5 minutes and serve.

x2 CHEESE PUFFS

Pre-heat broiler

Sesame Toast rounds (p. 145)

8	ounces sharp cheddar cheese
1	egg yolk
1/2	tsp. each salt and pepper
Dash of Worcestershire	
1	tsp. baking powder
1	T. mayonnaise
1	egg white, beaten very stiff

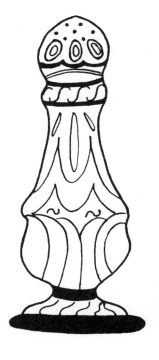

Steel Blade

Cut up the cheddar cheese in chunks and process with the steel blade until grated.

Add the rest of the ingredients, except the egg white and process a couple seconds.

Fold in the stiffly beaten egg white and mound on toast rounds. At this point, you may freeze them until you are ready to use or broil, not too close to the element, for 3-5 minutes or until puffed and browned.

x2 CRAB MOLD

Makes about 2 1/2 to 3 cups . . . . this is worth acquiring a fancy mold. Equally good made with salmon.

1	package unflavored gelatin (soften in 1/3 cup cold water, heat briefly, stirring to dissolve)
2	T. vermouth
2	tsp. horseradish
1/2	of a cucumber, seeded, cut in chunks
4	green onions
1	tsp. chives
1	tsp. freshly minced parsley
1/2	tsp. dill weed (only if you use salmon)
1/4	tsp. tarragon

Dash of salt and pepper

1	package frozen crabmeat
1	8 ounce package cream cheese

Steel Blade

Prepare the gelatin. Put everything but the crabmeat and the gelatin in the processor and process until smooth. Add the gelatin and the crabmeat and process by turning the machine on and off rapidly just to combine.

Pour into a wet mold, or an oiled one lined with cheesecloth. Chill 3-4 hours.

Garnish with fresh watercress, parsley or mint (for salmon) and serve with Sesame Toast Rounds.

Note: if you have any leftover, serve it for breakfast on an English muffin. Fabulous!

150

x2 SHRIMP BALLS

Makes 2-3 dozen

1 1/2	slices stale bread or rolls
1	tsp. each chicken bouillon powder and minced shallot
2	T. boiling water
5	water chestnuts
1	tsp. soy sauce
1/2	tsp. ground ginger
1	egg, separated
1/8	of a green pepper
Dash pepper	
1	pound shrimp, cleaned, peeled, (deveined but not cooked)

Peanut oil for frying

Steel Blade

Put the bread, bouillon, shallot, green pepper, water chestnuts and egg yolk in the processor bowl and process 5-10 seconds or until crushed together.

Add the shrimp and process again about 15-20 seconds or until minced and combined.

Beat the egg white until frothy, and add through the feeder tube with the machine running. If you have a pastry tube, force the mixture through it into little balls on wax paper or a plate rinsed with cold water.

Heat the oil, and fry the shrimp balls on both sides (they will usually turn themselves over) . . . takes about 2-3 minutes. Drain on paper towels and serve with Egg Roll Sauces (p. 100) or a Piquant Sauce.

Piquant Sauce:

Mix together:

1/2	cup catsup
1	tsp. lemon juice
1	T. horseradish

Try adding lobster or crab. Also try rolling in some bread crumbs before frying.

x2   OYSTERS ROCKEFELLER

To know how to eat is to know how to live

Escoffier

Pre-heat oven to 450°

Rock salt
2	dozen fresh oysters
8	sprigs fresh parsley
4	celery tops
3	"scrapes" lemon peel
1/4	tsp. freshly ground pepper
1/8	tsp. cayenne pepper
1/4	tsp. anise seed

Dash garlic powder
3	green onions
6	T. melted butter
1	package frozen spinach, cooked and well drained or
1	pound fresh spinach

Crumb mixture: (process together)

2	slices bread
1	ounce Parmesan cheese
2-3	T. butter

Steel Blade

Keep whole oysters in their shells or put in baking shells or ramekins on a baking sheet filled with rock salt.

Make the bread crumbs in the processor bowl with the steel blade and remove.

Put parsley, onion, lemon peel, celery leaves and spices in the work bowl and process until minced. Add the spinach and butter and process 10-15 seconds. Bake the oysters 5 minutes (edges will curl). Then divide spinach mixture on top, topping with a little crumb mixture. Return to oven at 450° about 5 minutes.

CREAMY MARINATED MUSHROOMS

This recipe was given to me by a dear English friend who intuitively knows how to make every meal a special occasion.

5   T. minced parsley
1   garlic clove
Juice from one lemon
2   T. oil
1/3   cup heavy cream
1   pound mushrooms
1/2   tsp. salt and freshly ground pepper
1/4   tsp. paprika

Steel Blade

Clean the mushrooms with a damp cloth and put in a large glass bowl.

Put the garlic clove and parsley in the processor bowl, using the steel blade, and process until minced. Add the seasonings and lemon juice and with the machine running, add the oil and cream.

Pour over the mushrooms and chill at least 4 hours, tossing a couple times.

Serve in a pretty glass bowl.

Note: If you have some left, slice them and saute in 1/2 of a stick of butter, and 2 T. port wine, and serve on some crusty French bread as a first course, or luncheon.

x2   CHEESE PUFFS WITH OLIVE BUTTER FILLING

Pre-heat oven to 425°

1	recipe Choux Pastry (p. 12)
3/4	cup Parmesan cheese (grated with steel blade)

Add the cheese after the eggs, making 40 miniature puff shells.

1	cup stuffed olives	4	T. butter
1	cup black olives	2	ounces cream cheese
1	T. mustard	3	T. mayonnaise

Steel Blade

Put all the ingredients in the processor bowl and process until combined (about 20 or 30 seconds). When the puffs are baked, pierce with a knife to let the steam escape. When cool, open and stuff with the olive mixture. You may heat 5 minutes before serving.

BEEF CANAPES

2-4   ounces cooked beef
Horseradish Butter (p. 67)
Pumpernickle or rye bread
Dill pickle
Red onion

Thin Serrated Slicing Disk

Cut the meat to lay in the feeder tube and using the slicing disk push it through. Remove. Then slice some onion strips and the dill pickle the same way. Cut the bread in bite size pieces and spread with Horseradish Butter. Put a slice of the beef on top, and then the pickle.

Suggestion: Try this with Liver Pate and a mushroom slice; smoked salmon and cream cheese spread with Mint Butter.

x2 STUFFED MUSHROOMS

Pre-heat oven to 400°

1	pound good size mushrooms
2	ounces Gruyere cheese
2	egg yolks
1	tsp. freeze dried shallot
1	tsp. minced parsley
1	piece of stale bread
2	T. liver pate
1	T. port wine
1/2	tsp. salt
Dash of pepper	
1/2	stick butter

Steel Blade

Cut the cheese in several pieces and process until 'grated' using the steel blade.

Wipe the mushrooms with a damp cloth and remove the stems, putting the stems in the processor bowl. Add the rest of the ingredients (except the butter) and process 10-12 seconds to combine.

Melt the butter, coat the mushroom caps, fill with the stuffing, and put them in a buttered baking dish.

Bake 10-15 minutes. They should not get too soft or soggy if you do not wash them with water or cook them too long.

x2 FRIED PASTRY APPETIZERS

These may be prepared ahead, but need to be fried within an hour of serving.

Pre-heat oven to 475°

1	recipe Basic Pastry (p. 9) chilled

1/2	pound shrimp (cooked and deveined) or
1	7 ounce can shrimp
4	ounces muenster cheese
1	stalk celery
4	green onions
1/4	of a green pepper
1	tsp. horseradish
1	T. catsup and mayonnaise

Beaten egg and 1 T. milk

Steel Blade

Roll the prepared pastry out on a floured board (fairly thin). Use plenty of flour on your hands. Cut out circles with a biscuit cutter, and brush with beaten egg and milk.

Put the onion, celery and green pepper in the bowl and process briefly. Put the rest of filling ingredients in the processor bowl and process by turning the machine on and off rapidly so the filling is coarsely chopped.

Put a spoonful of filling on each circle, covering it with another circle, and pressing the edges together. Seal with the egg wash.

Fry in hot fat, draining on paper towels. Sprinkle with some seasoned salt or Parmesan cheese.

Note: Try this filling in crepes or stuff inside some bread.

x2   ARTICHOKE PUFFS

4   fresh artichokes, cooked until tender
         (2-14 ounce cans may be substituted but fresh is better)
6   ounces Parmesan cheese
Several green onions
Several sprigs fresh parsley
1   tsp. lemon juice
1   cup mayonnaise

Steel Blade

If using canned artichokes, be sure to take the time to remove the feathery choke. If using fresh, scrape the edible portion from the leaves and remove choke from the heart. Whatever you do, do not put the leaves down the garbage disposal.

Put the cheese in the processor bowl, in chunks, and process first with on/off's, then run the machine to grate very fine. Leave the cheese in the bowl, add artichoke meat, green onions and parsley, processing to a puree. Add lemon juice and mayonnaise last, processing in briefly.

Mound on toast rounds or heat thoroughly and use as a dip. Dynamite!

x2   PIMENTO CHEESE

Being from Texas, it is difficult not to include Pimento Cheese . . . if I had a nickle for everyone who has asked me how to do this I'd retire to my kitchen and happily live on strawberry butter, croissants and champagne.

4   ounces processed Swiss cheese
8   ounces cheddar cheese
1   clove garlic
1   chunk onion
Dash of lemon juice
1   tsp. Worcestershire Sauce
1/2   cup homemade mayonnaise
Dash Tabasco
1/4   tsp. salt and pepper
Several pimentos including their juices

Steel Blade

Prepare mayonnaise and remove. In a dry bowl put the garlic, onion, lemon and Swiss cheese (in chunks) and process with on/off's to grate very fine. Add cheddar, processing in the same way. Add Tabasco, Worcestershire and process to pasty consistency. Add mayonnaise, salt and pepper, process with a couple of on/off's. Add pimentos last and process in with on/off's, then run machine a few seconds (they'll be diced throughout the cheeses). Serve with crackers as an appetizer or as a sandwich spread.

Fabulous grilled cheese: Spread the cheese on a slice of bread, top with another slice and saute in hot butter. Serve with jalapeno or pepper jelly. Try this with little Pain de Mie toasts for a terrific appetizer.

x2   CHUNKY GUACAMOLE

3   ripe avocados
1/2   of an onion or several small green onions
1   T. lemon juice
A couple of green chilies
2   tsp. piquant sauce or Tabasco to taste
1   tomato, cut into chunks
Salt and pepper to taste
Cilantro (optional)

Steel Blade

Put the onion directly into the bowl and run the machine to mince. Add chilies (on/off's).

Add lemon juice and avocados, in chunks, processing first with on/off's, then running the machine to puree.

Season to taste with piquant sauce or Tabasco, salt and pepper. Adjust to personal preference.

Add tomato, in chunks, processing with on/off's to dice and combine.

Note: Several sprigs of fresh cilantro, sometimes available, is a nice addition. Mince first with the onion. Chili powder (1/4 tsp.) is also a good addition. Leave the seed on top of the Guacamole if preparing ahead. It will help retard browning.

158

First Course and Salads

The dinner table was the altar of

the Gods of Friendship and Hospitality.

Plutarch

Fruits and vegetables are a beautiful part

of a meal when they are fresh, tender, and used

in exciting new ways.

Albert Stockli

JICAMA-MELON SALAD

1   jicama
1   cantaloupe melon
1   honeydew melon
Juice of one lime

Dressing:

6-8   ounces Ricotta cheese
1/4   cup sour cream
Juice and sections from 1/2 orange
1   T. brown sugar

Garnish:

Mint sprigs or smoked salted almonds

French Fryer, Steel Blade

Cut the melons and jicama to fit the feeder tube . . . about 1 1/2 inch strips. Using the French fryer and the pusher cut them into julienne strips. Be sure they are packed tightly in the tube. Remove to a bowl, toss together with the juice of one lime.

Change to the steel blade and process the ricotta cheese and orange juice and sections smooth. Add the sugar and sour cream and process briefly to combine. Pour over the fruit and chill. Garnish with mint sprigs or chopped (in the processor) smoked salted almonds. Fresh!

Note: Cucumber, seeds removed, may be substituted for the jicama.

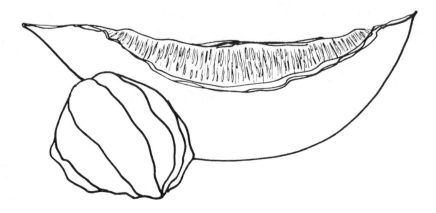

GREEN BEAN SALAD WITH BLUE CHEESE

2   cans of green beans or fresh cooked beans
1   head cauliflower
1   red onion
3   hard boiled eggs

3-4   ounces blue cheese
1   T. lemon juice
2   ounces cream cheese
1   cup sour cream
4   T. mayonnaise
1   tsp. honey
Salt and pepper to taste
Dash of lemon juice

Thin Serrated Slicing Disk, Steel Blade

If you have planned ahead, soak the green beans overnight or several hours in 1/3 cup each vinegar and oil plus some sugar, salt and pepper. Use 1 T. lemon juice over the onions and slice using the thin serrated slicing disk and toss with the beans. Cover tightly and stir every several hours (or when you think about it).

Cut the cauliflower into chunks that fit the feeder tube (flat ends against the blade) and slice with the thin slicing blade. Remove to a salad bowl. Use the same slicing disk and slice in the eggs (they'll be crumbled). Add to the salad bowl. Drain the beans and onions and toss with the other vegetables.

Use the steel blade and process blue cheese and cream cheese with on/off's. Add sour cream, mayonnaise, lemon juice, honey and seasonings, processing in briefly. Pour over the salad and serve on lettuce leaves or as is. This may be prepared ahead.

Everything I eat has been proved by some doctor or other to be a deadly poison, and everything I don't eat has been proved to be indispensable for life . . . But I go marching on.

Bernard Shaw

x2 WALDORF SALAD

Shows how the french fryer can be used to "dice".

		Dressing:	
2	apples	4	T. mayonnaise
4	stalks of celery	2	tsp. honey
1/2	Jicama (peeled)	2	tsp. lemon juice (or lime juice)
1/2	cup walnuts	1/4-1/2 tsp. salt	

French Fryer, Plastic Knife, Medium Serrated Slicer

Core the apples and cut into chunks. Peel the jicama and cut into chunks. Use the French fryer and load the feeder tube alternately with apple chunks, celery chunks and jicama chunks. The smaller the chunks, the finer the "dice" . . . if the pieces are as long as the feeder tube they will look like French fries. Push through rapidly, loading the feeder tube again. The nuts may be done with the vegetables also, or you may use the medium serrated slicer pushing them through by themselves after doing the vegetables.

Put in the plastic mixing blade, and all the dressing ingredients on top of the fruit and process with quick on/off's to mix everything together. Ready to serve . . . and all in one bowl.

Jicama may be omitted. Try adding a pear, melon chunks or seeded cucumbers with the apples.

CUCUMBER-ONION SALAD

3	cucumbers	1	tsp. sugar and 1/2 tsp. salt
1	small onion (whole)	1	cup sour cream
Lemon juice		Fresh parsley	
1/4	tsp. dill	Coarse ground pepper	
3	T. vinegar		

Slicing Disks, Steel Blade

Cut the round ends off the cucumbers and slice using the medium serrated slicer. Change to the thin slicer (use plenty of lemon juice with the onion) and load the onion through the bottom of the feeder tube. Slice with moderate pressure. Remove vegetables to a serving dish. Process seasonings and sour cream with quick on/off's, (steel blade) adding vinegar, and pour over vegetables. Cover and chill. Use the steel blade again to mince the parsley when ready to serve. Sprinkle over the top, adding freshly ground black pepper.

SHREDDED SQUASH SALAD

4   zucchini squash
1/2   cup walnuts
4   ounces Parmesan or Romano cheese
Romaine lettuce leaves

Lemon-Parsley Dressing (p. 167)

Julienne Blade, Steel Blade, Slicing Disk (Medium Serrated)

Wash the squash but do not peel. Use the steel blade and put cheese in the bowl in chunks. Process first with on/off's, then run machine to grate to a powder. Change to the slicing disk and slice in the nuts. Remove the nuts and cheese. Use the julienne blade and load the feeder tube with the squash stacked horizontally and shred in using firm pressure. If the skin gets stuck, bounce several times with the pusher to free up. Spread out on paper towel to remove excess moisture.

Use the steel blade and prepare dressing (see p. 167). Toss everything together and serve on Romaine lettuce leaves.

FRESH PINEAPPLE SALAD

1   head Boston or Romaine lettuce
1   fresh pineapple (small)
1/2   cup Pine Nuts (walnuts or toasted almonds)
1/2   of a fresh coconut
Salt
1   T. oil

Dressing:

1/2   tsp. salt
Several sprigs parsley
Black coarse ground pepper
1   T. lemon juice
2   T. vinegar
6   T. oil
1   shallot
Juice from the pineapple

Julienne Blade, Steel Blade, Slicing Disk

Tear the lettuce and place in a salad bowl.

Use the julienne blade and load the feeder tube with pieces of coconut wedged in horizontally for long shreds.

Change to the plastic knife and add pine nuts (or slice in walnuts with the medium or fine serrated slicer), 1/4-1/2 tsp. salt and 1 T. oil. Process with a few on/off's to combine, then spread on a greased cookie sheet and toast at 450° until golden (5-8 min.).

Remove pineapple meat from the shell. Load the feeder tube with large pieces and slice using the medium serrated slicing disk. Drain off the juice and add fruit to the lettuce.

Prepare the dressing (steel blade) by mincing shallot and parsley first, then adding remaining ingredients, process smooth and season to taste.

Add toasted coconut and nuts and toss with dressing at serving time.

Serving Suggestions:

Will serve about 6 generously. Very good with Roast Pork, Barbeque dishes. Try adding cubed chicken and cantaloupe for luncheon salad.

The table is the only place where a man is never bored during the first hour.

Brillat-Savarin

CARROT SALAD

1   pound cooked until just tender carrots
1/2   onion + lemon juice
1   green pepper
1   tomato
Optional: bunch of green onions (wedge between carrots to slice)

Dressing:

Fresh parsley
1   shallot
1/2   tsp. dry mustard
Dash pepper
1/2   tsp. salt
2   T. tomato paste
2   T. brown sugar (or honey)
4   T. vinegar
8   T. oil
Additional liquid for proper consistency

Medium Serrated Slicing Disk, French Fryer, Steel Blade

Slice the cooked carrots with the medium slicer using very firm pressure and transfer to a salad bowl. Load the feeder tube with onion and green pepper (use some lemon juice with the onion to cut the bitterness) and use the French fryer to dice. Prepare the dressing by mincing the shallot and parsley first, then adding all the seasonings and liquids, processing smooth. If quite thick you may need to add a little water. Pour over the salad.

Use the French fryer. Cut the tomato in chunks and process. Toss with the rest of the salad and chill overnight.

*Fruits and vegetables are an integral part
of a meal — use them when they are
fresh and experiment with new, fun ideas.*

GRAPEFRUIT APPETIZER

Colorful!

For 8

Pre-heat oven to 400°

4	grapefruits
1	pomegranate
3	T. currant Jelly
2	T. Grenadine syrup
1	tsp. arrowroot

Cinnamon sugar
1/4   cup sweet sherry

Pomegranates are ripe when they are reddish brown and dry . . . . they are a fall and winter fruit, and if you've ever had grenadine syrup . . . that's the flavor. Refreshing! Open the fruit and scoop out the seeds and juices. Put them in a saucepan with the arrowroot, which has been dissolved in the grenadine. Stir and thicken, then melt with the currant jelly. Set aside. (Thicken further if necessary).

Cut the grapefruits in half. With a knife, cut around the edges and membrane so the sections will spoon out easily. Pour off excess juice and divide the sherry between the fruits. Sprinkle with cinnamon sugar and bake for 10 minutes.

Spoon a generous spoonful of the pomegranate mixture over each fruit. Serve.

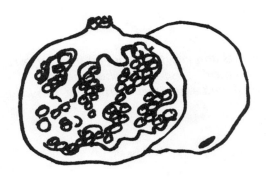

FRESH LEEK SALAD

Serves 4-6

2	bunches leeks
8	cherry tomatoes
2	hard boiled eggs
1/4	tsp. salt

Boston lettuce

Lemon-Parsley Dressing:

1	clove garlic
6-8	sprigs fresh parsley
1/4	tsp. each dill, dry mustard, pepper, salt
4	T. lemon juice
1	cup salad oil

Steel Blade

Boil the leeks about 5-6 minutes, tender but not too soft. Drain and rinse under cold water. Chill.

Cut the eggs in half and process until minced. Remove.

Put the parsley and garlic in the processor bowl and process until finely minced. Add the lemon juice and the rest of the seasonings, and with the machine running add the oil through the feeder tube. Set aside.

To assemble:

Put some lettuce leaves on each plate. Make a slice down the center of the leek, but not all the way through, and put two on each plate. Pour some dressing over each plate, and the chopped egg on top. Garnish with several cherry tomatoes.

> *All the goodness of a good egg cannot make up for the badness of a bad one.*
>
> Charles A. Dana

CEDAR KEY SALAD

There is a quaint, and very windblown little village on the west coast of Florida that many mid-Florida dwellers visit for fresh seafood. This is a variation of a salad that all the restaurants serve in one way or another.

For 8

1	head cabbage
1	large bunch green grapes
1	fresh pineapple (cut in chunks)
1	cup fresh Mayonnaise (p. 39)
1/2	cup peanuts
1 1/2	pints vanilla ice cream
1/2	cup diced dates

Steel Blade, Shredding Disk, Slicing Disk

Using the slicing disk, slice the cabbage and transfer to a large bowl. Push the grapes through the feeder tube to slice them. Add to the cabbage. Change to the steel blade, and process the pineapple. Add to the cabbage and grapes. Arrange them together on 8 salad plates.

Wipe out the bowl, then add the peanuts and process with the steel blade until finely chopped. Remove. Prepare the Mayonnaise and remove all but one cup. Add the ice cream in spoonfuls and process smooth. Add the peanuts, processing to combine together. Chill in the freezer and pour over the cabbage and fruit when ready to serve. Top with diced dates . . . . just a few for each salad.

Goes well with fish, chicken and fresh pork.

x2 FRESH PEAR SALAD

You may substitute canned pears, but fresh are better . . . . Buy pears a little bit green and let them ripen in your kitchen . . . . they'll have less bruises.

Serves 4

Boston Lettuce
4   ripe pears
1   3 ounce package cream cheese
1   3 ounce package Camembert cheese

Frosted grapes
Fresh berries

Dressing:

1   cup fresh Mayonnaise (p. 39)
3   T. honey
3   T. fruity white wine
1   tsp. fresh chives

Slicing Disk, Steel Blade

Wash the lettuce and arrange on the plates.

Cut the pears in half and remove the core. Trim off the round end so they lay flat against the blade. Slice through and sprinkle with lemon juice. Divide on top of the lettuce. Change to the steel blade and process the two cheeses together until very smooth. Divide among the pears. (Use a pastry tube if you have one.)

Using the steel blade, prepare the Mayonnaise, adding the honey and white wine after you have added the oil. Pour about 1 tablespoon over the cheese and pears.

Top with some fresh seasonal berries, and garnish with frosted grapes.

SHRIMP DE JONGHE

Pre-heat broiler

1	pound medium or large shrimp
1	stick of unsalted butter
1	hard roll
1	garlic sliver
1	shallot
1	T. Parmesan cheese (grated)
3	sprigs of parsley
1	cup of white wine

Steel Blade

> *Drink wine, and have the gout;*
> *drink no wine, and have the*
> *gout too.*
>
> 16th Century

Put the garlic and shallots into the processor bowl and mince. Put the hard roll into the processor bowl and process using the steel blade until it is in crumbs. Add Parmesan.

Add the butter, cut in several pieces and the parsley, processing until combined.

Clean the shrimp and remove the tails (or ask the fish market to prepare them). Simmer them in the white wine 3-5 minutes. Then transfer to four small shells, with the wine. Divide the butter mixture between the shells. When ready to serve, run under the boiler a few minutes until hot and bubbling.

Serve with some small toast rounds or rolls so you don't miss any of the sauce.

170

LAYERED SALAD

There is no way you can own a processor and not start creating layered vegetable salads . . . the vegetables look so marvelous cut very thin or shredded, you'll collect a variety of glass salad bowls. Here's one combination.

3	white squash, raw
6	carrots, partially cooked
1	cup cooked green beans
3-4	leeks, raw
1	bottle low calorie creamy Italian dressing
1	large fresh tomato
1	T. fresh minced parsley

Medium Serrated Slicing Disk, Steel Blade

Cook the carrots until just barely tender . . . . they should be slightly crunchy. Put them through the feeder tube using the slicing disk and slice. Remove.

Wash the squash, but do not peel, and put them through the feeder tube (they are small enough to fit on their side) Remove.

Slice the leeks. Cook the green beans until just tender. Rinse under cold water and drain.

Layer the vegetables in a glass bowl.

Put the tomato and parsley in the processor bowl using the steel blade and process until minced and crushed. Combine with the dressing and pour over the salad. Cover and chill.

"Paradise" comes from the Persian word for garden.

x2   JICAMA SALAD

This is one of those "prepare ahead salads" . . . an adaptation from a friend's kitchen.

Serves 10-12 people

1	cup mayonnaise
1/2	cup Parmesan cheese
1/2	cup sour cream

1	head iceberg lettuce
1	green pepper
2	leeks, whites only
1	jicama (use water chesnuts if you don't have this vegetable)
1	package frozen peas, thawed, not cooked
1/2	pound fresh white mushrooms, without bruises

Medium Serrated Slicing Disk, Steel Blade

Slice the lettuce with the slicing disk. Remove. Use the French fryer for the green pepper and peeled jicama. Stack the leeks vertically and slice with the slicing disk. Rinse under cold water.

Layer the vegetables in a large glass bowl starting with 2/3 of the lettuce, thawed peas, leeks, jicama, green pepper, then the remaining lettuce.

Prepare the mayonnaise, remove and mix with sour cream. Grate the Parmesan using the steel blade until finely grated, and mix with the dressings. Pour over the top, cover and refrigerate 3-6 hours.

*The only way to keep your health is
to eat what you don't want
drink what you don't like, and
do what you'd rather not.*

Mark Twain

CRISP VEGETABLE SALAD

This is best to do when asparagus is in season and fresh.

Serves 4

1	bunch fresh asparagus
1/2	head of cauliflower
1	bunch watercress

1/2	cup shaved almonds
2	T. butter

Cheese Dressing:

4	ounces Swiss cheese
1/4	cup vinegar
3/4	cup oil
1	egg white
1/4	tsp. salt pepper
1/2	tsp. dry mustard
1	tsp. minced parsley
1/2	tsp. freeze dried shallot
1/2	tsp. lemon juice

Slicing Disk, Steel Blade

Divide the watercress between four salad plates. Cook the asparagus until just tender but still a bit crunchy. Drain under cool water.

Divide the cauliflower into bunches and using the slicing disk, slice thinly. Arrange the two on a salad plate.

Put the shallot, cheese, and seasonings in the processor bowl using the steel blade and process until the cheese is grated fine. Add the oil, vinegar and egg white through the feeder tube with the machine running and process about 30 seconds. Divide over the vegetables.

Saute the almonds in the butter and divide on top of the vegetables.

FRESH GARDEN SALAD

There is nothing to quite equal a bowl of assorted greens.

1	head iceberg lettuce	Dressing:
1	head Boston lettuce	
1	head Romaine lettuce	Freshly ground pepper
1/2	pound mushrooms	1 clove garlic
1/2	red onion	3/4 cup oil
3	ounces Swiss cheese	1/4 cup red wine vinegar
2	stalks celery	1 egg white
		Dash salt
Croutons (optional)		1/4 tsp. dry mustard

Steel Blade, Medium Serrated Slicing Disk

Tear the Boston and Romaine into a salad bowl. Using the slicing disk, push the iceberg lettuce, cut into chunks, through the feeder tube. Add to the other lettuce and toss together.

Peel the onion, and push through the slicing disk. Cut the celery to fit the feeder tube and repeat, slicing it also. Clean the mushrooms, and slice the same way.

Toss the celery with the lettuce and put the mushrooms and onions in a shallow dish.

Change to the steel blade. Put the garlic, seasonings, and Swiss cheese, cut into chunks, into the processor bowl and process until very finely minced. Add the liquids through the feeder tube and process 20-30 seconds more.

Pour the dressing over the mushrooms and onions, adding some salt and freshly ground pepper. Toss with the lettuce when ready to serve.

FRESH TOMATO SALAD-SOUP

Prepare this when tomatoes are home grown and very good. If you prefer to make your own dressing rather than a bottled one, use oil and vinegar with a little fresh garlic.

12	large tomatoes
2	green peppers
3	red onions
1	pound mushrooms, cleaned
4-5	sprigs parsley
1	can beef consomme
2	T. dry sherry
1	bottle red wine vinegar and oil salad dressing

Croutons:

6-8	pieces French bread
1	stick butter, cut in chunks
1/4	cup Parmesan cheese
1/2	tsp. salt and pepper
1/4	tsp. each thyme and basil

Slicing Disk, Steel Blade

Cut the tomatoes in quarters and spread in a 9 by 13 pyrex dish. Cut the peppers in chunks, and slice by pushing through the feeder tube. Repeat with the onions and the mushrooms, and add to the tomatoes.

Put the parsley in the processor bowl, changing to the steel blade and mince. Sprinkle over the vegetables.

Pour the 3 liquids over all and toss lightly. Chill 3-4 hours, or overnight, covered.

Using the steel blade, process the cheese, seasonings and butter. Butter the bread on both sides, cut into large chunks and toast in 450° oven until lightly browned.

Serve the salad in a shallow bowl, with its juices, topped generously with croutons.

Serve with a fork and a spoon.

OYSTERS CREATION

Pre-heat oven to 400°

Serves 6

1 1/2	dozen oysters	1/3	cup Parmesan cheese
8	fresh artichokes, cooked tender	1/3	cup Gruyere cheese
2	leeks	1/2	cup White Sauce (p. 36)
1/2	tsp. salt and pepper		
1/2	stick butter		Tart shells (any pastry) or:
1	T. flour		Thick sliced French bread

Oyster liquid and white wine to make 1 cup

Steel Blade

Prepare and bake the tart shells or butter and toast the bread on both sides. Use the steel blade to grate the Parmesan.

Warm the wine and oyster liquid and simmer the oysters just a few minutes. Remove and put them in the processor bowl.

Boil the leeks in salted water 2-3 minutes, then add to the processor bowl. Remove the heart from the artichokes and add to the bowl. Process until all are minced and pureed (20 seconds or so). Add the flour and seasonings, and with the machine running, the wine and oyster liquid through the feeder tube. Remove.

Put the Gruyere cheese in the processor bowl and "grate" using the steel blade. Add the prepared White Sauce (p. 36), process to combine. Remove and mix with pureed mixture.

Spoon into the shells, top with the Parmesan cheese, and bake 10-12 minutes or until nicely browned.

If using the bread, heat the mixture in a saucepan, stirring all the time, and spoon over the bread, topping with the cheese. Run it under the broiler just a minute to melt the cheese.

dlc-7 When doing this in one bowl, change to the shredding disk (after pureeing leeks and artichokes) and shred in cheese. Change again to the plastic knife, add White Sauce and combine with the pulse.

MUSHROOM TART

Make this in individual tart shells, ramekins, or a large quiche pan . . . a little rich but absolutely marvelous.

Serves 8

Pre-heat oven to 375°

1   recipe Basic Pastry (p. 9)

1   pound mushrooms
1   cup heavy cream
1   stick butter
1   shallot
2   eggs, beaten
1/2   cup port wine
6   ounces Gruyere cheese

Vegetable Slicing Disk (Smooth), Steel Blade

Prepare the pastry and chill. Roll out on a floured surface and line the shells you decide to use.

Clean the mushrooms with a damp cloth and slice them by pushing them through the feeder tube. Do the shallot along with the mushrooms. Remove. Put the cheese (in chunks) in the bowl and process on/off to grate.

Melt half the butter in a heavy skillet and saute the mushrooms about 5 minutes. Add the cream, slowly, stirring briskly, then the port wine, and half the cheese, stirring all the time. Remove from heat.

Bake the shells for 10-15 minutes, pricking the bottom pastry first. They should be lightly browned.

Beat the eggs in the processor bowl using the steel blade. Add 1 T. flour, and with the machine running, add the rest of the butter (melted) through the feeder tube. Add to the mushroom mixture, fill the shells and top with the rest of the cheese. Turn the oven to 500° and heat the tarts until the cheese melts and is slightly browned (a few minutes).

x2 CRAB ALASKA

Very 'gourmet'.

Pre-heat oven to 350°

**Grapefruit or
English Muffins, halved**

2	6 ounce packages frozen crabmeat
6	sprigs fresh parsley
2	T. vermouth
1	8 ounce package cream cheese
1	tsp. lemon juice
1	T. horseradish
1	T. powdered sugar
1/2	cup sliced almonds

Meringue Topping:

3	egg whites
1/8	tsp. cream of tartar
1	T. sugar
2	T. mayonnaise

Steel Blade

To prepare the crab, drain and thaw, reserving the liquid for another time.

Put the parsley, cream cheese, horseradish, vermouth, sugar and lemon juice in the processor bowl and process until smooth. Add the crab, processing by turning the machine on and off rapidly to chop coarsely.

Mound the mixture on toasted English muffin halves or; prepare the grapefruit by removing the sections, scraping out the membrane, and folding the sections into the crab mixture. Re-stuff the grapefruit shell and heat in the oven for 10 minutes. (If you are using the muffins, heat for 10 minutes.)

Beat the egg whites until very stiff, adding the sugar after they first begin to stiffen. Very gently and quickly fold in the mayonnaise (the oil will make the egg whites change consistency so do this very rapidly). Divide on top the crab mixture, returning to the oven, turned up to 500°, until browned (5 minutes).

Garnish with the sliced almonds.

LATE SUMMER LAYERED SALAD

Serves 8-10

		Dressing:	
2	green peppers	Fresh basil and parsley	
1	red onion	Juice of one lemon	
1	cantaloupe melon	1	shallot
4	fresh tomatoes	1	T. red wine vinegar
		1/2	tsp. salt
		1/4	tsp. dry mustard and Hungarian paprika
		Coarse ground pepper	
		Juice from tomatoes and melon	
		6	T. oil

Medium and Thin Serrated Slicing Disk, French Fryer, Steel Blade

Use a 9 by 12 pyrex dish. Core the green peppers, cut off the round bottom and pack in the feeder tube so they fit quite firmly. Slice with the thin slicing disk and spread over the bottom of the dish. Cut the onion to fit the feeder tube and slice in the same manner. Remove and place on top of the peppers. Core the tomatoes, cut in half and slice with the medium slicer. Layer slices on top of the onion and reserve juice.

Cut the melon in wedges and use the French fryer. Load the feeder tube with chunks of melon that fill the tube laying horizontally. Put on top of the tomatoes. Drain and save juice.

With the steel blade mince the shallot. Add basil and parsley, processing to mince. Add remaining ingredients and process to combine. Toss with the vegetables.

179

CHEF'S SALAD WITH
ORANGE FRENCH DRESSING

Get out all your blades, a beautiful large glass salad bowl and invite your curious friends into your kitchen while you "dice and dump".

Sections from 3 oranges (save juice)
1/2	pound fresh spinach (tear by hand)
1	head iceberg lettuce (medium serrated slicing disk)
1	large chunk of ham (to fill feeder tube) (thin serrated slicing disk)
1/2	red onion (thin slicing disk)
1	green pepper (French fryer)
1	cantaloupe (French fryer)
4	pieces of crisp bacon (steel blade)

Using the blades marked, slice, dice and prepare everything, transferring to a large salad bowl. Cut the pepper and cantaloupe into chunks before loading the feeder tube.

Steel Blade

Orange Dressing:

1	shallot
Juice from the oranges	
Several sprigs fresh parsley	
1/2	tsp. salt
1/4	tsp. dry mustard
Dash pepper	
1	tsp. honey
1	egg
2	T. vinegar
6	T. oil
2	T. water
2-3	ounces Swiss or Gruyere cheese (in chunks)

Start the machine (steel blade) and drop the shallot through the feeder tube. Add parsley, seasonings and cheese processing to mince and combine. Add egg, honey and with the machine running, the juice, vinegar, water and oil through the feeder tube.

Main Dishes

. . . . .There's a fire softly burning

and supper's on the stove. . . . . . .

Hey, its good to be back home again. . . . .

John Denver

BEEF AND PASTA

1	recipe Basic Pasta (p. 10) or
3	cups (dry) Fettucine
1	clove garlic
1 1/2	pounds chuck, including some of the fat
2-3	Italian sausages
2	ounces tomato paste
1/2	pound fresh mushrooms
1/2	pound fresh spinach
1/2	cup cottage cheese

Fresh basil or 1 tsp. dried
Fresh parsley

1/2	of an onion
1	cup White Sauce (p. 36)
2	T. Demi-Glace (p. 63)

Salt and pepper to taste

1-2	T. each butter and oil
3	ounces Muenster cheese, <u>very</u> cold

*Steel Blade, Thin Vegetable Slicing Disk, Fine Shredding Disk
or Julienne Blade*

Prepare the Pasta using the basic recipe and a pasta machine. Or, boil packaged pasta until just tender . . . not too soft . . . rinse under cool water briefly.

Cut the meat into chunks, removing gristle, and put about half of it in the processor bowl (steel blade) to grind. Use on/off's (pulse) until coarsely ground. Process the rest of the meat, adding garlic, onion, parsley sprigs and basil. Remove and saute in 1-2 T. hot oil. Slice the sausages and add to the saute pan (medium serrated slicing disk).

Use the vegetable slicing disk and load the feeder tube with mushrooms. Process through, then remove to a saute pan and saute in 1-2 T. hot butter. Stir in tomato paste, Demi-Glace, and White Sauce. Add to the beef and keep warm.

Boil the spinach 2 minutes, rinse and drain. Process (steel blade) with several on/off's to chop . . . do not run the machine to puree. Add to the beef and mushrooms along with cottage cheese. Salt and pepper to taste, heat thoroughly and serve with the pasta.

Shred the cheese with the fine shredding disk or julienne blade and serve as you would Parmesan with spaghetti.

Note: Add a fresh diced tomato with the spinach. Cut the tomato in chunks and dice with the French fryer.

SPITZ'S SPECIAL CHILI

Margo Spitz, one of San Antonio's most charming television person-
alities, is responsible for this recipe. Every two to three weeks we
have some new fun with the Cuisinart during her show. One diced
onion was about all it took to get her hooked. Her enthusiasm for
good food (and the recipes loaded with sliced, diced and chopped
ingredients she loves to share) are delightful.

4-5	cups water	2	pounds pork shoulder
1/2	pound pinto beans	2	pounds chuck
6	cups canned tomatoes	2	T. salt
6	green peppers	1/3	cup chili powder
2	large onions (in chunks)	1 1/2	tsp. each pepper, cumin
2	cloves garlic		seed and Accent
2	T. oil		
1	cup loosely packed parsley		
1	stick butter		

Steel Blade, French Fryer

Wash the beans and soak overnight in the water. Simmer (in the same
water) about 40 minutes, adding additional water if necessary. Add
tomatoes, simmer 5 minutes.

Heat the oil and half the butter in a large saute pan. Use the French
fryer and dice the onions. Remove and saute. Change to the steel
blade and mince garlic (run the machine), then add green peppers
and process with rapid on/off's to dice. Add to the saute pan. Dry
out the bowl.

Cut all the meat into chunks and process (steel blade) in batches of
about 1 cup using on/off's 3-4 times to grind coarsely. Brown in
remaining butter. Add seasonings. Process parsley with steel blade
and add. Transfer to stock pot and simmer covered one hour.
Uncover, simmer an additional hour. Add more beef stock if it is too
thick. Serves about 10 people.

Margo suggests serving this with lots of grated cheese and additional
diced onions. I asked her if she served it this way before or after she
got her Cuisinart . . . she just smiled.

dlc-7 The new machine will process larger quantities of meat at one
time. You can grind 1 1/4 pounds of meat quite successfully at one
time. Use the pulse instead of the on/off's.

CHORIZO SAUSAGE

1 1/2	lbs. fresh pork, including all fat, gristle removed
1/2	lbs. additional meat (beef or veal)

1	clove garlic
1/2	tsp. allspice
2	T. mild chili powder
3	T. vinegar
2	tsp. cilantro
1	tsp. salt
1/4	tsp. pepper
1	tsp. oregano
1/2	tsp. ground cloves
1/4	tsp. pepper flakes

Steel Blade

Put the garlic and meats (in chunks) in the bowl about 1 cup at a time. Process with on/off's until desired texture. Process the seasonings with the meat. Combine meats together in a separate bowl and add vinegar. Form into patties and saute until cooked through.

TENDERLOIN IN MUSHROOMS
AND MADEIRA

A simple but very elegant dish. Serve with wild rice and fresh vegetable.

2	pounds tenderloin
1	pound mushrooms
2	shallots
1	stick butter
1 1/2	cups cream
1	cup Madeira
1 to 2	T. cornstarch
1/2	tsp. salt
1/4	tsp. pepper

Slicing Disk

Medium or Thin Serrated Slicing Disk, Vegetable Slicing Disk

Run machine (steel blade) and drop in shallots to mince.

Use one of the serrated slicing disks and slice meat. Saute meat and shallots in butter (rare) and remove.

Clean mushrooms and slice with smooth slicing disk. Saute, adding more butter if needed. Add seasonings and cream gradually, stirring to thicken. Add Madeira, mixed with cornstarch, bring to a boil and add tenderloin.

Serve immediately with rice.

STEAK AND KIDNEY PIE

A traditional Scottish Dish that the processor makes a breeze.

Pre-heat oven to 400°

2	recipes Puff Pastry (p. 11)
2 1/2	pounds chuck or stew beef
1/2	lb. lamb kidney
1	dozen oysters
1	onion
1 1/2	tsp. salt and pepper
2	T. flour

Some fat from the stew beef
1   cup beef stock

Egg wash:

1   beaten egg and 1 T. water

Steel Blade

Prepare the pastry ahead. Cut the meat and onions in large chunks, dust with flour, salt and pepper, brown in hot fat and simmer in the beef stock about an hour. Cool.

Put the meats, onions and the oysters in the processor bowl and process together using the steel blade until ground. If you wish it to be coarsely ground, process by turning the machine on and off rapidly.

Roll out the pastry, in two sections, on a floured surface. Line the bottom of a 10" pie plate with half of the pastry, pricking the bottom in a couple places. Spoon in the onion and meat mixture.

Top with the rest of the pastry, reserving some for decorations . . . . . (use your Scottish imagination)! Prick in several places and brush with the egg wash.

Bake for 25-30 minutes, or until pastry is done.

Note: You may substitute a basic pastry.

VEAL IN SEAFOOD SAUCE

Pre-heat oven to 350°

8	veal filets
Salt and pepper	
Flour	
1/2	pound shrimp pieces, cooked and deveined
1	6 ounce package frozen crabmeat, thawed
1	green pepper
1	large tomato
2	shallots
4-6	sprigs parsley
1	tsp. lemon juice
1	pound mushrooms
2	T. flour
1	cup milk
Reserved liquid from the crabmeat	
1/2	cup white wine
1	stick butter

Slicing Disk, Steel Blade

Pound the veal filets if they are not tender, then sprinkle them with salt, pepper and flour and saute them in half of the butter until the juice runs pink. Set aside to keep warm.

Clean the mushrooms with a damp cloth, then using the slicing disk, slice them by pushing through the feeder tube. Change to the steel blade (removing mushrooms from the bowl) and dice the pepper and shallot by using the on/off method of "chopping" with the processor. Saute the vegetables in the same pan as the veal, adding more butter if necessary.

Drain the liquid from the crab and add to the wine, and milk. Warm in a saucepan.

Cut tomato in quarters and process with French fry blade. Drain off juices and seeds.

Using the steel blade, process parsley and lemon juice. Add any remaining butter and flour. With the machine running add one cup of the warm liquid through the feeder tube. Transfer to the saute pan, with the vegetables, stirring over medium heat, adding the rest of the liquid. Stir and thicken. Add the crab, tomatoes, shrimp, and pour over the veal in a baking dish.

Bake covered, 10-12 minutes, or until heated through.

SUNDAY SUPPER

Fresh vegetables ... last night's ham ... and hard boiled eggs makes a lovely summer supper.

Pre-heat oven to 350°

1-2	cups ham
1	box Brussels sprouts (1 1/2 cups)
5-6	hard boiled eggs
1/4	tsp. dill
1	tsp. fresh minced parsley
1/2	tsp. pepper

1 1/2	cups Basic White Sauce (p. 36)
4	ounces shredded Gruyere cheese
1/3	cup Basic Bread Crumbs (p. 7)

Steel Blade, Medium Serrated Slicing Disk, Shredding Disk

Slice sprouts with slicing disk ... blanch 1 minute and rinse under cool water.

Using the shredding disk, shred the cheese. Remove and prepare the White Sauce by processing the flour and butter using the steel blade. With the machine running, add 1/2 cup of the warm milk, then the cheese, then the rest of the milk and seasonings. Transfer to a saucepan and stir until thickened. Add a little milk if necessary.

Prepare the crumbs.

Using the slicing disk, slice the ham and remove. Then slice the eggs, forcing them through the feeder tube standing them on end.

Layer everything in a buttered casserole adding the seasonings and topping with the crumbs. Bake 10-12 minutes or until heated through.

Serve with some fresh tomatoes.

MEXICAN PIZZA

There's nothing more fun or memorable for teen-agers (families too!) than gathering in the kitchen putting a pizza together. This is a very loose recipe and a great project when you first get your processor. Start by making the pizza dough and end with the cheese on top.
Pre-heat oven to 400°

Pizza Crust (p. 14)

The Sauce:

1	tsp. cornstarch
1	can chili, no beans
1	whole fresh tomato
1	can tomato paste
1	can enchilada sauce

The Fillings:
Cooked chicken or pork (Steel blade ... mince with on/off method or slice with serrated slicer)
Peppers (Steel blade, mince with on/off method or push through French fryer)
Tomatoes (French fryer to dice ... use firm ones)
Calabaza squash (Julienne blade ... then saute briefly and arrange pinwheel fashion)
Olives (Steel Blade or Slicing disk)
Onion (Vegetable thin slicer)
Mushrooms (Thin slicer ... cut off ends and lay in feeder tube ... saute briefly first)
Peanuts or raisins (Plastic Knife for coarse chop ... sprinkle over the cheese)
Cheddar or Monterey Jack cheese (Fine shredder ... use light pressure ... mound on top ... you'll love the way it looks ... ethereal!)

Steel Blade

Using the steel blade, put all the sauce ingredients in the processor bowl and process until smooth. Heat and thicken over medium heat in a saucepan.

Roll out the pizza dough to fit the pan you are using.

Using all the blades you have, choose some of the filling ingredients and have some fun shredding, chopping, and slicing, Put the cheese on top last and bake for 20-25 minutes.

Serve with shredded lettuce.

Nutritionally speaking this contains the basic four:
1) breads and grains, 2) fruits and vegetables, 3) dairy products,
4) meats. And it's as much fun to prepare as it is to eat.

The nuns in Mexico originated "Carne con chili" or, chili as it is known today.

STOVIES

Gravy and potatoes in a good brown pot — put them in the oven and serve them very hot!

Beatrix Potter

Try this when you have some lamb or beef to use. A Scottish dish for the meat and potato lover.

Pre-heat oven to 325°

1/2 to 1 pound meat		Chill raw meat until firm
5	peeled potatoes	before slicing . . . use
2	onions	serrated slicer only.
1/2	stick butter	
Salt and pepper		
1	cup chicken stock	

Slicing Disk

Using the slicing disk, slice the potatoes (cutting them to fit the feeder tube), the onion and the beef. Place the meat and the onion in the bottom of a deep casserole dish, and cover with the potatoes. Dot the butter all over the potatoes, sprinkle with salt and pepper, and pour the stock over all.

Cover and bake for 1 to 1 1/2 hours.

LAMB OR BEEF WITH OYSTER SAUCE

2	cups leftover beef or lamb
1	bunch whole green onions (white part)
1/2	pound mushrooms
1	green pepper

4	T. Oyster Sauce (p. 38)
1	tsp. soy sauce
1	tsp. cornstarch
1	T. water

Peanut Oil

Slicing Disk

Using the slicing disk, slice the beef or lamb. Repeat with the green pepper and mushrooms. Leave the onions whole or cut in half once.

Heat the oil. Stir-fry the vegetables separately a minute or so and remove. Add some more oil, heat, then add the meat and the rest of the ingredients, stirring until the sauce coats the meat. Add the vegetables, stir just a few seconds, remove and serve.

PROCESSOR TUNA FISH CASSEROLE

Serves 8

Pre-heat oven to 350°

1	T. prepared mustard
3	T. mayonnaise
1 1/2	cups Cheese Sauce (p. 37)
1	onion (in chunks)
4	stalks of celery
1/2	cup black olives
Several sprigs parsley	
2	7 ounce cans tuna fish or (leftover turkey or chicken)

Fettucine or other pasta

Steel Blade, Medium Serrated Slicing Disk

Prepare the Cheese Sauce. Process the onion with the steel blade (on/off's) to mince. Leave in the bowl. Stack the celery in the feeder tube (from the bottom) and slice. Remove and saute both in about 1-2 T. butter. Add to Cheese Sauce. Stir in mustard and mayonnaise.

Slice the olives. Prepare pasta and boil "al dente" (firm . . . not mushy soft). Drain and place in a casserole dish.

Stir in tuna (rinsed and drained) or turkey (slice with the serrated slicer) and transfer to the casserole dish on top of the pasta. Toss together gently. Top with Bread Crumb Topping (p. 7), adding additional parsley.

Bake about 15 minutes or until the top is browned.

RUEBEN FONDUE

Simply great . . . . you'll come up with all sorts of new combinations after trying this one.

Pre-heat oven to 350°

12 slices whole wheat or rye bread
Cooked corned beef (about one pound)
8   ounces Swiss cheese
1   large dill pickle
1 1/2 cups sauerkraut

1   stick butter
1   T. horseradish
1/2   tsp. dry mustard

6   eggs
3   cups milk
Salt and pepper

Steel Blade

Butter a large pyrex dish. Cut off the crust from the bread and reserve for future use. Put the butter, horseradish and dry mustard in the processor bowl using the steel blade and process smooth. Butter the bread on both sides generously.

Put the corned beef and pickle in the processor and process by turning the machine on and off rapidly to chop. Remove and add the cheese, cut in chunks, and process until grated.

Line the casserole dish with half the bread. Then spread with half the beef mixture, half the sauerkraut, half the cheese. Repeat.

Mix together the eggs, milk and seasonings and pour over the casserole. Depending on the size of the dish you may need to add more or less liquid.

Let it rest in the refrigerator overnight or 3-4 hours. Bake for 40-45 minutes.

You can slice raw meat (for stroganoffs, meat pies, etc.) if you freeze it until just firm . . . cut it first so it will fit the feeder tube.

STROGANOFF WITH VEAL OR BEEF

This is a good way to use up a roast . . . or start with raw meat. Chill the raw meat until firm before slicing.

1-2	pounds leftover beef, veal, or pork
1	pound mushrooms
1	onion
4	T. butter
1	garlic clove
1	T. demi-glace (p. 63)
1	T. tomato paste
2	T. currant jelly
3	T. flour
1/2	tsp. salt, pepper
1	T. fresh parsley
1	cup beef broth, warm
1/2	cup white wine
1	cup sour cream

Thin Serrated Slicing Disk, Steel Blade

Cut the cooked meat to fit the feeder tube, and using the slicing disk, slice by pushing through with the pusher fairly hard. Remove. Clean the mushrooms and slice in a similar manner. Repeat with the onion and set aside.

Change to the steel blade and put the garlic, tomato paste and meat extract in the bowl and process until the garlic is minced. Add the flour, seasonings and parsley, processing to combine. Then, with the machine running, add the warm broth through the feeder tube.

Heat the butter in a large skillet and saute the onion until translucent, then add the mushrooms and saute a few minutes. Add the contents of the processor bowl and the currant jelly. Stir until the jelly is nearly all incorporated, then add the sour cream and meat and adjust the seasonings.

Serve with rice.

> *A man seldom thinks with more a earnestness of anything than he does of his dinner.*
>
> Samuel Johnson

BAKED PORK CHOPS

Pre-heat oven to 350°

1/4-1/2 stick of butter
8   pork chops
"Some" flour, salt and pepper
1/2   of a head of red cabbage
2   apples, cored
1   large red onion
1/2   cup red wine
1   cup beef broth
1/4   cup vinegar
1   T. brown sugar

For the Sauce:

1/2   cup cream
1/2   cup currant jelly
1   tsp. cornstarch

Thin Serrated Slicing Disk, French Fryer

Sprinkle the chops very lightly with flour, salt and pepper. Saute in the butter and place in a deep baking dish. Using the French fryer, push the apples through the feeder tube, cut in chunks. Repeat with the onion. Remove.

Change to the slicing disk and slice the cabbage by cutting it to fit the feeder tube and forcing through with the pusher. Mound the cabbage, apples, and onion over the pork chops. Mix together the broth, wine, sugar and vinegar and pour over the vegetables. Cover and bake for 35-40 minutes.

Remove the pork chops to a serving dish. Surround them with the vegetables. Put all the juices (skim the fat) in a saucepan, adding the currant jelly and the cornstarch, dissolved in the cream. Heat and stir to thicken, then pour some of the sauce over the pork chops, passing the rest.

Serve with some rolls and a fresh green salad.

x2 PASTIES

There are as many versions of this Upper Peninsula dish as there are cities in Michigan . . . it is a cousin to the empanada in Chili, the burrito in Mexico, and the Scottish kidney pie. Also a marvelous base for your creativity in fillings and variety of pastry and preparation.

2   recipes Basic Pastry (p. 9)

3/4	pound lean beef		2	carrots
1/2	pound pork		1	tsp. salt
1	onion		1	T. fresh minced parsley
1	potato		1/4	tsp. red pepper flakes
1	zucchini squash			

1 beaten egg and 1 T. water

Steel Blade, Shredding Disk

Put the meat in the processor bowl with the squash, cut in chunks and process (on/off's) until ground. It may be raw or cooked, but remove any gristle or sinew if raw. Process in two batches. Add the seasonings, processing to combine. Remove.

Add the carrot, potato, onion and process until coarsely ground. Combine with the meat.

Roll out the pastry on a floured board and make 6 circles about 5 inches in diameter. Spread 1/6 of the filling in the center of each, brushing the inside with a little egg white first. Roll out 6 more rounds and place on top of the filling, using the beaten egg to seal the edge. Press together with a fork. With a knife make a pinwheel design on the top, beginning in the center, curving the line down to the edge. Brush with the egg wash and bake on a buttered baking sheet at 375° for 30 minutes. Dot with a little butter and serve.

Try different meats, mushrooms, vegetables . . . seafood . . . if you do not use potatoes, add 1-2 T. of flour.

dlc-7 If using the new larger capacity machine, you may prepare a double recipe of pastry at the same time (steel blade). The meat can be ground at one time.

PROCESSOR BEEF RANCHERO

When trying to figure out how to finance the first printing of my book, I decided to enter some recipe contests. It seemed logical that if one recipe could win a first prize, then a collection of recipes could sell a book. I went to New York the day my book went to press and came home with the down payment. Here's the processor version (which may have come first!). This is my idea of putting domestic skills to work in a career. Or, going from the frying pan into the fire.

2	1 1/2 pound flank steaks
3	tsp. instant meat tenderizer
1	6 ounce package Uncle Ben's Stuff 'n Such, Traditional Sage Flavor
1	egg, beaten slightly
1/2	pound ground pork sausage
1	medium green pepper, chopped
1/2	cup finely chopped onion
1	6 ounce jar stuffed green olives, sliced
1	10 1/2 ounce can condensed beef broth
1	medium ripe tomato, chopped
1	T. flour
2	T. cold water

Steel Blade

Pound the steaks thin enough to stuff and roll easily. Sprinkle both sides with tenderizer. Prepare Stuff 'n Such according to package directions (or you may substitute 3-4 slices of bread, processed with the steel blade to coarse crumbs, adding 2 T. butter, and 1/4 tsp. sage, thyme, salt and pepper, and 3-4 T. chicken stock). Add a beaten egg to the stuffing and place in a separate mixing bowl.

Prepare the sausage by cutting fresh pork, including fat, into cubes. Place in a dry bowl and process with a couple quick on/off's. Add onion (about 1/2 fresh), pepper (in chunks) and drained olives. Process with additional on/off's to desired textures. Saute this mixture in 2 T. butter until lightly browned.

Use the steel blade (on/off's) to chop the olives. Toss meat and stuffing together and spread over steaks, roll up and tie securely with string. Place in a baking dish and cover with the beef broth and tomato (dice by cutting into chunks and processing with the French fryer). Bake at 350° about an hour, basting occasionally.

Prepare sauce by bringing juices to a boil. Process 1-2 T. flour with 3 T. cold water and add 1/2 cup of the broth through the feeder tube. Transfer to saucepan, stirring to thicken and cook flour. Pour over beef. Serves 8-10.

ROASTS

The smells of your dinner

All sizzling and stewing

Will promise your family

a special dinner is brewing

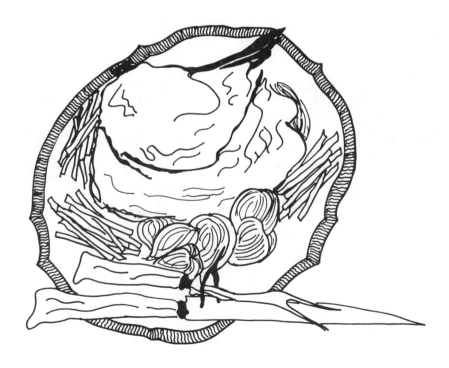

A word about Roasts. . . . .

There is nothing quite like a succulent roast surrounded by fresh vegetables or potatoes for hungry families or for special guests. Nor is there a more economical way to cook and while the roast is sizzling away you can devote a little time to some fresh, colorful vegetables.

Some suggestions for roasts, sauces to baste and serve them with, what to do with the bones, and how to get the most out of the beast follow: Look at it three ways:

1. The bone
2. The magnificent dinner
3. The many and varied meals to follow with the cooked meat and your imagination.

Many roasts are easily boned (have the butcher do it unless you're unusually adept with a knife). . . .use the bones to prepare some meat extract or beef broth. The broth is pretty simple. . . .just simmer the bone with enough water to cover it, adding water when needed, and some salt, for several hours.

With your processor, you can whip up all kinds of interesting stuffings to fill up the cavity the bone left. Or just tie it up and glaze or sauce it. Escoffier is reported to have said:

"A sauce must fit a roast
as a tight skirt fits a beautiful woman."

Save the fat drippings for Yorkshire Pudding.

When you cook meat with vegetables, process a combination of the vegetables (a cup or so) with some broth and the meat drippings . . . superb gravy.

198

STUFFED BREAST OF VEAL WITH ORANGE SAUCE

This may be served hot or refrigerated overnight and served cold. When I serve this cold, I serve it with Hollandaise or fresh Mayonnaise seasoned with minced parsley and basil.

Pre-heat oven to 400°

1	breast of veal, boned
	(Enlarge the pocket for stuffing or ask the butcher to do it for you)
1/2	pound shrimp, cooked and cleaned
1	cup fresh crab meat
1	pound fresh spinach, cooked and drained
1	garlic clove
1/2	tsp. each salt, rosemary
1/2	pound mushrooms
1	egg
1/2	cup cooked rice

Coarse ground pepper
2-4   T. cream
Optional: 1/2 cup nuts (pecans, almonds)

Steel Blade

Use the steel blade to mince garlic. Add shrimp, spinach, rice, seasonings and crab. Combine with on/off's. Change to the medium slicing disk and slice in the mushrooms. Insert the plastic knife and mix in the egg and enough cream to moisten the stuffing.

Stuff the veal, close opening with needle and thread, brush with some oil and put in a pre-heated oven. Turn the oven down to 300° after the first 15 minutes. Cover and bake 20 minutes per pound. Bake extra stuffing in a casserole at the same time, covered with a bread crumb and butter topping. (Add a little extra liquid.) Bake about 35 minutes.

If serving the roast hot, add 2 cups beef stock (preferably made with the removed bone), deglazing the pan, scraping up all the juices. Let this boil 2-3 minutes. Stir in 2 T. Demi-Glace (p. 63) and the juice from a lemon and half an orange. Season with salt, pepper and thicken with about 1 T. arrowroot (dissolve in some of the broth before adding). Let the sauce come to a boil and simmer gently 5-8 minutes.

BEEF WELLINGTON

The one you make at home will be superior to the one in the fanciest restaurant. It's one of the the most elegant things you can serve. . . . .

> *Skillful and refined cookery has always made its appearance during the most glorious epochs of history*

> Tendret

The pastry is very flexible. I've tried them all and usually rely on the Puff Pastry (p. 11) for the bottom crust and the Croissant Pastry (p. 316) for the top crust.

2	recipes of Puff Pastry (p. 11)
1	recipe of Croissant Pastry (p. 316)
2	beaten egg yolks and milk

(You'll have some left over. . .all to the good. . .either let one of your kitchen enthusiasts make up some pastry shells or freeze it.)

1	whole tenderloin (Ask the butcher to trim it for you but keep the trimmings.)
1	recipe Duxelles (p. 65)
4	ounces pate de foie gras (Unless goose livers are common around your house buy this in the gourmet section of the grocery store.)

Marinade (p. 63)
Sauce from the Marinade using Madeira (p. 64)

The day before:
Make the Marinade and immerse the beef. Let it sit overnight.

Prepare the pastry, complete the turns and chill.

In the morning, remove the tenderloin from the Marinade, tie the loose ends together and bake it in a pre-heated oven at 425° for 20 minutes. Cool and refrigerate, prepare the Madeira Sauce (p. 64). Refrigerate.

About 2 hours before you plan to bake the Wellington (not before that) remove the beef from the refrigerator, being sure all the fat is trimmed away. Prepare the egg wash and mix the Duxelles and pate together.

Roll out the bottom pastry on a floured surface so the meat will fit inside, (about 1/4 inch thick), trimming away what you do not need. Brush the inside with a little of the egg, then spread with the Duxelles and pate. Put on a baking sheet.

Roll out the Croissant Pastry, so it will fit the top and come over the edge so you can seal it to the bottom. Do this with a fork and a little of the egg mixture. Prick some holes in the top, and using the extra pastry cut out some leaves or other decorations and fasten them with a little water. Refrigerate.

Pre-heat the oven to 425°. Brush the top crust with the beaten egg and milk and bake (on the middle rack) for 25 minutes or until the top is nicely browned. Turn the oven down to 350° after the first 15 minutes. Let it cool before carving.

Serve on your most elegant platter, pass the heated sauce.

Suggested vegetables:

Parsley buttered potatoes
Grilled tomato halves
Fresh green vegetable

A man must take the fat with the lean.

David Copperfield

RUMP ROAST

This is an excellent way to prepare it and both the sauce and the meat are great for future dishes.

Pre-heat oven to 350°

1	**5-6 pound rump roast**
1	**recipe Oyster Sauce (p. 38)**
1	**cup beef broth plus 1/2 cup water**

Freshly ground pepper
1   **T. oil**

Steel Blade

Grate fresh pepper all over the beef, rub in with the oil. Put on the top broiler pan, putting 1 cup beef broth and the water in the bottom.

Turn the oven down to 300° when you put the roast in.

Prepare the Oyster Sauce, and after 30 minutes, pour it all over the beef. Baste from time to time and bake 20-25 minutes per pound. (Medium-rare, but use a meat thermometer to be sure.)

Remove the roast and let it sit a while before slicing. Thicken the basting sauce if you want it thicker, and serve with the roast.

Par-boil some potatoes and onions, and roast with the beef.

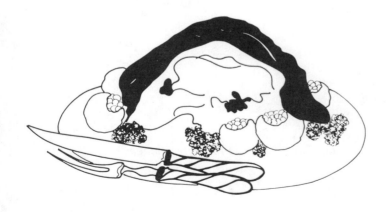

WHOLE FRESH HAM

Try this for your Easter Feast—it's almost worth getting a smoker to do one! Marvelous the first day, and you'll find so many ways to enjoy the meat the next day and the next.

Pre-heat oven to 400°

Sauce:

4	T. soy sauce
1/2	cup canned pineapple
1/2	tsp. ginger
1/2	cup vinegar
1/4	cup brown sugar

Steel Blade

Put the above ingredients in the processor bowl and process until minced. Pour over the fresh ham and cook in the smoker, or roast in your oven, 30 minutes to the pound, and baste often. Turn the oven down to 325°.

The next day:

Slice very thin in the processor using the slicing disk. Immerse and heat in your favorite bar-b-que sauce, serve on French bread or hamburger buns or use in:

1. Salads
2. Sweet-sour pork

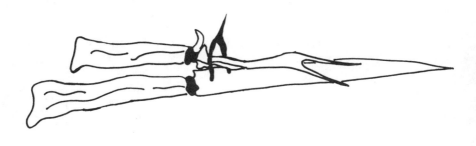

—Memories are like a fine brandy —
the warmth remains long after the liquid is gone—

203

BONED PRIME RIB

Ask the butcher to bone the roast and be sure he gives you the rib section.

Pre-heat oven to 450°
2   ribs from the rib section
1/2   Duxelles (p. 65)
1/4   Pate (p. 65)
1/2   of an onion
2   pieces stale bread
1   egg
1/2   tsp. salt, pepper, thyme
1   T. fresh parsley

1   T. oil
Garlic and pepper

Steel Blade

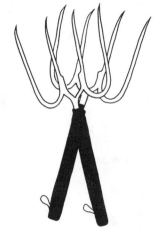

Use the rest of the rib section for another dinner or use to prepare some broth and meat extract.

Trim the lean meat from the 2 ribs and put in the processor bowl . . . along with the onion. Process with the steel blade until ground (takes a couple seconds). Add the Pate, Duxelles, salt, pepper, thyme, egg, parsley and stale bread. Process until combined. Prepare the Yorkshire Pudding batter (p. 26) and let stand. Force the stuffing into the cavity left by the bone and tie securely with string. Rub the roast with oil, pepper and garlic. Put in a 450° oven turning it down to 350°. Use a meat thermometer to insure the proper cooking time.

When the meat is 30 minutes from the end of the cooking time, remove some drippings and prepare the Yorkshire pudding. If you do not have 2 ovens, bake when the meat is done, or turn the heat up and bake directly in the roasting pan.

Surround the meat with fresh cooked vegetables, and serve with horseradish.

Poets, philosophers and artists have been interested in the art of food preparation for centuries.

BONED, STUFFED LEG OF LAMB

Stuff it and roast it, baste it with care,
Carefully then some gravy prepare,
Around your kitchen savory odors will tell,
Whatever is cooking, is doing well

Anonymous

Pre-heat oven to 450°

1	leg of lamb, boned (ask your butcher to bone it)
6	artichoke hearts, sliced
1	cup prepared wild rice (if you do not have wild rice, use the mix)
1/2	cup almonds
4	green onions

Salt, pepper
Some string
Fresh parsley

1/2	stick butter, melted
2	stalks celery

Glaze:

1	8 oz. jar currant jelly
1	clove garlic
1	tsp. rosemary
2	T. sherry
2	T. beef broth

1	cup beef broth

Fresh mint leaves

Instructions on following page.

Creating a new dish is like moving into a new house. . . . .start with a basic plan and then make it distinctively yours, with all the things you like.

Steel Blade, Medium Serrated Slicing Disk

Prepare the wild rice and take out one cup.

Put the artichoke hearts in a bowl with the wild rice. Put the parsley, onions and almonds in processor bowl (steel blade) and use on/off's to chop coarsely. Use the slicing blade to slice celery. Mix together and add melted butter.

Melt the currant jelly in a saucepan with 1 clove garlic, rosemary, sherry, and 2 T. beef broth. Remove the garlic.

Trim the fat from the inside of the lamb and make a cavity for the stuffing . . . do this with a lot of confidence . . . once its tied together and cooked it will be great but it is a bit awkward to work with. Stuff with as much of the rice mixture as you can, and tie together with some string. Put in a roasting pan and coat with the glaze (use half of it). Mix the rest of the glaze with 1 cup of beef broth in a saucepan.

Put the roast in a pre-heated oven, turn the heat down to 300° and bake for 20-25 minutes a pound. Use a meat thermometer, cook medium rare. Baste occasionally . . . use more of the sauce if necessary. When done, transfer the roast to the serving platter and let it rest before carving. Meanwhile strain off the fat and add the meat juices to the sauce, snip the mint with some scissors, and add to the sauce. Bring it to a boil, pour a little over the roast and pass the rest.

BONELESS PORK ROAST

Pre-heat oven to 450°

1	pork roast, boned

Glaze:

1	8 oz. jar apple jelly
1/2	cup beef broth
1	T. horseradish
1	T. vinegar

Heat the glaze until the jelly melts. Pour half of it over the roast and bake 30 minutes per pound. Reduce the heat as you put the roast in to 350°. Baste occasionally.

At the end of the baking time separate the drippings from the fat and add the drippings to the sauce along with 1 cup water. Heat in a saucepan and serve with the roast.

Variation: Try cutting a cavity down the center of the roast and stuffing it with:

1/2	cup sausage
1	apple
1	onion
1	green pepper

Combine the stuffing in the processor bowl, force into the cavity and tie together with some string. (Use the steel blade)

Make a glaze with:

1	jar currant jelly
1/2	cup red wine
1	T. orange juice concentrate

Melt the jelly, wine, and orange juice together and spoon a little over the roast. After the roast has baked 30 minutes, add a little water to the bottom of the pan and baste the roast occasionally. When it has finished baking, separate the fat and drippings, adding the drippings to the rest of the jelly mixture. Heat and gradually stir in I cup heavy cream. Pass the sauce separately.

Serve with rice and green peas.

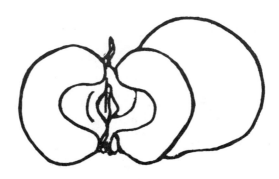

x2 STUFFED EYE OF ROUND ANTONIO

Pre-heat oven to 450°

1	3-4 pound eye of round
1/2	pound Chorizo Sausage (p. 184), cooked
1/2	cup stuffed green olives
1	green pepper
1	ripe tomato (large)
1	egg
1/2	calabaza squash
1/2	onion
1	cup beef broth
1	T. tomato paste
2	pieces stale bread

Steel Blade, French Fryer

Cut a deep slit down the center of the roast. Put the sausage, olives, onion, pepper, egg and bread (in pieces) in the processor bowl, using the steel blade, and process by turning the machine on and off several times until everything is coarsely chopped.

Cut the squash and tomato in chunks. Use the French fryer and "dice". Drain off juice and add chunks to stuffing. Pack into cavity and tie securely with string. Combine juices from vegetables with broth and tomato paste.

Pour a little of the sauce over the meat and bake 15 minutes per pound (medium rare). Turn the oven down to 350° when you put the meat in.

Put the meat on a serving platter. Transfer all the liquids and any loose stuffing to the processor bowl and process a few seconds. Heat to a boiling point with the rest of the sauce and pass separately.

Serve with some flour tortillas, and a fresh fruit or vegetable salad.

Shallots freeze well. . . . .when a recipe calls for one minced shallot, mince several in the processor and freeze. . . . .the same with onions.

Fish
Seafood

Little fishes in a brook,

Father caught them on a hook,

Mother fried them in a pan

Johnny eats them like a man

Nursery Rhyme

CREAMY CALVADOS FILETS

Flounder, sole or turbot (about 2 pounds)
Salted water
1	lemon
2	apples
2	cloves garlic

White Sauce Mix (p. 35) using 1/3 cup Calvados for part of the liquid
2	leeks
3	stalks celery
1	carrot
1	small squash
2	T. butter
1/2	cup heavy cream

Julienne Blade, Steel Blade

Soak 1-2 pounds filets in salted water for about an hour. Drain well and poach over simmering water (fish poacher or Wok). Put cut up apples, pieces of lemon and several slivers of garlic into the poaching liquid. Poach until done, about 10-12 minutes. Remove and keep warm on heatproof platter. Prepare the White Sauce using the strained poaching liquid and Calvados for the liquid (recipe on p. 35). Use the formula for a medium sauce and prepare about 2 cups.

Use the julienne blade and stack the vegetables horizontally in the feeder tube. Remove after shredding to a cloth and squeeze out some of the moisture (gently). Saute in butter just a minute or so. Do not let them get limp. Stir in cream, then White Sauce.

To serve, pour hot sauce over the fish and garnish with watercress or parsley.

People who appreciate gastronomic miracles never worry about their insides while they eat — any more than a man worries about his heart while making love.

Louis Vaudable

RED SNAPPER WITH BROWN SAUCE

Simple but memorable.

Fritter Batter (p. 28)

1	cup Basic Bread Crumb mixture (p. 7)
2	pounds red snapper filets
6	artichoke hearts (fresh if possible)

Brown Butter Sauce (p. 41)

Hot oil for frying

Steel Blade

Prepare the Fritter Batter and the Bread Crumb mixture. Process the crumbs to a very fine stage. Cut the filets into serving size pieces.

Dip the filets into the batter, draining off the excess. Then dust with the crumbs and fry in hot oil. Adjust the oil temperature if they brown too quickly. They'll take 5-6 minutes to cook through. Drain on paper towels and keep warm in the oven while preparing the Brown Butter Sauce.

Serve with an artichoke heart on top of each filet, pouring the sauce over the top.

Note: When you prepare the artichoke hearts fresh, scrape the meat from the leaves after cooking until tender and save for soup or to add to sauces as a thickening ingredient.

x2   VEGETABLE SHRIMP LOAF

A low calorie dish that seems very rich . . . also very good cold, and has a texture like a pate.

Pre-heat oven to 325°

1	cup Brussels sprouts
1/2	head of cauliflower
1	pound shrimp
1	slice bread
1/4	of an onion
1/2	cup milk, scalded
3	egg yolks
1	3 oz. package cream cheese (low calorie)
2	tsp. lemon juice
1	tsp. chicken broth
1	tsp. fresh minced parsely
1/4	tsp. red pepper flakes
1/2	tsp. salt and pepper
1/4	tsp. imitation butter flavoring
1/4	cup grated Parmesan cheese

Steel Blade

Cook the vegetables until tender. Boil the shrimp 3-5 minutes and devein.

Put the cooled vegetables, bread, onion, egg yolks, cream cheese and all the seasonings except the cheese in the processor bowl and process until pureed and smooth. With the machine running, add the milk through the feeder tube. Remove.

Add the shrimp to the bowl and process until finely chopped (just a couple seconds.) Add to the vegetable mixture and pack into a loaf pan (which has been buttered) and bake in a shallow pan of water for 30-35 minutes.

Unmold and serve with either sauce:

Skinny White Sauce (p. 43) adding:

1	anchovy	2	green onions
1	fresh tomato (in chunks)		Several sprigs fresh parsley

212

Use the French fryer to dice tomato. Remove, adding to White Sauce. Use the steel blade to mince parsley. Add anchovy, process on/off several times. Add to sauce and heat thoroughly.

Other Sauces:

Herbed Mayonnaise (p. 39)
Hollandaise (p. 40)

SHRIMP WITH TOMATOES AND COGNAC

2	large firm tomatoes
2	pounds shrimp (heads on if possible)
1	large onion
1	large green pepper
1/2-1	pound mushrooms
2	T. flour
1/3	cup cognac
1	cup heavy cream
1	stick butter
2	shallots
2	T. oil
Lots of fresh parsley	

Steel Blade, French Fryer, Thin Vegetable Slicing Disk (Smooth Edge)

Clean the shrimp very well, being sure all the sand is washed off. Boil in enough water to cover along with juice from a lemon, some celery tops, leeks, salt, pepper and thyme. After 3-5 minutes remove, clean, devein and peel. Let the shrimp water boil about 10 minutes, removing scum. Keep shrimp on warm buttered platter.

Use the steel blade and mince the shallots. Leave in the bowl. Change to the French fryer and process onions and peppers (in chunks). Saute in sizzling oil and butter. Remove with slotted spoon. Use the smooth slicing disk and slice the mushrooms. Saute. Add cream, slowly, stirring to thicken. Simmer 5 minutes. Heat cognac, pour over cooked shrimp and ignite. Combine flour with 1/2-1 cup of the shrimp water (strained) and add to mushrooms. Use the French fryer to dice the tomatoes (cut into chunks) and add to pan. Process the parsley to mince. Pour sauce over the shrimp and top with chopped parsley. Serve with fresh hot bread and a marvelous white French wine.

SHRIMP IN BROWN BUTTER SAUCE

Pre-heat oven to 350°

2-3   pounds fresh shrimp (in shells)
Brown Butter Sauce (p. 41) made with 2 whole fresh lemons,
         including pulp
1   tsp. liquid smoke
1   tsp. Worcestershire sauce
Lots of fresh parsley
Coarse ground black pepper and sea salt
French bread

Steel Blade

Clean the shrimp very well and mound in a large baking dish (shells on).

Prepare a double recipe of the Brown Butter Sauce adding the liquid smoke and Worcestershire sauce. Grind pepper and salt all over shrimp, cover with sauce.

Bake at 350° for 20-30 minutes. Serve with freshly minced parsley and plenty of hot French bread. Use gigantic napkins or bibs and let everyone peel their own. Needless to say, a good dish for an outdoor casual supper.

BOUILLABAISSE

Joseph Thackery has described Etienne-Marcel (gourmet extraordinary) as "loquacious as a lobster" and says when he was asked about the contents of his bouillabaisse he replied ". . . not that it's any of your damn business but let me tell you — I would not mind eating my grandmother, God Bless her, if she were properly cooked in white wine and seasoned with garlic, fennel, and saffron."

This is a quick and easy way to prepare bouillabaisse . . . not authentic . . . but served with a smile, a robust wine, and a large bib for everyone, makes for a grand meal.

214

A total of 3 pounds white fish (flounder, sole, haddock, or cod)
1 lobster or 4-6 frozen lobster tails
1 pound shrimp, cleaned and deveined
1 1/2 pound scallops

6	large fresh tomatoes
1	10 ounce bottle of clam juice
1	can clams, and their liquid
2	cups white wine
4	cups water
2	onions
4	stalks celery
1	cup fresh parsley
2	cloves garlic
2	bay leaves, crushed
4	T. flour

Juice from one lemon
1   tsp. saffron and thyme
A pinch fennel seeds
1   tsp. freshly ground pepper
2 to 3 T. oil

2 loaves French bread
1 to 2 sticks butter

Steel Blade

Put the 10 ounce can of clam juice in a large stock pot with 2 cups of the water and 1 cup white wine. Boil, add shrimp for 6 minutes. Remove.

Put the tomatoes, cut up, in the processor bowl and process until minced and pureed. Add to the stock pot and heat over medium heat.

Put the garlic, onion, celery (cut in chunks), in the processor bowl and mince. Saute in a small skillet with the oil, and add to the stock pot.

Put the seasonings, flour, lemon juice, and 1/2 cup of the liquid from the pot in the processor and process 30 seconds, returning to the stock pot.

Poach the fish filets in the remaining wine and water, along with the lobster and scallops. Remove and set aside with the cooked shrimp.

Add the poaching liquid to the stock pot and simmer 20 minutes, partially covered. Add the canned clams and their juice.

Cut and butter the bread and heat in a hot oven (450°). Add all the fish to the stock pot, removing the lobster from the tails. Serve in shallow bowls, spooning the soup over a piece of crisp French bread.

Serve with a tossed green salad and end with a spectacular ice cream dessert.

FILET OF SOLE IN BEER

This is as good with red snapper, whitefish, or halibut . . . the recipe inspired in an effort to find a use for bits and pieces of shrimp that the fish market sells for half the price of whole shrimp.

1	stick butter
2-3	pounds filet of sole
1	green pepper (in chunks)
1	onion (in chunks)
2/3	cup sliced almonds
1	pound shrimp pieces
1	T. oil
1	fresh tomato (diced with French fryer)
1	tsp. Hungarian paprika
1/2	tsp. red pepper flakes
1	tsp. lemon juice
1	T. fresh minced parsley
1/2	tsp. salt and pepper
2-4	T. flour
1	cup stale beer
1	cup cream
1/2	cup sour cream

Steel Blade, French Fryer

Melt the butter in a heavy saucepan. Saute the fish on both sides quickly . . . it should flake with a fork but not get mushy. Be careful not to overcook. Remove to a platter to keep warm.

Using the French fryer, dice the green pepper and onion. Saute them and the almonds separately and remove to another plate. Clean and devein the shrimp, and add them to the saute pan with a little oil and saute until they turn pink . . . remove and put with the vegetables.

Using the steel blade process flour and seasonings with 1/2 cup beer. Add cream to the saute pan, gradually, stirring to thicken. Add contents of the processor bowl plus remaining beer. When thickened, add vegetables, sour cream and tomatoes. Coat the fish with sauce and serve.

FLOUNDER BAKED IN A MOLD

Pre-heat oven to 350°

Prepare a large baking dish, fill it with some water and put it in the oven.

2	pounds flounder
1	cup White Sauce (p. 37)
1/2	cup heavy cream
3	egg yolks
1/4	tsp. dry mustard
1	T. flour
1/2	tsp. nutmeg
4	green onions
1/3	cup cooked spinach
1	tsp. lemon juice
1/2	tsp. salt pepper
3	T. soft butter (melted)

The center:

1	package frozen crabmeat, thawed and drained
1	3 ounce package cream cheese
1	tsp. horseradish
1	tsp. lemon juice
2	T. flour
1	T. soft butter (melted)

Steel Blade

Butter a loaf pan.

Poach the flounder in a fish poacher in lightly salted milk five minutes. (Save the milk and use it to make the White Sauce.) Remove, cool slightly, put it in the processor bowl and puree using the steel blade. Remove to a mixing bowl.

Cook the spinach and drain well. Prepare the White Sauce. Put the spinach in the processor bowl with the onions and process until minced. Add the flour, seasonings, and lemon juice, and with the machine running, add the cream, melted butter, and egg yolks. Process a few seconds and pour over the fish, adding the White Sauce and mixing all together.

To prepare the center:

Put the cream cheese, flour, horseradish, and lemon juice, in the processor bowl and process smooth; add the melted butter through the feeder tube with the machine running. Add the crab and process by turning the machine on and off just a few seconds.

Pour the fish mixture into the mold, filling half way. Mound the crab mixture down the center, and pour the remaining fish mixture in the mold. Rap it sharply to remove any air bubbles and place in a pan of water in the oven and bake one hour. Cover after 20 minutes.

Let it sit a few minutes before unmolding on a serving platter.

Surround with fresh greens or grilled tomato halves.

Serve hot with warmed Hollandaise (p. 40) or:

Chill, unmold and serve cold with Herbed Mayonnaise (p. 39).

LOBSTER AND SCALLOPS IN CREAM SAUCE

*The art of cooking and dining can provide a lifetime
of the highest aesthetic enjoyments.*

Albert Stockli
Ladies Home Journal

Serves 4

1	package frozen lobster tails or fresh lobster to equal 1 1/2 cups	French bread, spread with:	
1	pound scallops	2	T. Parmesan
1	garlic clove	1/2	stick butter
1	shallot	1/4	tsp. chervil
1/4	of an onion		
4	T. melted butter		
4	T. flour		
1	cup white wine		
1 1/2	cups half and half		
2	cucumbers, peeled and seeds removed		
5	stalks celery		
4	carrots, peeled		
1/2	tsp. salt and pepper		
1	T. fresh minced parsley		
3	T. butter		
2	T. oil or:		
4-5	T. Clarified Butter (p. 2)		

Steel Blade, Medium Serrated Slicing Disk, French Fryer

Use the steel blade and mince the garlic, onion and shallot. Remove and saute in 3 T. butter plus 2 T. oil (or use Clarified Butter p. 2).

Use the French fryer and load the feeder tube with chunks of peeled, seeded cucumber. Push through to dice. Add to the saute pan along with washed, drained scallops and saute 2-3 minutes. Add drained frozen lobster, heat through and remove from heat.

Bring drained liquid, wine and half and half to a boil. Combine flour and butter in the processor bowl (steel blade) and process to a paste. With machine running, add 1 cup of hot liquid through the feeder tube, then transfer to the rest of the liquid stirring until thickened. Prepare the rest of the vegetables.

219

Change to the slicing disk and slice the carrots and celery by pushing through the feeder tube and boil until tender. Remove and drain.

Add the vegetables and seafood to the sauce, heating thoroughly for 2-3 minutes. Mince parsley (steel blade), add last.

Prepare the herb butter using the steel blade, and spread on the French bread, toasting both sides under the broiler.

Serve with the seafood.

Fish and visitors smell in
three days

Benjamin Franklin

L'hote et le poisson en trois
jours sont poison.

French Proverb

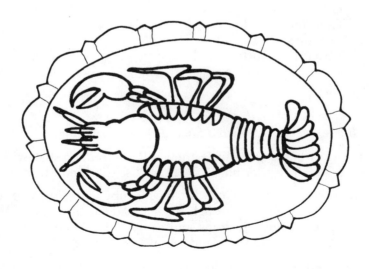

When cooking vegetables or fish undercook rather than overcook.

SEAFOOD WILD RICE CASSEROLE

1	package Wild Rice Mix
1/2	cup wild rice
1	stick butter
4	T. flour
1	lemon
1	cup white wine
1	package frozen crab (including liquid)
1/2	pound fresh shrimp
1 1/2	T. tomato paste
1	bunch green onions
1	pound fresh mushrooms
1/2	tsp. each salt and chervil
1	T. diced pimento
1/2	of a green pepper
Several	sprigs fresh parsley
8	ounces cheddar cheese

Steel Blade, Slicing Disk

Cook the wild rice mix according to the package directions, increasing water by 1 cup and adding the wild rice. Remove from heat when nearly all the liquid is absorbed and set aside. Thaw the frozen crab.

Rinse off the fresh shrimp. Bring about 2 cups water and 1 cup wine to a rolling boil. Add half of the lemon and the shrimp. Return to a boil and boil 3 minutes. Remove shrimp but save the cooking liquid, continuing to boil and reduce to about 2 cups. Peel and devein the shrimp.

Clean the mushrooms with a damp cloth and use the slicing disk to slice. Remove. Use the steel blade (rapid on/off's) to mince the onion and green pepper. Saute with the mushrooms in 1/4 stick butter. Process the rest of the butter and flour to a paste (steel blade) and add 1 cup hot shrimp water through the feeder rube to combine. Return to the remaining broth, stirring to thicken. Add to vegetables with tomato paste, stirring 4-5 minutes over medium heat.

Process pimento (steel blade) in a dry processor bowl and add to the sauce with undrained crab, shrimp, juice from a lemon half, stirring together.

Using the shredding disk, and slight pressure, shred the cheddar cheese . . . remove . . . use the steel blade to mince the parsley. Assemble the dish in the following manner. First the rice in a buttered 9 by 13 dish, then half the cheese, the creamed fish mixture, parsley, and the rest of the cheese. Either freeze until another time or bake at 375° 15 minutes or until heated through

After a good dinner one forgives everyone —
even relations.

Oscar Wilde

Poultry

"....And...without any strife he cut

up the goose with a carving knife

And they never had such a supper in their life

And the little ones chewed on the bones. . . . ."

"The Fox"

CHICKEN BREASTS IN BRANDY

Serves 6

6-8	chicken breasts (boned and skinned)
1	pound fresh mushrooms
1/4	medium size onion or 2 shallots
1	stick butter
1	T. Demi-Glace (p. 63)
1	T. tomato paste
1	cup heavy cream
1	cup chicken broth

Salt and pepper
Generous sprig fresh tarragon or 1 tsp. dried
A little flour
Brandy

Steel Blade, Slicing Disk (Smooth Vegetable)

Heat half the butter in a large skillet and brown the chicken. This takes very little time . . . 4-5 minutes each side. Remove to a platter to keep warm. Add the rest of the butter to the saute pan.

Mince onion (or shallot) with the steel blade. Clean the mushrooms and slice with the slicing blade. Remove and saute with onion. Add cream, slowly, stirring while it thickens. Mix 1 T. flour with the broth and add to the pan. Add the seasonings, tomato paste, stirring constantly. Adjust seasonings to taste and if the sauce is not thick enough (should be like heavy cream . . . not thick like gravy), add additional flour mixed with some broth.

Warm the brandy and ignite . . . pour over the chicken. Return the chicken to the saucepan and coat with sauce. Simmer gently 5-8 minutes.

Serve with fresh green vegetables (peas, asparagus, broccoli).

Note: Substitute frozen orange juice concentrate or the juice from a lemon for the tomato paste for a different flavor. This is also a lovely way to prepare veal filets . . . especially with orange sauce and orange flavored brandy.

CHOCOLATE CHICKEN

This is a variation of a classic recipe.

Pre-heat oven to 350°

Breasts, thighs, and legs of two chickens
"Enough" flour to dredge chicken

1/4	cup Clarified Butter (p. 2) or oil
1	onion
1/2	cup almonds
1/4	cup peanuts
1/4	cup raisins
1	T. flour
1	T. sesame seeds
1/4	tsp. each cinnamon, cloves, cumin, anise
1/2	tsp. salt
2	tsp. cocoa
2	cups chicken broth
1/2	cup sour cream

Steel Blade

Dredge the chicken in the flour and saute in the Clarified Butter. Drain on paper towel and put in a large baking pan. Pour one cup of the stock in the pan and bake for 30-40 minutes. Warm the rest of the stock.

Put the onion, nuts, raisins, spices, flour, and cocoa in the processor bowl with the steel blade and process smooth. Add the warm broth through the feeder tube with the machine running. Transfer to a saucepan to stir and thicken over medium heat. Add the sour cream.

When the chicken is done, transfer to a serving platter, garnish with shredded lettuce and pour the sauce over the chicken.

Serve with warm tortillas.

CHEESY CHICKEN CRUNCH

Pre-heat oven to 350°

Chicken breasts, thighs and legs for 6 people

2	T. lemon juice
6-8	pieces stale bread
4-6	ounces Parmesan cheese
1/2	cup almonds
4	T. sesame seeds
1	tsp. salt and pepper
1	tsp. freshly minced parsley
1	stick butter, in chunks
2	beaten eggs

Steel Blade

Sprinkle the lemon juice over the chicken pieces. Put bread, cheese, almonds, sesame seeds, seasonings, in the processor bowl and using the steel blade, process until crumbs. Add the butter, in pieces, processing with on/off's.

Roll the chicken in the beaten eggs and coat well with the crumb mixture. Mound any remaining mixture over the top . . . you'll have quite a lot . . . it will adhere to the chicken during the baking. Bake in a baking pan 40 minutes, or until nicely browned on top.

CHICKEN WITH CREOLE SAUCE

Pre-heat oven to 350°

2 fryers, cut up
Smoked sausage, about 1/2 pound
Rice to serve 8

1	cup Parmesan cheese
1	T. minced parsley
1	T. chicken stock
2	T. butter
3	T. cream
2	cups Creole Sauce (p. 38)

Thin Serrated Slicing Disk

Cut the sausage so it will fit into the feeder tube and slice with the slicing disk very thin. Put over and around the chicken.

Add a small amount of water to the pan, just to cover the bottom. Pour the Creole Sauce over the top and bake, covered, for 30 minutes. You do not need to simmer the sauce first, just prepare it according to the directions and add to the pan. Uncover the chicken after 30 minutes and continue baking 10-15 minutes.

Prepare enough rice for 8 people. After it has cooked, stir in the cheese, grated in the processor bowl using the steel blade, along with the parsley, butter, and cream. Put in a casserole and keep warm or pack into a decorative mold (oiled) and keep warm in a pan of hot water until ready to serve.

Transfer the chicken to a serving platter. Arrange the sausage over the top. Put the sauce and contents of the baking pan into the processor bowl and process with the steel blade a few seconds. Bring to a boil in a saucepan and pour some over the chicken, passing the rest.

STIR FRY CHICKEN WITH NUTS

3-4	chicken breasts
1	green pepper
3	stalks celery
1/2	pound mushrooms
1	cup fresh pea pods (or garden fresh lima beans)
1	tsp. soy sauce
2	T. cornstarch
1	tsp. sugar
6	T. chicken broth
1/2	tsp. cardamon
3/4	cup cashews, almonds or peanuts

Peanut oil

Slicing Disk

Using the slicing disk, slice the chicken. If you use raw meat, freeze until firm. Repeat with the celery, green pepper, and mushrooms.

Cut the little ends from the pea pods ... just the brown part. Dissolve the cornstarch in the broth.

Heat the oil in a wok or heavy skillet. Stir fry the vegetables separately, adding a little salt each time. Add more peanut oil as needed.

Stir-fry the chicken with the spices, seasonings, cornstarch, and broth, adding the vegetables and coating them with the sauce.

Remove to a serving dish, mounding the nuts on top.

TURKEY AND HAM BAKE

Pre-heat oven to 350°

1/2	cup cooked ham
2	cups leftover turkey
3	cups cooked rice
1	cup sour cream
1	T. steak-type sauce
1	apple
1	green pepper
2	stalks celery
1	bunch green onions
1/2	tsp. salt
1/4	tsp. cayenne pepper
4	ounces cheddar cheese

Steel Blade, French Fryer

Mix the steak-type sauce with the sour cream. Prepare the rice and fold in half of the sour cream. Put it in the bottom of a buttered casserole dish, about 8 x 10.

Cut the apples, onion and pepper into chunks. Using the French fryer to dice, push the vegetables through the feeder tube. Put on top of the rice.

Changing to the steel blade, put the turkey, ham, and seasonings in the processor bowl and process by turning the machine on and off rapidly until coarsely ground. Put on top of the fruit and onion. Mix the remaining rice and sour cream together and put on top.

Using the steel blade, grate the cheese by cutting it in chunks and putting directly into the processor bowl. Add to the casserole and bake for 25-30 minutes.

CHICKEN ENDIVE BAKE

This is a recipe from my sister, who is a marvelously creative cook.

Serves 4-6

8	boned chicken breasts
10	heads endive
8	slices ham
1/2	cup liver pate
1/2	cup flour
1/2	tsp. salt, pepper
2	tsp. savory
1/2	stick butter
2	T. oil
1/2	stick butter
1/4	of an onion
1	clove garlic
1/4	tsp. salt, savory
1	T. fresh minced parsley
1	cup chicken broth
2	T. each brown sugar and orange juice concentrate
2	ounces sherry

Steel Blade

Put the flour, salt, pepper, savory in the processor bowl and process using the steel blade. Remove and use to dredge the chicken breasts. Saute the breasts in the butter and oil.

Wash the endive, removing any brown leaves.

Spread some liver pate (a small amount) on each piece of ham and roll around a chicken breast. Then place in a buttered casserole dish or baking pan with the endive. Dot the endive with the remaining butter.

Put the parsley, onion, brown sugar and garlic clove in the processor bowl and process until minced. Add the seasonings and orange juice. Process again.

229

Warm the chicken broth in the pan you used to saute the chicken and stir over medium heat, incorporating the juice and flour from the chicken. Add the contents of the processor bowl, and the sherry. Stir and simmer 5 minutes, then pour over chicken.

Bake 30 minutes, covered. Serve from the baking pan and plan on French bread so you won't miss any of the sauce.

CHICKEN IN A PASTRY CASE

Prepare the pastry a day ahead . . . this is elegant!

Pre-heat oven to 375°

2	recipes Puff Pastry (p. 11) (or) Croissant Pastry (p. 316)

8	chicken breasts, boned
1/2	of a stick of butter
1/2	cup ham
1/4	cup liver Basic Pate (p. 65)
1/4	cup Duxelles (p. 65)
4	green onions
1/2	cup almonds

Sauce:

1	cup currant jelly
2	tsp. good quality beef bouillon powder
1	T. orange juice concentrate
1/2	cup water
1/4	cup port wine
1	beaten egg

Steel Blade

Prepare the pastry and let it chill.

Pound the chicken breasts to flatten; then saute in hot butter on both sides and drain on some paper towel (just a few minutes).

Put the ham, green onions, and almonds in the processor bowl with the steel blade and process until the meat is ground. Mix with the Pate and Duxelles. (If you do not have the Duxelles made up, add 1/2 pound fresh, cleaned mushrooms to the processor bowl with the meats and the onions.)

Roll the pastry out on a floured board, working quickly, into 8 squares large enough to accommodate the chicken breasts, and encase them. Leave a little pastry for decoration. Place a breast on each square, spread some of the Pate and Duxelles mixture on top, and fold up the pastry to enclose. Cut out some designs with the reserved pastry, place on the top, brush with the beaten egg (or egg and some cream if using Croissant Pastry) and bake 25-35 minutes. If the pastry browns too rapidly, cover with some foil.

Melt the currant jelly with the rest of the sauce ingredients. Spoon a teaspoon over each chicken case after the first 20 minutes of baking time, and return to the oven.

Serve the chicken, passing the rest of the sauce.

The magnificent meal is one of the most successful door openers in the world.

Florence Pritchett Smith

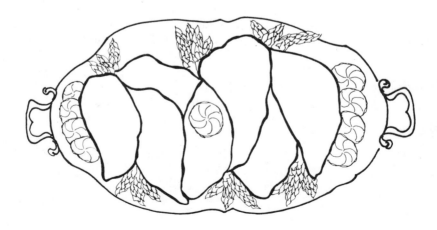

CURRY

You'll need a fresh coconut to make the coconut milk in the recipe . . . use the coconut meat for the curry condiments.

2 whole chickens
2-3 cups of the cooking stock

1	cup Coconut Milk (p. 22)
6	T. butter
6	T. flour
1	T. curry powder
1/2	tsp. salt
1	tsp. cardamon
1/2	tsp. ground ginger
1	tsp. coriander
1/4	tsp. nutmeg and paprika
1/4	of an onion

Steel Blade, Slicing Disk

Boil two chickens in enough water to cover them (about 6 cups) and reserve the stock. Put the onion and all of the spices in the processor bowl, and combine using the steel blade. Add the flour and butter, processing to combine. Add 1 cup of the warm chicken stock through the feeder tube, with the machine running, then transfer everything to the stock.

Remove the meat from the chicken, cool, and slice with the medium serrated slicing disk. Add the Coconut Milk and heat thoroughly. Serve with rice and curry condiments, which you can have all sorts of fun slicing, chopping, and grating with the processor. Suggestions: peanuts, almonds, coconut, bacon, raisins, hard boiled eggs, fresh parsley.

Serve with an avocado and citrus salad.

When I demanded of my friend what viands he preferred, he quoth: "A large cold bottle, and a small hot bird".

Eugene Field

CHICKEN WITH CHILIES

3-4   zucchini squash
Chicken breasts or meat from a broiler
Chili poblano peppers (use green peppers if not available
        or canned green chilies)
1/2   cup black olives
2   fresh tomatoes
2   cups White Sauce (p. 35 or 36)
2   shallots
1   T. diced pimento
Freshly ground black pepper
Several sprigs fresh parsley
Salt to taste

Steel Blade, Julienne Blade, Medium Serrated Slicing Disk

Bring some water to a boil, add a dash of salt, oregano, celery tops and 1/2 onion. Add chicken. Bring water back to a boil and simmer until tender. Remove chicken, cool and remove the meat from the bone. Boil the broth 15 minutes to reduce. Strain.

Mince the shallots (steel blade) and saute in 1 T. butter. Prepare a white sauce using chicken broth and 1/2 cup cream for the liquid. Make the medium thick sauce (see p. 35, 36).

Use the French fryer to dice the tomatoes. Cut into chunks before loading the feeder tube. Drain off juice (reserve for another use) and add to sauce.

Use the medium slicing disk to slice the poblano chilies. Stack firmly in the feeder tube. Use the same disk to slice the olives. Combine with the sauce, and shallots. Add a generous amount of coarsely ground black pepper. Use the same disk for chicken. Remove.

Use the julienne blade and load the unpeeled squash (horizontally) to shred. Use a clean dishcloth to wring out some of the moisture and saute briefly in 2 T. hot oil.

Use the steel blade to mince the parsley. Add to sauce along with pimento and chicken. Serve the creamed chicken on top of the squash, "spaghetti" style.

Note: This is particularly good with a Rich White Sauce prepared from Choux Pastry (see pages 12 and 13). Use the amount made with 1 cup leftover pastry, adding chicken broth (hot) instead of cream.

CHICKEN CHILI CASSEROLE

This is easy to do (and if you're not a purist you can use cream of chicken soup instead of preparing the sauce).

1	recipe Choux Pastry (p. 12) adding:
3	ounces Swiss or Gruyere cheese

Leeks, carrot, onion, bouquet garni for boiling chicken

4	chicken breasts
2	cups White Sauce with Chicken Broth (p. 36)
1	green pepper
1	bunch green onions
2	zucchini or Mexican squash (or another summer squash)
1/2	tsp. chili powder

Juice from 2 lemons
Salt and pepper to taste
Fresh parsley

2	avocados, medium ripe

Steel Blade, French Fryer, Slicing Disk

Boil the chicken reserving the broth for the sauce. I usually enrich this by reducing it to half the volume, skimming the fat and adding more rich stock to make about 2 cups. Cool the chicken, then place in the feeder tube and slice using the medium slicing disk (the one that comes with the machine). Remove.

Now use the French fryer and put the green pepper and squash through (cut in chunks) . . . remove. Use the steel blade with an on/off method to mince the green onions, then prepare the white sauce processing butter and flour, adding hot liquids through the feeder tube (1 cup only . . . then return to a saucepan with the rest). When thickened, add seasonings, chicken, squash and green pepper. Remove from heat and add lemon juice.

Prepare the choux pastry. Before adding the eggs, use the shredding disk and shred in the cheese . . . replace the steel blade and add the eggs, processing in well. Let this sit about 10 minutes, then remove in tablespoonfuls to a greased cookie sheet making a circle. Dash on a few drops of cold water and place in a preheated 450° oven. Bake 15 minutes, then turn oven down to 375° and continue baking 20-25 minutes until well browned. Poke in several places with a knife to let the steam escape and return to oven, turned off 10-15 minutes. Split by cutting the tops off. Reheat 5 minutes before serving.

When you are ready to serve, mince the parsley with the steel blade. Heat the chicken mixture and add the avocado, cut in chunks and the parsley. Spoon into the puff shell ring, put on the tops, and serve.

Vegetables

"Mary, Mary, quite contrary,

How does your garden grow. . . . . ?"

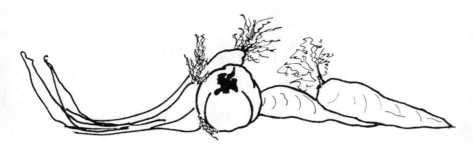

A Word about Vegetables . . .

The fresh vegetable is enjoying a renaissance of its own. People are planting gardens . . . physicians and nutritionists are extolling the virtue of fiber in raw vegetables . . . fortunately you don't need an expensive health food store, as the corner grocery has all the basics and then some.

The food processor allows you to get into the fresh vegetable world with ease . . . it will process all those skins (that's where a lot of the good vitamins and fiber are) and pureeing releases the flavor of many vegetables. Proof that good nutrition and gourmet fare go hand in hand is epitomized by the highly acclaimed "Le Petit Gourmet" restaurant in Chicago. Their motto "Good Food is Good Health" is demonstrated by their devotion to freshly prepared fruits and vegetables. The customers are only aware of the marvelous taste.

Joan Bronte, author of "Vittles and Vice" says:

Eat and be Glamorous

Brillat-Savarin, French politician and gourmet said:

Tell me what you eat and
I shall tell you what you are.

A KINGS' CABBAGE

The time has come, the walrus said,
to talk of many things
of shoes — and ships — and sealing-wax —
of cabbages — and kings. . .

Lewis Carroll

1	head cabbage
2	cups of fresh peas (or 1 package frozen)
1	onion
1/2	stick butter
4	ounces of cream cheese
2	ounces grated cheddar cheese
1/2	tsp. salt and pepper
1/4	tsp. dill, tarragon

Slicing Disk

Put the cabbage in the feeder tube and slice with the slicing disk. Put it in boiling salted water for 2-3 minutes.

Boil the peas. Be careful not to overcook . . . even fresh peas need very little cooking. Drain.

Put the onion through the feeder tube using the slicing disk. Remove and saute in half of the butter. Put the cream cheese in the processor bowl using the steel blade, with the rest of the butter, processing until smooth. Add to the onions along with the seasonings. Stir in the cabbage, and remove to a serving platter, putting the fresh peas on top with the grated cheddar cheese.

237

HARVEST QUICHE

This quiche is so versatile . . . . an excellent dish for a fall or winter luncheon, a hearty first course to preceed a fish meal, or a light supper with a green salad and white wine.

Pre-heat oven to 375°

1	recipe Basic Pastry (p. 9)

10 inch pie pan or quiche pan
1 1/2 onions
Assorted squash, two only:
      Zucchini
      Crook-neck
      White squash

6	ounces Gruyere cheese
2	cups half and half
1/2	cup white wine
3	eggs
1/2	tsp. each salt, pepper and nutmeg

Steel Blade, Shredding Disk, Thin Slicing Disk

Prepare the pie pastry and line the pan. Prick the bottom and chill until ready to use. Pre-bake 12-15 minutes at 375°.

Slice the onions with the thin slicing disk. Use the shredding disk for the squash.

Use the steel blade to grate the cheese. Place chunks directly in the bowl and use on/off's. Add eggs and seasonings, process to combine. Add 1 1/2 cups of the milk, process to combine, then add to remaining milk and wine in a 4 cup measure.

Place onion and squash in the pre-baked shell. Sprinkle with a couple dashes of cayenne pepper and 1-2 T. minced parsley. Pour the cheese mixture over the top. Dot with some extra butter.

Bake for 30-35 minutes or until browned, and the pie is "set".

Try slicing raw potatoes with the thin slicing disk and frying in hot oil . . . homemade potato chips . . . fun!

VEGETABLE GARDEN CASSEROLE

Pre-heat oven to 350°

1/4	cup oil
1	eggplant
4	fresh tomatoes
4	zucchini squash
2	white squash, (or one calabaza)
1	green pepper
4	stalks celery
1	onion
1	cup seedless grapes
4	carrots (peeled)
1	cup loose fresh parsley
1	T. sugar
1	tsp. each basil, salt, oregano
2	tsp. beef bouillon powder
1	cup Parmesan cheese, grated

Steel Blade, Medium Serrated Slicing Disk, French Fryer

You'll need a large casserole.

Use the slicing disk to slice green pepper and celery. Use the French fryer and process the tomatoes (cored and cut into chunks), onions, and squash. Remove.

Peel the eggplant, carrots and cut in large chunks. Dice with the French fryer. Remove and saute in the oil. Use the slicing disk for the grapes, pushing with firm pressure so they are not too thin.

Using the steel blade and a dry bowl, add 3-4 ounces of Parmesan cheese, in chunks and process to a powder. Remove. Mince the parsley (steel blade). Add seasonings, sugar and process on/off to combine.

Layer the casserole in the following manner: 1/2 the eggplant, 1/3 of the tomatoes and seasonings, squash, grapes, 1/3 of the tomatoes and seasonings, carrots, eggplant and remaining tomatoes and seasonings. Bake 30 minutes, covered.

Uncover, adding the grated cheese on top and bake an additional 15 minutes.

COOL AND CREAMY MUSHROOMS

1 1/2 pounds mushrooms
1   T. fresh minced parsley
1   cup lightly cooked peas
1/2   of a green pepper
1   bottle low calorie creamy Italian dressing
1/4   cup vinegar
1   shallot

Slicing Disk, Steel Blade, French Fryer

Clean the mushrooms. Using the slicing disk, lay the mushrooms on their side in the feeder tube and slice. Remove and put half in the bottom of a glass bowl, saving the rest. Then dice the green pepper by putting through the feeder tube cut into chunks and using the French fryer. Put on top of the mushrooms.

Change to the steel blade and mince the parsley. Spread over the green pepper, then add the peas, then the rest of the mushrooms.

Put the shallot in the processor bowl and process until the shallot is minced. Add the dressing and vinegar processing just enough to combine. Pour over the mushrooms and chill 3-4 hours (or overnight).

FETTUCINE SQUASH

Serves 8

4-5   zucchini squash
1   pound mushrooms (clean with a damp towel)
6   ounces Parmesan or Romano cheese
1/2   cup cream
1   stick butter
Salt and pepper
Several sprigs fresh parsley
1/2   cup walnuts (optional)

Julienne Blade, Steel Blade, Thin Vegetable Slicing Blade

Put chunks of Parmesan cheese directly into the bowl (steel blade) and process with on/off's, then run the machine to grate to a powder. Remove. Change to the julienne blade and load the feeder tube with squash, horizontally. Shred in all the squash. Remove to a tea towel and gently squeeze out excess moisture.

240

Use the thin slicing blade and slice the mushrooms. You can go to a lot of trouble cutting the round ends off but I usually just load the feeder tube and slice away. Heat half the butter and briefly saute the squash. Remove to a platter and cover with cheese while warm. Keep warm.

Add more butter to the pan and when quite hot, add mushrooms to saute. Grind coarse salt and pepper over them. When hot and simmering, add cream, slowly, to keep the pan from cooling off. Stir until cream is thickened.

Use the steel blade to mince about a cup of fresh parsley. (If using walnuts, slice with the medium slicer.) Stir into simmering sauce and pour over the squash and cheese.

Serve with chicken, veal, steaks or as a first course.

CREAMY VEGETABLE CASSEROLE

Pre-heat oven to 350°

4	assorted squash
4	carrots
1	box Brussels sprouts
1	onion
1/2	stick butter
1	cup sour cream
1/2	tsp. seasoned salt
1/4	tsp. pepper
1/2	cup Parmesan cheese
1	cup Basic Bread Topping (p. 7)

Slicing Disk, Steel Blade

Cut the squash to fit the feeder tube and slice with the slicing disk. Repeat with the onion, carrots, and Brussels sprouts, removing the vegetables after they are sliced and keeping them separate. Boil the carrots 5 minutes. Boil the squash and sprouts together 2-3 minutes. Toss together in a mixing bowl.

241

Melt the butter, and toss with the vegetables.

Using the steel blade, grate the Parmesan cheese and mix with the sour cream and seasonings. Combine with the vegetables and put in a buttered 9 by 13 pyrex dish.

Prepare the Crumb Topping (p. 7), put on top of the vegetables and bake for 20-25 minutes.

FRESH CHILLED CAULIFLOWER AND BEANS

1	red onion
1	head cauliflower, partially cooked
2	cups cooked green beans
1	bottle low calorie creamy Italian dressing
3-4	sprigs parsley

Steel Blade, Slicing Disk

Clean the cauliflower and separate into flowerettes that will fit on their side in the feeder tube, and slice using the slicing disk. They will look like little trees. Remove, and slice the onion.

Layer the flowerettes, onion and beans in a glass bowl.

Change to the steel blade and put the parsley in the processor bowl, and process until minced. Add to the salad and toss with the dressing.

Add shrimp or tuna fish for a light luncheon salad.

x2 STUFFED ONION CASES

Pre-heat oven to 375°

8	medium sized onions

Boil the onions until just tender when pierced with a fork. (About 10 minutes.) If they get too soft, they are impossible to deal with. Cut a "v" out of the center, scooping out the rest with a sharp knife or grapefruit spoon. Fill with either stuffing:

Puree of Peas:

2	cups fresh peas, including pods (use frozen if not available)
1/4	of a head of lettuce
2	T. butter (melted)
3	T. cream
1	tsp. mint jelly

Salt and pepper to taste

Boil the peas until tender. Put in the processor bowl with the lettuce, using the steel blade and process until fairly smooth. Melt the jelly and butter together, and add with the cream, processing a second or so. Season to taste and stuff the onions. Bake 10 minutes just to heat through, or refrigerate. Set them out an hour before baking and bake about 15 minutes.

Green Beans:

2	cups fresh beans (use frozen if not available)
1/4	cup almonds
2	T. butter (melted)
3	T. cream

Salt and pepper to taste

Boil the beans until just tender. Put in the processor bowl with the almonds, melted butter and cream and process until smooth. Salt and pepper to taste, and stuff the onions. Bake until heated through, about 10 minutes, or refrigerate until ready to use. Set them out an hour ahead and bake 15 minutes.

Top with cheese or seasoned bread crumbs.

x2   POTATO PUFFS

1	cup Choux Pastry (p. 12)
	Additional salt
1	egg yolk
1/2	tsp. nutmeg
1	tsp. minced parsley
	Dash of pepper
4-5	medium size potatoes

Steel Blade, Shredding Disk

Either prepare or warm the choux pastry and place into the bowl with egg yolk and seasonings. Use the shredding disk and shred in the hot cooked potatoes... push in plastic knife, being careful not to get any food down the center stem, and process on-off to combine.

Let the batter rest a few minutes, then fry by spoonfuls in hot oil until browned. Sprinkle with grated Parmesan cheese if desired as they drain on paper towels. Serve at once. If you cut the Parmesan into chunks and grate using the steel blade they look especially nice.

GREEN RICE DISH

Combination of vegetables and rice in a creamy sauce. Good to have with a Roast Lamb or chicken.

Pre-heat oven to 350°

1	package fresh spinach
1	package Wild Rice Mix
1	cup Basic White Sauce (p. 36)
1	ripe avocado (peeled and seeded)
4	green onions
1	fresh tomato, in chunks
1	tsp. lemon juice
1/2	tsp. nutmeg

Topping:

1	cup bread crumbs
1/2	cup walnuts
1/4	cup grated Parmesan cheese
3	T. butter

Steel Blade

Prepare the wild rice according to the package directions.

Cook the spinach 3-5 minutes in boiling water. Rinse under cold water. Prepare the White Sauce, thicken over the stove and cool slightly.

Put the onions, spinach, avocado, and tomato in the processor bowl and with the machine running, add the White Sauce through the feeder tube. Check to see if it's all combined... you may have to turn the machine on and off a few times to finish processing.

Add to the wild rice in a greased casserole dish.

Put the nuts in the processor bowl and process until finely chopped. Then add the bread (or crumbs) and the cheese. Add butter and process in with on/off's. Put on top of the casserole.

Bake until heated through (10-15 minutes), or freeze and re-heat for 25-30 minutes.

> *All human history attests that happiness for man . . .*
> *the hungry sinner . . .*
> *Since Eve ate apples,*
> *Much depends on dinner!*
>
> Lord Byron

TOMATO TOM GRATIN

Pre-heat oven to 425°

Serves 6-8

6	slices bacon, fried crisp
1/2	cup mayonnaise
2	green onions
1	anchovy
1	shallot
1	T. capers
1	T. spinach (optional)
6	tomatoes (firm)
4-5	slices bread
Fresh basil	
Fresh parsley	
Dash of sugar, pepper	
1	stick butter

Medium Serrated Slicing Blade, Steel Blade

Core the center of the tomato, cut in half vertically, slice off the round end and place in the feeder tube (from the bottom) with the flat surface against the blade. Push through to slice. Repeat, slicing all the tomatoes. Remove and wipe out the bowl.

Process 2 slices of bread with some parsley to coarse crumbs. Add half the butter, in chunks, and process in with on/off's. Layer in the bottom of a rectangular buttered pan. Top with the sliced tomatoes. Sprinkle with sugar and pepper. Put the crisp bacon and basil in the bowl (steel blade) and process with on/off's to dice. Sprinkle over the tomatoes. Process anchovy, capers, shallot, green onions (and spinach). Add mayonnaise last and process in with a couple on/off's. Divide on top of the bacon.

Process the remaining bread, parsley and butter to crumbs and put on top of the casserole. Bake at 425° about 15 minutes (or until browned). If the tomatoes are quite juicy, increase the bread crumbs.

x2 APPLE POTATO BAKE

How do you divide two apples among
six people?
. . . Make Applesauce!

Pre-heat oven to 350°

For 6

2	apples
1	acorn squash
3	large potatoes
1	onion
3	ounces cream cheese
1/4	tsp. nutmeg
Salt and pepper	
1	T. butter
3	T. milk

Process together using the steel blade:

1/2	cup walnuts
2	slices bread
2	T. butter

Steel Blade

Cut the squash in half, turn upside down in a shallow pan of water. Bake at 350° about 20 minutes or until soft. Peel the potatoes and boil in salted water 20 minutes or until tender. Cut in chunks.

Put the potatoes, onion, cream cheese and the seasonings in the processor bowl and process until combined. Remove to a bowl.

Discard the seeds from the squash, scoop out the meat and add to the processor bowl with the cored apples. Process until smooth and combined. You may need to scrape down the sides of the bowl. Melt the butter and milk, adding through the feeder tube with the machine running. Add to the potato mixture and transfer to a shallow, buttered baking dish. Add the topping and bake 10-12 minutes or until heated through.

x2 STUFFED TOMATOES

Arnold Shircliffe, the former head of the Wrigley Building restaurant, has praised the tomato . . . .

> *Tomatoes are great when made into soup, add pep to an egg dish, give folks an appetite to eat fish, are tangy and colorful as the chief ingredient of a sauce . . . are healthful as a vegetable or salad . . . have so much color and beauty they can compete with a bouquet of flowers as a decorative item for the table.*

Pre-heat oven to 350°

To prepare the tomatoes: Remove the core and discard. With a grapefruit spoon, remove the pulp (save to use in sauces and dressings). Drain upside down. Stuff with either filling:

Spinach:

1   package fresh spinach
1/2   cup sour cream
2   T. butter
3   green onions
1/2   cup grated Parmesan
Dash of garlic powder
Salt and pepper to taste
Basic Bread Topping (p. 7)

Steel Blade

Cook the spinach by boiling 3-4 minutes. Drain and rinse under cool water. Press out all the liquid. Put in the processor bowl with the green onions, seasonings and butter, adding the sour cream and cheese last. Stuff the tomatoes and top with the Bread Topping. Can be made ahead and refrigerated, but set them out an hour before baking. Bake 15 minutes, or until heated through. Do not let the tomatoes get soggy. This will fill 6-8 tomatoes.

Eggplant:

		Topping:	
1	eggplant, peeled	2	pieces of bread
1/2	of an onion	3	T. butter
3-4	T. butter	Several sprigs parsley	
1/2	tsp. salt and pepper		
1/3	cup sour cream		
3	ounces Parmesan cheese		
1/2	tsp. basil and oregano		

Steel Blade

Use the steel blade with on/off's to mince the onion. Peel the eggplant and cut it into chunks. Salt and let stand 10-15 minutes. Saute in butter with the onion until tender. Put the Parmesan cheese, in several chunks, in the bowl (steel blade) and process to a powder. Add eggplant and onion, processing to puree. Add seasonings, sour cream and process in. Fill tomatoes.

In a dry bowl, process parsley and 2 pieces of bread, until in crumbs. Add 3 T. butter, processing in with on/off's. Put on top of the tomatoes and bake 10-15 minutes at 375°. If prepared ahead, and refrigerated, remove from the refrigerator and let tomatoes come to room temperature before baking. If baked too long, the tomatoes get soggy and are difficult to serve.

MASHED POTATOES

Pre-heat oven to 350°

4-5	baking potatoes	Cheese Options:
1	cup lima beans (cooked)	Monterey Jack
4	ounces cheese (optional)	Blue cheese
1	tsp. fresh minced parsley	Gruyere or Swiss
1	T. butter	
3	T. milk	
1	T. mayonnaise	
1	tsp. salt	
1/2	tsp. pepper	
1	tsp. freeze dried chives	

6   slices bacon, fried crisp, broken in chunks

Steel Blade, Plastic Knife, Shredding Disk

Bake the potatoes until they are tender (about 45 minutes at 400°) and boil the lima beans 5-6 minutes. Fry the bacon crisp. Scoop out the hot potato meat from the potato, saving the skins.

Put the lima beans and parsley in the processor bowl and process by running the machine to mince. Put on the shredding disk and put half the potatoes (hot) in the feeder tube. Shred in. Remove the disk and put butter, milk, mayonnaise and remaining seasonings on top. Replace shredding disk and shred in the rest of the potatoes. Remove shredding disk and use the plastic knife to mix together with the on/off method of processing. This gives a light potato . . . using the steel blade alone works but it is difficult to control texture. In other words, gluey potatoes often are the result. Remove potato mixture.

Clean the bowl and shredding disk and shred the cheese by pushing through the feeder tube with light but steady pressure. Remove. Use the steel blade with an on/off method to coarsely chop the bacon.

Re-stuff the potatoes, sprinkling with bacon and mounding the cheese on top. Bake about 15 minutes at 350° or until the potatoes are heated through and the cheese is melted.

To make a double recipe with a processor just make two batches and put them together in the cooking or baking dish . . . it will still take less time!

x2 POTATO PLUS PANCAKES

With your fun machine you can now compete with the shredded potato patties the convenience food restaurants charm your children with . . . only you can shred in some extra vegetable vitamins and create a nutritionally dense pancake.

2	green onions
3	medium size potatoes, peeled
2	winter squashes (unpeeled)
1	medium size apple (optional)
2	eggs
4	T. flour
1	tsp. salt

Dash of pepper and nutmeg
Several sprigs of parsley

Clarified Butter (p. 2) or oil for frying

Steel Blade, Shredding Disk, (Plastic Knife)

Use the steel blade and mince the parsley and onions with the seasonings. Add flour and eggs, process in. Use the shredding disk and shred in vegetables and apple. Remove disk and push in plastic knife and process on/off to combine.

Heat the butter or oil in a skillet. Let the batter rest 5-10 minutes, then drop by large spoonfuls and fry until browned and crisp on both sides. Drain on paper towels.

Serving Suggestions:

Mince the green onion tops with the steel blade and combine with sour cream . . . serve on the pancakes.

Mince peelings from half a lemon with 1 tsp. sugar. Add juice from the lemon, 1 T. cornstarch and 1 T. butter, processing smooth. Pour 1/2 cup hot chicken broth through the feeder tube, then combine mixture over medium heat with an additional cup of chicken broth. Stir to thicken and serve with the pancakes.

Sprinkle with Parmesan cheese.

Note: When eggplants are in season, try this using 2 eggplants instead of apple, squash and potato.

250

JULIENNE OF VEGETABLE CASSEROLE

Serves 6

Pre-heat oven to 375°

6	medium potatoes
4	stalks of celery
2	leeks
3	anchovy filets
1	cup heavy cream
4	T. butter
3	ounces Gruyere or Swiss cheese

Pepper, nutmeg

Julienne Blade, Steel Blade

Wash the leeks as well as possible, and layer horizontally in the feeder tube. Push through (julienne blade) firmly. Remove to a colander and rinse off the rest of the dirt.

Use the julienne blade and stack the potatoes and celery (horizontally) in the feeder tube and push through. Remove and wipe out the bowl.

Use the steel blade, and put drained, dry, anchovies and cheese chunks in the bowl. Process with on/off's, then run machine a few seconds. Add butter and process in with on/off's, then cream, processing smooth.

Layer all the vegetables in a buttered baking dish. Sprinkle generously with coarsely ground pepper and nutmeg. Pour cream and cheese mixture over all and bake at 375° about 30 minutes. Top should be browned and cream all absorbed. Check during baking and add additional cream, if necessary.

Some people have food but no appetite; others have an appetite but no food. I have both. The Lord be praised.

Oliver Cromwell

EGGPLANT CREOLE

Serves 6

Pre-heat oven to 350°

1	eggplant
5	T. butter
3	T. flour
1	tsp. salt
1	T. brown sugar
1/2	tsp. each ground cloves and crushed bay leaf
3	tomatoes
1	onion
1	green pepper

Crumb Topping:

1 1/2	pieces bread
2-3	ounces Parmesan or Swiss cheese
2	T. butter

Steel Blade, French Fryer

Peel the eggplant and dice by cutting in chunks and processing with the French fryer. Sprinkle with salt and let stand about 20 minutes. Process the onion and green pepper the same way. Saute in 1-2 T. butter and remove with a slotted spoon.

Pat eggplant dry, dredge with flour and seasonings. Add the remaining (3 T.) butter to the saucepan. Brown eggplant in hot butter.

Process tomatoes (in chunks) with the French fryer and add to eggplant along with reserved vegetables. Put in a buttered gratin dish. Process crumb topping. Use the steel blade to grate Parmesan first, then process in butter and bread with on/off's. Transfer to casserole and bake at 350° 30 minutes.

Note: This is also a good breakfast dish. Cook the casserole, covered, omitting topping. Poach 3-4 eggs until the whites are nearly set. Transfer to the top of the casserole after it has baked 30 minutes, cover with the bread-cheese topping and run under the broiler (8 inches away) just long enough to brown.

DESSERTS

Tis the dessert that graces
all the feast

For an ill end disparages
all the rest . . . .

Dr. William King
circa 1700

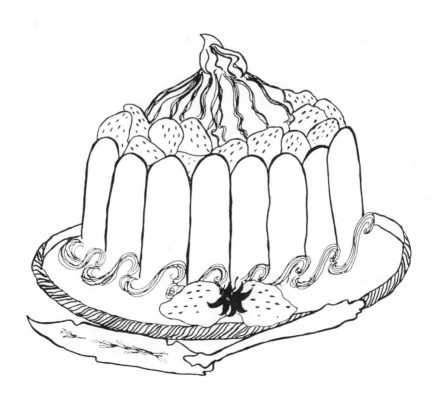

BAKED ALASKA

Pre-heat oven to 450°

Anyone who has an adequate freezer can make a Baked Alaska . . . it really is one of the most beautiful and delicious desserts. It also lends itself to the imaginative cook. Try using a variety of molds and cake crusts. Or pack the ice cream into a decoratively cut orange, grapefruit, or pineapple shell. If you have a big freezer, and a large crowd, fill a watermelon shell with a variety of ice creams. I could fill an entire cookbook with different combinations, but will restrain myself and offer just one, leaving the rest to you and your family's imagination.

Crust:

1   recipe Coconut Crust (p. 5), adding
1   small package lady fingers

Follow the directions for the Coconut Crust (p. 5) adding the lady fingers to the processor bowl with the coconut.

Filling:

1   pint pistachio ice cream
1   pint strawberry ice cream
1   small jar chocolate fudge topping

Mound the pistachio ice cream on the bottom, intersperse with the topping, then mound the strawberry ice cream. Press it down a bit, cover, and freeze very firm (a little dry ice is a big help).

Meringue Topping:

3   egg whites
1/4   tsp. cream of tartar
3/4   cup sugar plus 1/8 tsp. salt

Beat the egg whites with cream of tartar until they begin to stiffen. Gradually add the sugar and salt and beat until very stiff. Mound on top of the ice cream (or use a fancy tipped pastry tube) and run in a 450° oven 5 minutes.

x2 BAKLAVA

This is neither difficult or time consuming . . . . only the name sounds difficult . . . . It's a wonderfully different little pastry you may serve as a dessert or with coffee and fruit.

Pre-heat oven to 350°

1	pound filo pastry
1	pound Clarified Butter (p. 2)

1	cup walnuts
1 1/2	cup almonds
1/3	cup sugar
1/2	tsp. cinnamon
1/4	tsp. ground cloves
1/4	tsp. grated lemon peel

Syrup:

3/4	cup sugar
1	cup honey (natural, unrefined)
3	whole cloves

Juice from one lemon and some of the peel

2	ounces Curacao liqueur

Steel Blade

The pastry is bought in sheets . . . . its easy to work with and if it breaks or cracks, just fit it together . . . . the butter will seal it. Clarify the butter, and brush a large cookie sheet with sides, with butter.

Put the nuts, sugar and spices in the processor bowl and process until ground fine.

Spread 2 sheets of the pastry in the pan, and brush with the clarified butter. Repeat, buttering after every other one until you've used 10-12 sheets. Spread with 1/3 of the nut mixture.

Layer 10-12 more sheets of pastry, buttering between every other one, and spread with another third of the nut mixture. Repeat. End with about 4-6 sheets of pastry, buttering again between every other one, (sounds rich doesn't it?) If you have some pastry left, freeze it . . . . it makes a great egg roll wrapper.

Butter the top, and with a very sharp knife, cut through the top layer as you plan to cut it when it is baked. (Diamonds are traditional.) Bake for 40-45 minutes. If the top browns too rapidly, turn the oven down to 325°. Leave it in the oven for 30 minutes after it has finished baking, with the door ajar.

Prepare the syrup by boiling all the ingredients together, stirring until the sugar dissolves. Remove from heat, turn the heat down to very low, and simmer the syrup for 20 minutes. Remove the cloves and lemon peel. Pour all over the Baklava.

Cool 24 hours (if you can wait that long) . . . Cut along your markings.

Louis XIV, a dedicated gourmet, insisted all his mistresses be skillful cooks. Could this be the origin of:

The way to a mans heart is through his stomach.

GRAND MARNIER TORTE

Learned men vied with each other to write about an art that procured such enjoyment.

Plato

This is a most grand dessert. Don't let the Puff Pastry deter you. The processor does the mixing in 3 minutes and all you have to do is remember to roll and turn it a few times.

Pre-heat oven to 425°

The Pastry:

2 to 3   recipes Puff Pastry (p. 11)
1   beaten egg

Roll out the pastry and using a plate as a pattern, cut out three circles. Put on 3 baking sheets, pricking several places with a fork, brushing with the egg, and baking for 12-15 minutes. They should be lightly browned.

The Custard Filling:

Birds Custard Powder using:

2	cups half and half
1/2	cup sugar
2	eggs
1/3	cup Grand Marnier
1/2	cup heavy cream
1/2	package unflavored gelatin

or prepare the following:

2	cups half and half
5	egg yolks
1/2	cup sugar
1/4	tsp. salt
1/3	cup Grand Marnier
1/2	tsp. vanilla
1/2	cup heavy cream
1	package unflavored gelatin

Steel Blade, Plastic Knife

Prepare the Bird's custard powder according to the package directions, using the 2 eggs, half and half, sugar and liqueur in the recipe. Soften gelatin in 1/4 cup cold water, then heat to dissolve. Chill with the cream.

Or, prepare a custard according to the preceeding recipe by:

Scalding the half and half. Beat egg yolks with the sugar and salt in the top of a double boiler. (Or, with the steel blade, transferring to a double boiler.) Add scalded half and half, stirring constantly, and cook over simmering water until very thick. Add vanilla, liqueur and cool. Prepare gelatin by softening in 1/4 cup cold water, heating to dissolve and chilling with the cream.

In both custards, whip the gelatin and cream before it "sets". Pour through the feeder tube (machine running) using the steel blade and process until thick. Fold into either prepared, chilled, custard.

Icing:

Process **1 egg white** until foamy. Add **1 cup confectioner's sugar, 1 tsp. vanilla** and **1 T. boiling water.** Process until smooth adding more boiling water in droplets if needed (steel blade).

Chocolate:

Process **4 ounces semi-sweet chocolate** until chopped (steel blade). Bring **1/2 cup water, 2 T. butter, 1/3 cup sugar** to a boil for 1-2 minutes. Pour through the feeder tube (machine running). Add **1/2 tsp. vanilla** and cool the sauce.

To assemble:

Divide the custard between the layers. Pour the white icing over the top and chill. Drizzle chocolate over the top while it is still warm enough to "pour".

Decorate the plate with marzipan leaves or flowers . . . or use some candied violets.

A little beaten egg white brushed on top of pastry keeps it from browning too fast.

FLAMBÉING

You'll be simply delighted

as your guests faint and swoon

When your dessert is ignited

and they all reach for their spoon,

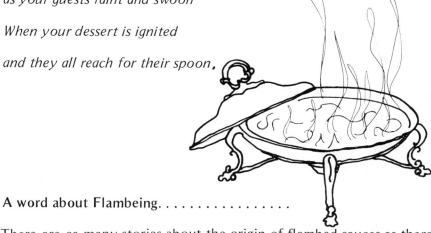

A word about Flambeing. . . . .

There are as many stories about the origin of flambed sauces as there are varieties. The one I like the best deals with the origin of Crepes Suzette. As the story goes, the sauce, while being prepared for King Edward VII of England, accidently caught fire. The chef carried the flaming pan to the King and served the crepes as the fire subsided . . . . just as though he planned it that way. Showmanship!

It seems a paradox to discuss an anti-climactic possibility, however, to avoid a failure in igniting just be sure to have the proper alcoholic content. 80-90 proof seems to be the minimum. Be careful not to add too much liqueur to the sauce too fast or the result may be more spectacular than you planned. Better yet . . . . see if you can interest your husband in the task. Most men have a bit of the "showman" in their souls, and have great fun performing at the table. (While you can take care of other things in the kitchen).

You'll need a portable burner, a large shallow copper pan, and a serving cart for all the ingredients.

If you are preparing the dessert in the kitchen and wish to carry it flaming to the table, you can do so by soaking some sugar cubes with a little food coloring (just for color) and ignite the sugar. Be careful they do not touch the dessert. Or you can insert a broken egg shell half in a meringue topping, fill with brandy and ignite as you bring it to the table.

FLAMING MANDARIN CHOCOLATE CREPES

Hurray for Baskin Robbins for creating this ice cream which inspired this dessert. If you cannot find it, or it's not in season, use orange juice concentrate (2 T.) mixed with chocolate ice cream (1 quart).

8   crepes
1   quart Mandarin chocolate ice cream

At the Table:

Flambe pan and burner
1/2   cup sugar
1   whole orange, cut in half
1   stick butter
Mandarin orange sections
1   jigger each: Triple-Sec, 90 proof brandy, Kirsch or rum

Prepare the ice cream and the crepes as far ahead as you like, filling the crepes, then freezing. (Sprinkle them with powdered sugar when serving.)

Melt the butter in the flambe pan and get it sizzling. Gradually add the sugar, stirring in. Squeeze in the orange juice, stirring. Add the orange sections, heat until bubbling. Add more sugar if you like. Add the liqueurs last, the lesser proof ones first . . . then ignite if they do not do so spontaneously.

Pour the sauce over the crepes with great flourish!

If you want to do this the easy way, in the kitchen, combine the following in a saucepan, heat to a boil, cool slightly, and serve on the crepes.

1   jar orange marmalade
1/2   cup Mandarin orange sections
1/2   of a stick of butter
2   T. orange juice concentrate
1   tsp. vanilla
Liqueurs

Variation: Instead of filling the crepes, try folding them in quarters and deep fat fry. Put 3-4 fried crepes on a plate, with a generous scoop of ice cream in the center.

CHOCOLATE COCONUT FLAN

This is the epitome of what you can do with a fresh coconut.

Pre-heat oven to 350°

1	cup sugar, for a 4-5 cup mold
1	whole small coconut, including its liquid
1	cup sweetened condensed milk
3/4	cups whole milk
6	eggs
3	T. cocoa
1/2	cup sugar
1/4	tsp. salt
1	tsp. vanilla
1	tsp. rum flavoring

Steel Blade, Plastic Knife

See page 22 about processing a coconut. After peeling the skin and removing the meat, put the meat in the processor and using the steel blade, grate very fine. Put it in a saucepan with the 3/4 cup milk and the coconut liquid and boil for 3-4 minutes, stirring all the time. Add the condensed milk, bringing to a boil, then set aside to cool.

Put the sugar (1 cup for the mold) in a heavy saucepan over medium to medium-high heat and watch it closely until it begins to turn amber. Turn the heat down and stir constantly until it is all caramelized (just a few seconds). Coat the mold.

Put the eggs in the processor bowl using the plastic knife and process 30-40 seconds more. Change to the steel blade and add the sugar, salt, cocoa, vanilla, and rum flavoring. Add 1 cup of the coconut mixture and process about 30 seconds. Combine with the rest of the coconut-milk mixture and pour into the prepared mold.

Place the mold in a pan of water and bake for about an hour . . . . a knife inserted should come out clean when it is done. Let it cool 5 minutes, then unmold on a serving plate.

x2 NUTRITION COOKIES

Pre-heat oven to 350°

1	stick butter or margarine	**Topping:**	
1/2	cup powdered sugar		
1	ripe banana	1/2	cup Natural Cereal (p. 3)
1	cup snipped dates	1/2	cup powdered sugar
1/2	cup nuts	1/4	cup nuts
1	cup flour	1/3	cup shredded coconut
1	tsp. vanilla		

Steel Blade

Put the butter, vanilla, sugar and banana in the processor bowl with the steel blade and process 10-15 seconds or until creamed.

Add dates and nuts, processing on/off to chop. Then add flour, processing to combine.

Remove from the bowl and chill about an hour.

Put the coconut, cereal, sugar and nuts in the processor bowl and process until ground fine.

Shape the cookies into flat circles and dredge with the topping. Bake 15-20 minutes.

x2 CONTINENTAL DESSERT

The Europeans traditionally end their meals with fresh fruit and assorted cheese. Let this one be your centerpiece.

1	8 ounce package cream cheese
1	3 ounce package soft Camembert
1	cup Ricotta cheese
1/2	cup sour cream

Fresh berries (or) sliced fruit
Frosted grapes
Cookies

Steel Blade

Prepare a heart shaped mold by lining it with cheesecloth.

Put the assorted cheeses in the processor bowl using the steel blade and process smooth. Add the sour cream last, processing just briefly to combine. Pack inside the mold and chill.

Prepare some frosted grapes and cookies . . . or use the packaged "Pirouettes".

Unmold the cheese and surround with fruit.

Try this on Valentines Day.

x2   GLAZED MINIATURE CREAM PUFFS

All's well that ends well

Shakespeare

Serves 10

1	recipe Choux Pastry (p. 12, 13)
	(make 40 small puffs)

1	recipe Italian Creme (p. 21)
1/2	cup apple jelly
1	T. rum

Custard Sauce:

2 1/2	cups half and half (scalded)
1/2	cup sugar
2	egg yolks
1	whole egg
1	tsp. vanilla
1	envelope unflavored gelatin

Steel Blade

Process egg yolks, gelatin, egg and sugar until very light.

Scald half and half. Add 1 cup (very hot) through the feeder tube, machine running. Transfer to a double boiler and stir until very thick. Cool.

Prepare the puffs according to the recipe. Remove any uncooked dough in the center. Prepare the Italian Creme, cool and when 1-2 hours from serving time re-crisp the puffs in a 400° oven 5 minutes, cool slightly and fill with creme. When ready to serve, re-heat 10 minutes, coating tops with apple jelly, melted with 1 T. rum.

Serve filled cream puffs with chilled custard. Before using the custard, re-process a few seconds with the steel blade to restore consistency.

A l'oeuvre on connait l' artisan.

French Proverb

The workman is known (judged) by his work.

Catherine de' Medici, queen of Henry II, brought her Florentine chefs to France and introduced many cakes, pastries and pastry creams.

CHOCOLATE SUNDAE CAKE

A must for chocolate lovers. Try it two ways.

Pre-heat oven to 350°

	I			II	
1	cup flour		1	cup flour	
2/3	cups sugar		2/3	cups sugar	
2	T. cocoa		2	T. cocoa	
1/2	tsp. salt		1/2	tsp. salt	
2	tsp. baking powder		2	tsp. baking powder	
2	T. butter		2	T. butter	
3/4	cup figs or dates (optional)		1/2	cup crushed	
1/2	cup milk			Peppermint candy	
			1/3	cup coconut	
			1/2	cup milk	

Steel Blade

Using the steel blade, process the fruits (or candy & coconut). Add the first six ingredients to the processor bowl and using the steel blade, process until combined. Add the milk, and process a few seconds more. Spread into a deep buttered souffle dish.

1/2	cup brown sugar		1/2	cup brown sugar	
1/4	cup white sugar		2	T. white sugar	
3	T. cocoa		4	chocolate mints	
1	tsp. vanilla		3	T. cocoa	
1	cup boiling water		1	cup boiling water	

Put the first four ingredients in the processor bowl and using the steel blade, process 10 seconds. Put over the cake. Pour the boiling water over the top.

Bake for 40-45 minutes at 350°. Cool and serve with:

Topping:

	I			II	
2	tsp. orange juice concentrate		1	pint vanilla ice	
2	tsp. Curacao			cream	
1	tsp. vanilla		1/3	cup Creme de	
1	pint vanilla ice cream			Menthe	

Process the topping in the processor using the steel blade until smooth. Pour over each serving. This is enough topping for four modest servings.

STUFFED PEARS ALASKA

Pre-heat oven to 450°

4	slices pound cake
2	fresh, ripe pears

Italian Creme (p. 21) or

Process together using the steel blade:

2	coconut macaroons
1/4	cup almonds
4	T. sherry

Meringue:

3	egg whites
1/8	tsp. cream of tartar
1/2	cup sugar

Toast the pound cake, and trim to fit a pear half leaving some space around the edge.

Poach the pears, cut in half, turned upside down in a mixture of white wine and water, in a shallow pan. Simmer about 5-8 minutes or until just tender.

Core, leaving a generous hole for the filling, and place on the pound cake. Fill the hole with the Creme, or macaroon mixture and prepare the Meringue.

Beat the egg whites until stiff with the cream of tartar, adding the sugar gradually until it forms stiff peaks. Cover the pears, and immerse an egg shell filled with brandy if you wish to flambe (p. 259). Bake for 5 minutes or until the Meringue is browned.

Serve with a choice of Chocolate Sauce or Vanilla Custard Sauce. See pages 257 or 264 for sauces.

x2 COFFEE CRUNCH CUSTARDS

Serves 6

1	square unsweetened chocolate
1	package Bird's instant custard powder
1	cup each strong coffee and milk
3	T. Tia Maria or Kahlua
1/2	cup sugar
1	whole egg
3-4	chunks of peanut brittle
1	cup heavy cream

Steel Blade

Heat the milk, coffee, sugar and liqueurs to a boil. Put the chocolate in the bowl and run the machine to crush (start with on/off's). Add 1/2 cup hot liquid through the feeder tube, with the machine running, then whole egg and custard powder, processing in. Add another 1/2 cup of liquid, process in, then transfer to the saucepan to stir until thickened. Chill.

In a clean bowl (steel blade), run the machine to crush the peanut brittle in the same way as the chocolate. Remove. Run the machine adding cream slowly through the feeder tube. Add vanilla and sugar (to your preference) when almost thick. Watch . . . it can turn into butter quickly.

Fill glass dishes 3/4 full with cooled custard. Add a generous spoonful of cream and crushed brittle.

Note: Use the custard on page 270 if you do not have Bird's custard powder.

Coffee should be black as Hell,
Strong as Death and
Sweet as love.

Turkish Proverb

STRAWBERRY DESSERTS

Curly Locks! Curly Locks!

Wilt thou be mine?

Thou shalt not wash dishes,

Nor yet feed the swine,

But sit on a cushion

And sew a fine seam

And feed upon strawberries,

Sugar and Cream!

x2 FROZEN STRAWBERRY JAM

This will keep 2-3 weeks in the refrigerator or freeze.

1	cup strawberries
2	cups sugar
2	tsp. lemon juice
1	tsp. orange juice
1/3	bottle liquid pectin

Steel Blade

Put the washed, hulled berries in the processor bowl and process using the steel blade until crushed . . . takes just a few seconds. Add 2 cups of the sugar, process to combine. Combine the pectin and juice and add to the mixture, processing until all combined. Put into clean jars, and cover tightly. Let sit at room temperature for 12-24 hours (until set).

x2 STRAWBERRY BUTTER

Try this on your toast or waffles!

1	stick butter
1	8 oz. package cream cheese
1	cup powdered sugar
1	tsp. vanilla
1	cup strawberries (fresh or frozen drained)

Steel Blade

'Cream' the butter, cream cheese and sugar using the steel blade. Add the vanilla, processing until combined. Add the berries and process by turning the machine on and off rapidly.

God could doubtless have a better berry, but doubtless he never did.

Johnathan Swift

FRESH FRUIT TRIFLE

This is the queen of desserts . . . light . . . fruity . . . beautiful to look at and melts in your mouth. Tradition calls for raspberry jam, but with a wealth of fresh fruits it seems a shame to use preserves.

Spongecake (or)
Angel food cake (about half of a prepared cake)
3   large macaroons
1/4   cup Natural Cereal (p. 3)
1/4   cup sweet sherry
1 to 2 boxes fresh strawberries or raspberries
1   tsp. orange juice concentrate
1   T. orange marmalade
1   recipe Vanilla Custard
1 1/2 cups whipping cream
2   T. powdered sugar
1   tsp. rum flavoring

Slicing Disk, Steel Blade

Cut up the cake and put it in the bottom of a deep glass bowl. Put the macaroons in the processor bowl and "crumble" using the steel blade. Add the Natural Cereal, and process a few seconds to combine. Pour the sherry over the cake, then the macaroon mixture.

Wash the berries . . . if using raspberries, just pour the orange juice, melted with the marmalade, over the macaroons. If using strawberries, remove the stems, and using the slicing disk, slice them in the processor, then pour over the juice and marmalade. Chill until ready to assemble.

Prepare a Vanilla Custard .

Vanilla Custard:

2   T. cornstarch
1/4   tsp. salt
1/2   cup sugar
4   eggs

2   cups half and half
1   tsp. vanilla
1   tsp. rum flavoring

Put the eggs, sugar, salt and cornstarch in the processor bowl and process 10-15 seconds. Warm the milk. Add 1 cup through the feeder tube, process again.

Add to the rest of the milk, stirring until it is thickened. Do not boil. Chill.

Whip the cream by running the machine (steel blade) and pouring cream through the feeder tube, slowly. When very thick (almost immediately) add powdered sugar and rum flavoring.

To assemble, put the fruit on top of the macaroons. Beat the chilled custard by returning it to the processor bowl using the steel blade and process a few seconds. Pour over the fruit, then top with the whipped cream.

Trifles

It has been said that when 19th Century English tourists went to Italy they longed for their *fruit and cream*. Italians preferred rum to sherry and *Zuppa Inglese* was the result. Trifle originates from the Spanish cake *bizcocho*, or *spongecake* which was soaked in sherry and served with cream. First it was called *Drunken Cake*, then *Tipsy Cake*, and finally *Trifle*. Interestingly enough, Trifle in America became *Boston Cream Pie*. Nutritionally speaking, the combination of fruit and cream is the proper combination to utilize nutrients.

STRAWBERRIES AND CREAM

. . . . And let your various creams incircl'd be
With swelling fruit just ravish'd from the tree.

Dr. William King
Circa 1700

For 6

3 pints strawberries, cleaned and left whole

1	quart vanilla ice cream
1	ounce Amaretto liqueur
1	ounce Tia Maria (or Creme de Cocao)
1	ounce Curacao
1	tsp. vanilla flavoring

Steel Blade

Let the ice cream sit out while you wash and hull the strawberries. Put the ice cream, in scoops, in the processor bowl and process smooth. Mix together the liquids, and add them with the machine running. Store in the freezer until using. If if hardens, just process it smooth again.

Pour over the berries when serving.

The strawberry grows underneath the Nettle
And wholesome berries ripen best
Neighbor'd by fruit of lesser quality.

Shakespeare

STRAWBERRY ICE CREAM TORTONI PIE

Crust:

2	cups Natural Cereal (p. 3)
1/2	cup almonds
1/2	cup pecans
1/2	stick butter

Steel Blade

Combine the cereal and nuts in the processor bowl. Add the butter, melted, through the feeder tube and spread in a 10 inch pie plate. Chill in the freezer.

2	pints strawberries
1	T. orange juice concentrate
2	ounces Curacao
2	egg whites
2	T. powdered sugar
1/8	tsp. cream of tartar
1/2	envelope gelatin
1/4	cup whipping cream

4	coconut macaroons (large)
1	T. Amaretto liqueur
1/4	cup sweet sherry
1	quart French vanilla ice cream

1	cup whipping cream
1	T. sugar
1	tsp. vanilla

Sliced almonds
Currant jelly

Slicing Disk, Steel Blade

Wash the berries. Slice 4 in half, coat with melted currant jelly and reserve to decorate the top.

Put the rest of the berries in the feeder tube and slice using the slicing disk. Remove to a bowl and soak in orange juice concentrate and Curacao. Prepare the gelatin according to the package. Chill with the cream.

Whip the egg white and cream of tartar very stiff, adding the sugar gradually. Whip the cream. Fold the berries into the cream, then into the egg whites and chill in the pie crust shell. Put in the freezer. Wait until firm to prepare the rest.

Using the steel blade crush the macaroons in the processor bowl. Soak them in the liqueur and sherry. Stir into the softened ice cream, and mound on top of the strawberries.

Whip the cream, adding the sugar and vanilla, and spread on top of the pie. Freeze. If you have a pastry tube, make a ruffle a round the edge. The "final touch":

Make some daisies using the glazed berry halves as centers and the sliced almonds as the petals.

Desserts can be lovely and sensuous things

Morrison Wood

One cup of strawberries supplies the entire day's need for Vitamin C and 8% of the U.S. RDA for iron.

Try dipping strawberries into cheese or chocolate fondue.

VERY BERRY ICE CREAM PIE

1 Coconut Crust (p. 5)

Filling:

1	3 ounce package cream cheese
1/2	cup powdered sugar
2	tsp. orange juice concentrate
1	T. orange liqueur
1	T. grated orange rind
2	T. butter
1	quart strawberry ice cream

Topping:

1	carton whipping cream
1	cup coconut
1/2	cup almonds
1/4	of a stick of butter

Steel Blade

Prepare the crust in the processor bowl. Prepare the coconut, almonds and butter for the topping by processing with the steel blade and put on a separate cookie sheet. Bake 15-20 minutes at 325°. Put the cream cheese, butter, sugar, orange rind, orange juice and seasonings in the processor bowl with the steel blade and process smooth. Spread over the chilled crust. Mound the ice cream on top.

Whip the cream with sugar and vanilla. Sprinkle the toasted coconut mixture on top.

Serve with a chocolate sauce or fresh strawberries, sliced in the processor.

Wait to wash and hull the berries until just before using . . . the caps help preserve the berries as well as protect the flavor and nutrients.

CREAM CROWDIE

This is a variation of a Scottish dessert . . . don't wait for dessert to try it!

Serves 4

1	cup whipping cream
1	pint vanilla ice cream
1	T. sugar
2	T. dark rum
1	cup Natural Cereal (p. 3)

Fresh seasonal berries (raspberries, blueberries, strawberries)

Steel Blade

Wash the berries and divide among 4 bowls. If you use strawberries, slice them first using the slicing disk.

Using a chilled bowl, beat the cream until stiff with the sugar.

Put the ice cream, in spoonfuls, into the processor bowl with the rum and process smooth using the steel blade. Fold into the whipped cream and pour over the berries. Top with Natural Cereal.

PEACHES AND CREAM

Serves 4-6

Pre-heat oven to 400°

10-12	**fresh peaches**
2	**T. butter**
6-8	**macaroons**
2	**slices white bread**
4	**T. cold butter (in pieces)**
1/3	**cup sweet sherry**
2	**T. Amaretto liqueur**
2	**cups sour cream**
1/2	**tsp. vanilla**
2	**T. powdered sugar**

Medium Serrated Slicing Disk, Steel Blade

Butter a baking dish approximately 8 by 10.

Peel and core the peaches, saving the peelings, and slice in with the slicing disk. Sprinkle with sherry.

Use the steel blade, with on/off's, to process macaroons and bread to crumbs. Add butter and process with on/off's. Cover the peaches and sprinkle with a little granulated sugar. Place in a 400° oven for 15 minutes or until the top is browned.

Put the peach peelings in the processor bowl with Amaretto, vanilla and a small amount of additional sugar. Process to puree. Add sour cream, combining with a few on/off's.

Serve the dessert warm with the cream.

DATE RUM ICE CREAM PIE

Resist everything but temptation.

Ginger-Spice Crust (p. 6) or
Macaroon Crust (p. 280)

1	cup dates
1/4	cup dark rum
1	quart coffee ice cream
1/4	cup pecans
1	cup whipping cream
3	T. sugar
1	tsp. vanilla
1	tsp. rum flavoring

Steel Blade, Shredding Disk

Prepare the crust according to the directions on page 6 or page 280.

Use the steel blade and put the dates and pecans in the bowl with 1-2 T. sugar. Dice using on/off's. (An alternate method, for very finely diced dates and nuts is to use the shredding disk alternating nuts and dates in the feeder tube.) Remove.

Soften the ice cream and fold in dark rum and diced dates and nuts. Mound in the crust and re-freeze.

Whip the cream (steel blade) by running the machine, pouring the cream through the feeder tube. It will be thick by the time you've finished pouring. Add the remaining sugar and vanilla, process in. Mound on top of the frozen pie or pipe decoratively through a pastry tube using a star tip.

Decorate with chocolate curls. If you have the julienne blade, try alternating a few pecans and chocolate chunks in the feeder tube and shred in. Great texture for decorating the top.

Note: Try with raisins . . . or another flavor of ice cream . . . swirl in some fudge topping.

 **CARROT PIE**

*And when she peeps out there is noboby there
but a present of carrots put down by the stair.*

Beatrix Potter

Pre-heat oven to 350°

1/2	cup almonds	4	graham crackers
1/2	cup pecans	1/2	stick butter
10	gingersnaps	1/2	cup coconut (optional)

Steel Blade

Process the nuts first, (until ground), then add the cookies and crackers, broken in several pieces. With the machine running, add the melted butter and process until combined (just a few seconds). Press into a 9 or 10 inch pie plate and bake for 10 minutes before filling. Cool.

Filling:

1	pound carrots
1	6 ounce can pineapple and its juice
3	eggs
2	T. brown sugar
1	14 ounce can sweetened condensed milk
1	3 ounce package cream cheese
1	tsp. cinnamon and nutmeg
1/2	tsp. salt
1	tsp. vanilla

Steel Blade

Cook the carrots until tender. Rinse and cool. Put them in the processor bowl with the cream cheese and process using the steel blade until pureed. Remove to a large bowl. Add the eggs, sugar, seasonings, and pineapple, processing just a few seconds to combine. With the machine running, add the milk through the feeder tube. Add to the carrots in the bowl, stir together, and put in the prepared crust. Bake 35-40 minutes.

FANTASTICALLY RICH CHOCOLATE PIE

Crust:

4	egg whites
1	cup almonds
1/2	cup sugar

Dash each salt and cream of tartar

Filling:

1 1/2	sticks unsalted butter
1	cup sugar
3	squares semi-sweet chocolate
3	large eggs
1	tsp. vanilla

Steel Blade

To prepare crust, beat egg whites in a copper bowl until stiff. If you do not have a copper bowl, use salt and cream of tartar. Use the steel blade to grind the almonds and sugar very fine. Fold quickly into whites and spread into an 8 inch pie plate. Bake at 350° 25-30 minutes or until lightly browned.

Put chocolate pieces in the processor bowl (steel blade) and process first with on/off's, then run the machine to grind very fine. Melt half of the butter until sizzling hot, and add through the feeder tube, machine running. Add 1 egg, processing smooth. Remove chocolate mixture. Process remaining butter and sugar until very light. Add vanilla and chocolate mixture, running machine until smooth and light. Add eggs, one at a time, processing until all the sugar is dissolved. Some people have told me they get a lighter mixture by changing to the plastic knife when adding eggs . . . I'm not entirely convinced. Light or not, the mixture is worth writing home about.

Decorating and Creative Additions:

Whip 1 cup heavy cream stiff. Use the steel blade and slowly pour cream through the feeder tube with the machine running. When thick, add 1 T. green Creme de Menthe and 3 T. powdered sugar. Spread or pipe decoratively over chilled pie. Grate additional chocolate with the julienne blade and sprinkle over the top. Or, grind some candy canes (steel blade) to a powder and sprinkle over the top. Or, decorate with candied cherries and marzipan leaves.

MACAROON PIE

After demonstrating one afternoon I had little paper plates full of ground nuts, shredded dates, cracker crumbs plus some egg whites leftover from making Hollandaise. This dessert was the result . . . surprisingly, it tasted very much like a specialty of one of my favorite restaurants in New Orleans.

6	egg whites
Dash of salt and cream of tartar	
12	saltine crackers
8	pitted dates
1/2	cup pecans
1	cup almonds
3/4	cup sugar
1	tsp. vanilla

Shredding Disk, Steel Blade

Beat the egg whites until stiff in a copper bowl or metal mixing bowl using a dash of salt and cream of tartar.

Use the steel blade and grind the almonds. With the machine running, add crackers and sugar. Remove steel blade and use the shredding disk. Load the feeder tube alternately with dates and nuts beginning with the nuts. Shred in using a "bounce" with the pusher if they seem to stick.

Fold the contents of the processor bowl, plus vanilla, into the egg whites. Gently spoon into a 9 by 9 square pan or 10 inch pie plate. Bake at 350° about 30 minutes (lightly browned). Turn the oven off and leave in about 10-15 minutes.

Serve with whipping cream or French vanilla ice cream.

Cookery must have an audience to be appreciated.

> Grimod de la Reyniere
> Publisher, one of the first gourmet magazines

ALMOND APPLE PIE

Almond Pastry (p. 358) or:
Basic Pastry (p. 9)

3   apples
Italian Pastry Creme (p. 21) or:
Quick Almond Cream (p. 20)
3-5   T. sugar
Lemon juice
Powdered sugar
Whipping cream

Steel Blade, Thin Slicing Disk (Smooth or Serrated)

Prepare the pastry and pre-bake at 375° for 15 minutes, in an 8 or 9 inch pan.

Use the thin slicing disk. Cut the apples in half. Remove core (not necessarily the peel), cut off the round edge and slice in lovely, uniform slices. Repeat until all are sliced. You will love the way they look!

Spread about 1/2 cup of the pastry creme on top of the baked crust. Arrange the apples in a decorative fashion, pinwheel for round pan, or, if using a rectangular pan, in rows. Sprinkle with lemon juice and 3-5 T. sugar. Bake 30-35 minutes at 350°. Cool and dust with powdered sugar before serving.

Serve with whipped cream, cream fraiche, sour cream, or, just as is.

Note: Try adding 3-4 T. apple brandy with the lemon juice.

My idea of retirement is a house with a big kitchen where I can cook and eat and get fat.

Juliette Prowse

x2 SHOO-FLY PECAN PIE

Pre-heat oven to 425°

1	recipe Cream Cheese Pastry (p. 10)

1/2	cup raisins
1/2	cup pitted dates
1/2	cup pecans
1/3	cup molasses or dark Karo syrup
1/4	cup rum
3	T. hot water
1/4	tsp. baking soda
2	eggs (optional)
3/4	cup sifted flour
1/2-3/4 cup pecans	
1/2	tsp. each cinnamon, nutmeg
1/4	tsp. ground ginger
6	T. butter
1/2	cup dark brown sugar

Steel Blade, Shredding Disk

Prepare the pastry adding 1 T. sugar. Pre-bake at 375° until lightly browned (10-12 minutes).

Put the flour, seasonings (cinnamon, nutmeg, ginger), 1/2-3/4 cup pecans and brown sugar in the processor bowl (steel blade) and process on/off to combine. Add butter, in pieces, and process a couple times on/off (pulse) to make a coarse, crumbly texture. Remove.

Use the shredding disk and fill the feeder tube with 1/2 cup dates and nuts, loading the nuts first. Shred in using light pressure, "bouncing" with the pusher if things seem to stick. Add hot water, molasses (or Karo), rum, raisins and soda. Let soak about 30 minutes. Add 2 eggs (optional) and process on/off a couple times to combine.

Pour the date-raisin mixture into the pre-baked crust. Put the flour mixture on top.

Bake at 425° 10 minutes, reduce temperature to 325° and bake an additional 15-20 minutes. Rich . . . however, serve it with ice cream anyway.

APPLEJACK BUNDT CAKE

Pre-heat oven to 350°

3	apples (small to medium)
1/4	cup white seedless raisins
2	cups sugar
3	eggs, separated
3/4	cups cooking oil
1/3	cup apple brandy (heated)
2 1/2	cups cake flour
1	tsp. each cinnamon, nutmeg
1/4	tsp. ground cloves
1/2	tsp. salt
1	T. baking soda

Steel Blade

Soak the raisins in the apple brandy. Put flour, spices, baking soda and salt in the bowl (steel blade) and process on/off to sift. Remove.

Put the apples, cored but not necessarily peeled, in the bowl and process to mince. Add raisins and liqueur and process by running the machine to grind the raisins. Add egg yolks, sugar and oil, processing by running the machine to combine thoroughly. Remove half this mixture to a large mixing bowl. Beat the egg whites in a copper bowl until stiff.

Remove the steel blade and insert the plastic knife. Add flour mixture and process in with several on/off's . . . just enough so that the flour disappears. Add a couple spoonfuls of the egg whites, processing in the same way. Transfer to the mixture in the mixing bowl, stirring in, then fold in the remaining egg whites. Pour into a well greased bundt pan and bake at 350° for about one hour. Cool 5-8 minutes and remove from the pan.

When cool dust with powdered sugar. Serve with whipped cream or cream fraiche . . . or the Sweet Sherry Sauce (p. 47).

dlc-7 When preparing this recipe with the large capacity machine, it is possible to do the entire recipe in one bowl. After combining the eggs, sugar and oil with the apples, you need not empty half the mixture to another bowl. Add the flour mixture, processing in with on/off's just until the flour disappears. Add a few scoops of the whites, processing in the same way. Remove and fold (by hand) into the remaining whites and bake as directed.

x2   FRESH LEMON-COCONUT CRUNCH CAKE

While I'm not totally opposed to using convenience foods, I do think one abandons them when "in to" processor cooking. However, I'm almost always asked how to do a cake mix, or, if the machine can "handle" a cake mix.

1   lemon cake mix
Peelings from a fresh lemon
1/2   cup heavy cream
Water, reduced by 1/3 cup (the amount called for in the mix)
2   tsp. juice from the lemon
1   T. granulated sugar

Topping:

1/2   of a fresh coconut
8-10   lemon candies (hard)
3   T. butter (soft)
1-2   T. granulated sugar
Remaining juice of the lemon

Steel Blade, Shredding Disk, Plastic Knife

Use the steel blade and run the machine, adding the cream through the feeder tube. Stop processing when stiff. Remove and wipe out the bowl. Put the peelings into the bowl and run machine to mince. It may be necessary to add additional sugar (about 1 tablespoon) to aid mincing. Add 2-3 eggs (as called for in the mix directions) and run machine to beat very well. Then dump the dry ingredients on top and add the liquid (as called for in the mix) on top of that. Process by on/off's until the flour is mixed in. Add cream, processing in with on/off's. Pour into a greased 9 inch springform pan and bake according to the package directions.

Put the candies into a dry bowl (steel blade) and process on/off to break up. Run the machine after well broken up to crush. Then use the shredding disk and pack the feeder tube with the coconut chunks. Shred in. Remove disk and put in plastic knife. Add soft butter, sugar and lemon juice, processing on/off to combine. Spread evenly over warm cake and return to oven, turn on the broiling element and toast several minutes until browned. Cool before cutting and serve with whipped cream, ice cream or lemon sherbert.

dlc-7 When using the DLC-7, you may prepare any of the bundt cake mixes (or variations on packaged mixes) easily in one bowl.

My fruit is better than gold, yea than fine gold.

Proverbs 8:19

ORANGE CANDY CAKE

This is one of two recipes shared by Margo Spitz, San Antonio's talk show hostess with whom I "process" every other week. After she had her processor a week she was getting out all her recipes formerly considered too much trouble . . . this is one of her favorites and one we prepared for her birthday on television.

Pre-heat oven to 300°

1	stick butter or margarine	Icing I:
1	cup sugar	
3	eggs	2 cups confectioner's sugar
1/2	cup buttermilk	1 egg white
1 1/2	tsp. baking soda	1 T. each lemon and
1/2	lb. orange candy pieces	orange juice
1/2	lb. pitted dates	"Enough" hot, boiling water
1/4	of a fresh coconut (about	1/2 (or the rest of) the coconut
	2/3 cup shredded)	
1	cup pecans	Icing II:
2	cups cake flour	
1/2	tsp. salt	Juice from an orange
Peelings from half an orange		4 T. butter
2	tsp. vanilla or	1/3 cup sugar
	1 T. orange liqueur	1/3 cup orange liqueur
		Fresh orange slices
		Cherries

Steel Blade, Shredding Disk, Julienne Blade

Use the steel blade to process flour, nuts and salt with a couple on/off's. Remove.

286

Process candy pieces, chunks of coconut and dates in several batches, along with a couple tablespoons of the sugar to aid chopping. Remove to a large bowl. Dust with some flour.

Process (steel blade) the orange peelings with a little of the sugar. When minced, add butter, in chunks, plus remaining sugar, processing until well mixed. Add eggs, vanilla or liqueur, processing smooth and light. Stir baking soda into buttermilk and add to the mixture. Combine with an on/off (or pulse). Add flour all at once and combine with a couple on/off's (pulse) . . . very brief processing. Stop processing even though a little flour remains on the top of the batter. Remove and stir gently into diced fruits. Pour into a well greased bundt pan and bake for about 90 minutes. Test with a toothpick to be sure the center is done. Cool 5-10 minutes, then unmold on a rack.

Icing I:

Use the shredding disk or julienne blade and load the coconut horizontally in the feeder tube with pieces as large as possible (load from the bottom). Remove for decoration.

Process the egg white (steel blade) until foamy. Add powdered sugar and fruit juices. Add boiling water, in 1 tablespoon amounts, through the feeder tube, with the machine running, until a proper glaze consistency. Pour over the cake when completely cooled and press coconut shreds into the icing.

Icing II:

If you have prepared the cake in a decorative mold (like the Kugelhopf) it looks lovely to coat with a clear glaze and decorate with thinly sliced orange sections and candied cherries. Heat the butter until sizzling. Add orange juice and sugar. Return to boiling point, boil one minute, then add liqueur. Let simmer a few minutes, then pour over the warm cake.

Use the serrated slicing disk. Cut the orange in half (horizontally), then cut off the round end so you have a flat surface against the blade. Pack from the bottom of the feeder tube so it fits firmly and slice through. Drain excess juice on a paper towel and arrange around the edges of the cake with cherries.

dlc-7 You may prepare a double recipe in the same manner. This is a help during the holidays and this is one "fruitcake" everyone will enjoy. Dice the dates, fruits and coconut in at least 3 batches . . . exact amounts of all three are flexible. You will be very pleased with the texture of the coconut with the new shredding disk. A double recipe will fill a bundt pan plus the Cuisinart Kugelhopf mold.

FRESH ORANGE CAKE

If you have the little round Pain de Mie, this is a wonderful recipe for it. Use the Fresh Orange Glaze and decorate with fresh sliced strawberries, slivered almonds or at Christmas, frosted cranberries.

Peeling from 1 naval orange (be careful to avoid white part)
2   tsp. orange juice concentrate (frozen)
1   T. orange marmalade
1 1/2 cups sugar
2   sticks unsalted butter
4   eggs
2   cups cake flour
2   tsp. baking powder
1   tsp. vanilla

Fresh Orange Glaze:

Sections from the orange
Triple-Sec liqueur
Powdered sugar
Some of the peelings

Steel Blade

Process the peelings by putting directly into the processor bowl using the steel blade. Process on/off several times to get started, then add sugar and process continuously until well minced. Add the orange juice, vanilla, marmalade and butter (in chunks). Process on/off to break up the butter, then process smooth. Add the eggs 2 at a time, processing in very well. Combine baking powder and flour and add directly into the bowl. Process on/off several times . . . be careful not to over-process . . . just let the flour disappear. Put batter into a well greased (about 8 by 10) pan and bake 35 minutes. Check with a toothpick. Let cool a few minutes before removing from the pan. If using the round Pain de Mie, use 1 cup of the batter. Use 1 1/3 cup for the oval. Bake 30 minutes at 350°.

Glaze: Soak the orange sections in the liqueur. Process smooth with some of the grated peelings, adding enough powdered sugar to make a glaze.

Some of the most memorable and fond occasions are with friends and family . . . and a culinary feast.

x2 DARTH VADAR CHOCOLATE CAKE

This is an old recipe with a new name which is perfectly delicious. You may substitute shredded zucchini for the sauerkraut.

Pre-heat oven to 350°

1	stick butter
1 1/2	cups sugar
3	large eggs
2	cups flour
2	tsp. baking powder
1	tsp. baking soda
1/2	tsp. salt (only if using squash)
1	cup Hershey's cocoa
8	ounces sauerkraut, washed and drained (or an equal amount of shredded zucchini)

Frosting:

6	ounces semi-sweet chocolate
1	stick butter
6	T. evaporated milk
1	tsp. vanilla
2-3	cups confectioners sugar
1	cup walnuts or pecans

Steel Blade, Shredding Disk

Combine dry ingredients (except sugar) with the steel blade and remove. Shred the zucchini, measure and return to the bowl. Or, drain sauerkraut and place in the bowl using the steel blade. Add butter, in pieces, and run the machine to mince and cream together. Add sugar and eggs, processing until light and well creamed.

Add dry ingredients and process (or pulse) with a few on/off's. Process very briefly, just enough so the flour disappears.

Grease and flour a 9 by 12 pan or 2-8 inch cake pans. Bake for 35-40 minutes. Cool before frosting.

Prepare frosting by heating butter and milk together, bringing to a boil. Put the chocolate pieces in the processor bowl (steel blade) processing first with on/off's, then running the machine to grind. Add hot liquid through the feeder tube (machine running). Add enough powdered sugar to make a smooth, spreadable frosting. Chop nuts using the steel blade with a couple of on/off's and press into icing while still warm.

x2   BUTTERSCOTCH DATE BARS

Pre-heat oven to 350°

1	stick butter
1	cup brown sugar
1	egg
1	cup flour
1	cup pecans
1/2	cup pitted dates
1/4	of a coconut
1	tsp. baking powder
1/4	tsp. salt
1	tsp. vanilla

Steel Blade, Shredding Disk

Put the flour, baking powder and salt in the bowl (steel blade) and sift with a few on/off's . . . if you wish pecans chopped fine, do at this time with the flour. Remove.

Use the steel blade to cream butter, sugar and egg. Change to the shredding disk and load the feeder tube with dates, nuts and coconut. Shred in, using a "bounce" with the pusher if at all sticky or difficult to push through.

Change to the plastic knife and mix in flour and vanilla. Use a couple on/off's to mix in flour.

Spread in a 9 inch square pan and bake 30 minutes at 350°.

x2   CHEWY CITRUS BARS

Pastry:

1 3/4	cups flour
1/2	cup filberts or almonds
1/2	cup powdered sugar
4	ounces cream cheese
1 3/4	sticks butter
2	tsp. lemon juice

Filling:

Peelings from a lemon (lime or orange)
Juice from 3 lemons (6 limes or 2 oranges)

4	eggs
2	cups sugar
3	T. flour
1/2	tsp. baking powder
1/2	of a fresh coconut

Steel Blade, Shredding Disk (or Julienne Blade)

Put the nuts in the bowl (steel blade) and grind to a powder. Add flour, sugar, cream cheese and butter in chunks. Process with on/off's to combine. When in a crumbly texture, add lemon juice and process again. If it seems dry, add a few drops of cold water but do not process to make a pastry ball. Pat into a 9 by 12 baking pan and bake at 350° for 20-25 minutes (lightly browned). Cool.

Process the citrus peelings with a few tablespoons of the sugar to mince very fine. Add juices, sugar and eggs, processing until very light and well mixed. Add flour, baking powder and process in with on/off's. Change to the julienne blade (or shredding disk) and shred in the coconut. Spread on top of the baked crust, blending the coconut into the batter as you remove with a spatula. Bake for 25 minutes at 350° or until "set". The top will be slightly crusty . . . too attractive to cover with anything but a rosette of processor whipped cream.

For quick results, start the machine running (steel blade) using a chilled bowl. Pour the cream slowly through the feeder tube. By the time you've emptied the carton it will be stiff. Add a tablespoon or two of powdered sugar for added stability and pipe through a pastry tube.

Note: When preparing this recipe in the new larger capacity machine, you may make a recipe that will fill an average size jelly roll pan which will yield about 48 citrus bars. The baking time is approximately the same but check after 20 minutes. The center should be "set".

QUICK NAPOLEONS

Mock Puff Pastry (p. 11)

Custard Filling (p. 258) or use
Birds Custard Powder with
    1 3/4 cups half and half
    1 whole egg
    3 T. sugar
    1/4 cup heavy cream

Confectioner's Sugar Glaze:
    1 cup confectioner's sugar
    "Enough" hot water

Instant Chocolate Sauce:
    4 squares semi-sweet chocolate
    1/3 cup water
    1/4 cup sugar

Steel Blade

Roll out the prepared pastry about 1/8 inch thick and cut into rectangular sections about 1 inch by 2 inches. Bake at 425° until puffed and browned . . . about 15-20 minutes. Cool.

Scald the half and half. Process the egg, custard powder and sugar together, adding 1 cup of the hot liquid through the feeder tube. Return to the rest of the half and half and stir to thicken over medium heat. If it lumps a bit don't be concerned, just give it the steel blade treatment a few seconds. Chill very cold before using. Prepare the icing adding additional water if necessary.

Boil together the water and sugar 1 minute and process the chocolate pieces with the on/off (or pulse) method to break up. Then run machine to mince very fine. Add the hot liquid through the feeder tube with the machine running.

Fill a pastry bag and using the star tip pile the chilled custard onto half the rectangles of pastry. Cover with the remaining pieces (like a sandwich). Heat the glaze so it pours easily and coat the tops. Refrigerate to set the icing, then drizzle with chocolate. Makes about 10

The whole of nature is a conjunction of the verb eat, in the active and passive.

William R. Inge

Breads and Pain de Mie

Without bread, without wine, love is nothing.

French Proverb

TIPS ON MAKING PROCESSOR BREAD

1. Add the last cup of flour in most breads in small amounts . . . you want a ball of dough to form but too much flour can cause "tough" results. Some doughs need to be quite soft and will not form a ball of dough.

2. Doughs rich with butter and eggs will cause the machine to slow down and probably cut off. Your Cuisinart has an automatic safety mechanism which will protect the motor from any damage . . . the machine will start again when the motor cools off. When adding additional flour, take care not to add too much or a stiff dough will be the result. If the machine continues to cut off, remove the dough and let it rise. You may then knead some by hand, though with many of the soft doughs or batter breads this is not really necessary.

3. The DLC-7 has a plastic dough mixing blade for bread recipes with over 3 1/2 cups of flour. All bread recipes doubled in the DLC-7 are marked with this blade.

A loaf of bread, the walrus said, Is chiefly what we need; Pepper and vinegar besides, Are very good indeed.

Lewis Carroll

x2  BASIC YEAST DOUGH I

Pre-heat oven to 350°

This dough is easy to mix and requires very little kneading. Perfect for rolls . . . after it has risen once you may chill or freeze.

1	package dry active yeast
1	T. sugar
1/2	tsp. salt
1	cup milk (120-130°)
1/2	stick butter
1	egg (for rolls)
2 3/4-3	cups unbleached flour (more or less)

Steel Blade

Heat the milk and sugar to 130° . . . stir in butter to melt. Check temperature to be sure it is above 120°.

Put the dry yeast and flour in the processor bowl and use the on/off method to process once. Add egg and warm milk with the machine running. Process with on/off (or pulse), adding more flour if necessary. What you want is a smooth, elastic ball of dough. Do not run the machine to knead but be sure the "dough ball" has formed. Remove and place in a bowl with 1 tsp. oil, turn over, cover and let rise in a warm place until doubled. It will rise fairly quickly (30 minutes).

Punch the dough down on a floured surface. Prepare to make bread, rolls or Pain de Mie loaves. The second rising is also short (20-25 minutes) and the bread should not be allowed to over-rise or it will collapse when baking. Glaze with melted butter, egg wash (beaten egg and milk) or water plus a dash of salt and cornstarch (crispier crust). Do not glaze if using the Pain de Mie pans.

Baking Times:

Bread (1 loaf):   35-40 minutes at 375°
Rolls: 20-25 minutes at 350°
Pain de Mie: 30-35 minutes at 350°

Acorns were good until bread was found.

Francis Bacon

x2 BASIC YEAST DOUGH II

1	package dry active yeast
1	tsp. sugar
1/4	cup warm water (105-115°)
2	T. butter
1	cup warm milk (beer, water or other combinations of liquids)
1/2	tsp. salt
3	cups flour (about)

May be whole wheat, rye, or any combination.

Steel Blade

Dissolve the yeast in warm water letting it sit until it becomes foamy. This is proofing the yeast.

Put 2 cups of the flour (4 cups for the DLC-7) plus salt and butter (in chunks) in the bowl and process with on/off's (or pulse) until combined. Add yeast mixture and milk, processing smooth. You may need to scrape down the sides of the bowl.

Add remaining flour in 1/3 cup amounts, processing in between additions until you have a ball of dough that will form around the top of the blades. Knead by running the machine continuously about 30-40 seconds. The dough should be smooth and elastic.

Remove and place in an oiled bowl, cover and let rise until doubled. Punch down and place on a floured board and use for a loaf of bread, rolls, or Pain de Mie.

The second rising will take about 30-40 minutes. Bake according to directions:

Bread (1 loaf):	35-40 minutes at 375°
Rolls:	20-25 minutes at 350°
Pain de Mie:	30-35 minutes at 350°

Add wheat germ, a handful of nuts, shredded cheese, unprocessed bran . . . experiment!

UNUSUALLY GOOD VARIATIONS USING BASIC DOUGH

x2 LEMON COCONUT

Basic Bread I or II

Peelings from a lemon
Juice from the lemon plus coconut milk and water
      to make all the liquid
3   good size chunks of fresh coconut or:
      2/3 cup shredded

Process the peelings with the coconut (steel blade). Leave in the bowl and add flour. Prepare bread according to the directions in the basic recipe and bake as directed for Pain de Mie pans or loaves.

x2 GRANOLA RAISIN

Basic Bread I or II (especially good using whole wheat flour)

2/3-1	cup Natural Cereal (p. 3)	
1	cup white seedless raisins plumped in 1/2 cup boiling water	
Water from the raisins plus enough milk to make up the liquid (in the Basic Recipe)		
3	T. butter	
Brown sugar and cinnamon		

Topping:
5   T. brown sugar
1   T. cinnamon
3   T. Natural Cereal
2   T. butter

Egg Wash:
1   egg
1   T. water

Prepare the bread as in basic recipe. Plump the raisins in 1/2 cup boiling water (10-15 minutes). Drain and use the water as part of the total liquid. When preparing the bread for a loaf pan, roll out the length of the pan and spread with a thin coating of soft butter. Sprinkle with cereal (use a little extra cinnamon sugar if you like) and raisins. Roll up and place in a greased loaf pan. Cover and let rise again until almost doubled. Brush with an egg wash. Prepare topping by combining brown sugar, cinnamon and cereal with the steel blade. Add butter in two pieces and process with on/off's to cut in evenly. Sprinkle on top of the bread and bake at 350° 35-40 minutes.

Note: You may add cereal directly to the batter instead, when adding the additional flour. Use only 1/2 cup.

x2 WHOLE WHEAT DATE NUT BREAD

Pre-heat oven to 375°

1	package dry active yeast
1/4	cup warm water
1	tsp. sugar
1/4	tsp. salt
2	cups whole wheat flour
1	cup (about) unbleached flour
7/8	cup warm water
2-3	T. butter
6-8	pitted dates
1/2	cup pecans or walnuts

Steel Blade, Shredding Disk

Dissolve the yeast in warm water and sugar and let it sit until it foams (about 10 minutes). Use the shredding disk and fill the feeder tube alternately (nuts first) with dates and nuts. Shred in. Put in the steel blade. Add whole wheat flour, salt and butter. Combine with a couple on/off's (or pulse). Add yeast and warm water, processing to a "batter" consistency. Add additional white flour until a ball of dough forms on top of the blades. If the machine stalls, wait a few minutes and add additional flour when starting it again. If you have trouble doing this, remove a little bit of dough, add flour in small amounts, and process until a ball of dough comes together.

Run the machine about 30 seconds to "knead". The dough should be smooth and elastic in appearance. Put it in an oiled bowl, cover, and let it rise until doubled (1-1 1/2 hours). Remove, punch down on a floured surface and form into a single loaf or prepare for the Pain de Mie pans (see directions p. 305). Let the formed bread rise again until nearly doubled. Brush with an egg and water glaze and bake 35-40 minutes.

The first Baking Contest was in ancient Greece.

x2 ALMOND BREAD

Pre-heat oven to 375°

1	package dry active yeast
2	cups all purpose flour
About 1 cup whole wheat flour	
1/3	cup almonds
4	T. butter
1	T. sugar
1/2	tsp. salt
1	cup milk (120-130°)

Beaten egg and water
1   T. each untoasted wheat germ and almonds

Steel Blade

Put the almonds and 1/2 cup of the all purpose flour in the bowl and process until the almonds are very finely ground. Add the remaining all purpose flour, salt, dry yeast and sugar. Process to combine with a couple on/off's. Add butter, in pieces, and process in with on/off's. Add the milk, process in by running the machine. Add the whole wheat flour in thirds, processing until a ball of dough forms on top of the blades. Add additional flour if necessary. You do not need to run the machine to "knead" more than 10 seconds or so.

Remove dough and place in an oiled bowl, cover with a damp cloth and let rise in a warm place until doubled. Punch down on a floured board, shape into a loaf, place in a buttered loaf pan and let rise again until almost doubled. This second rising will take 20-25 minutes. Brush with beaten egg and water, then sprinkle with the wheat germ and almonds (processed together with the steel blade). Bake at 375° 35-40 minutes. Remove from the oven and brush with a little melted butter while hot.

dlc-7 When doing this with the DLC-7, process almonds and flour with the steel blade. Use the plastic dough mixing blade to complete the recipe.

Note: If you have Almond Paste, you may substitute 1/2 cup for the almonds, butter and sugar. "Cut in" with the flour before adding milk. You may prepare this in the Pain de Mie pans but omit glaze and topping.

x2 WHOLE WHEAT CHEESE BREAD

This is prepared by "proofing" the yeast and kneading with the processor.

1	package dry active yeast
1/2	cup warm water (105-115°)
1/2	cup stale beer (at room temperature)
2	T. molasses
1 3/4	cups whole wheat flour
1	cup (more or less) unbleached flour
1/2	tsp. salt
1	T. dried minced onions
3	ounces Swiss cheese
3	T. unsalted butter

Steel Blade, Shredding Disk

Dissolve the yeast in warm water and molasses. Let it sit until it foams. Put the cheese through the shredding disk and remove. Put 2 cups of the flour, seasonings and butter in the bowl (steel blade) and process with on/off's to cut in the butter.

Add the yeast, beer and cheese, processing to a batter. Add the remaining flour in 1/3 cup amounts, processing in between until the dough gathers up in a ball on top of the blades. Knead by running the machine about 30 seconds.

Remove and place in an oiled bowl (1 tsp.), turn over, cover and let rise until doubled (1 1/2 hours). Prepare for a loaf of bread or Pain de Mie loaves. The prepared dough needs to rise again until doubled. Bake at 375°.

Baking times:

Pain de Mie: 30-35 minutes at 350°
Single loaf: 35-40 minutes at 375°

Bread, cheese and kisses.

16th Century

This dough makes little rolls that are a real treasure. It is also an excellent dough for encasing special meat mixtures, seafood-cheese mixtures . . . or you may use it to encase a Beef Wellington.

Pre-heat oven to 475°

1	envelope dry active yeast
1/4	cup warm water (110-115°)
1/4	cup warm milk (110-115°)
1	T. sugar
1	stick butter
3	large eggs
1/2	tsp. salt
2-2 1/2	cups all purpose flour
2	egg yolks beaten with 2 T. milk

Steel Blade

Dissolve yeast in the warm water with sugar, milk and 1 T. of the flour. Let it stand 10-15 minutes. Put the butter in the processor bowl, using the steel blade, and "cream" by processing 10-15 seconds. Add three eggs and process smooth. Add 2 1/4 cups flour to the bowl, with the salt, and process to combine. It should look smooth and elastic.

Add the yeast mixture and run the machine to combine. Add remaining flour and process, scraping the sides of the bowl occasionally. Stop processing if the machine slows down. The dough should be **very** soft and will not form a ball of dough. If the Cuisinart cuts off (a safety mechanism), remove the dough to rise. Your machine will start again in a few moments.

Put the dough in a buttered bowl, cover it with oiled wax paper, and let it rise at room temperature, away from drafts, for about 2-3 hours. If it rises over the top of the bowl, punch it down. After 2-3 hours, stir through the dough briskly and quickly. Knead briefly (with floured hands), then cover with a damp cloth and refrigerate overnight.

If you plan to make rolls, allow one and one-half hours for preparation, rising, and baking. If you plan to use it to encase something, eliminate 45 minutes rising time.

Rolls: Flour your hands, roll the dough into balls that will fit the bottom of a small brioche tin, or muffin tin. Mark an X across the top, and make a gentle indentation. Roll a smaller ball, set lightly in the indentation. Cover with oiled wax paper, and let rise in a warm place an hour. Brush lightly with the egg yolk and milk and bake for 12-15 minutes.

When baking rolls (or bread) turn oven down to 400°, put rolls (or bread) in, bake until lightly browned.

      Rolls: 12-15 minutes

      Bread: 20-25 minutes

For a Pastry Case:

Reserve a little of the dough for decorations. If you plan to encase a 4 pound tenderloin (as in Beef Wellington) you will need a double recipe.

Roll out the chilled dough on a floured board to about 1/4" thick. Brush it all over the inside with the egg yolk and milk mixture. Put in the meat, stuffing, or whatever, roll it up or seal the edges, make a hole in the top for the steam to escape, cover with oiled wax paper and let it rise about 15 minutes.

Bake at 375° for 25-30 minutes or until nicely browned on top.

It is important that the dough for Brioche be very SOFT. The chilling period makes it easier to handle the dough. Traditionally a "sponge" is prepared (the yeast mixture plus about 1/2 cup of the flour) first and added to the dough after "the sponge" rises.

This traditional German coffee cake is very light and airy in texture when prepared with one rising. If you prefer a finer texture, let the dough rise in a separate bowl for this first rising, then punch down and let it rise a second time in the mold.

1	package dry active yeast
1/4	cup warm water
1	tsp. sugar
3	cups flour (about)
1	T. sugar
3/4	cup lukewarm milk (110°)
2	large eggs
4	T. butter
1/4	tsp. salt
3/4	cup raisins and currants

For the Mold:

Lots of butter
1	tsp. sugar
1/2	cup almonds

Topping:

Confectioner's sugar

Steel Blade, Plastic Mixing Blade

Scald the milk and stir in the butter to melt. Combine yeast, 1 tsp. sugar and 1/4 cup warm water in a measuring cup. Let it stand until foamy (about 10 minutes).

Put 2 cups flour, sugar and salt in the bowl and process to combine. Add eggs, milk and yeast mixture processing to a batter. Add additional flour until a **soft** ball of dough comes together. This is a dough much like a Brioche, which is heavy with butter and eggs. It will not be possible to form a ball of dough without adding too much flour. If the machine slows down or cuts off, remove the dough and knead briefly by hand. (It does get kneaded some in the mixing.) Before removing dough, add dried fruits and process in.

Generously butter the Kugelhopf mold. Combine sugar and almonds together with the steel blade and use to dust the inside of the mold. Spoon the batter in, cover with oiled wax paper and let rise in a warm place (about 80°) an hour or until doubled.

Bake at 350° 50-60 minutes. Cover with foil if the top gets too brown. Cool a few minutes, remove from the mold and place on a rack. Dust with confectioner's sugar.

Of the female gourmand . . .

Her eyes sparkle, her lips glossy, her conversation agreeable, and all her movements graceful . . . with so many advantages, she is irresistable.

Brillat-Savarin

PAIN DE MIE

Cuisinart makes two, hinged, little bread pans for making cakes, yeast and quick breads. The Pain de Mie pans come with excellent bread recipes and complete instructions for their use. Measure amounts exactly to insure success (as well as a clean oven).

I would suggest preparing the pans with a vegetable coating spray prior to baking. Avoid soap or harsh abrasives when cleaning. When the pan has been used several times it will "season" and clean up easily with water.

When slicing the bread in the feeder tube use the medium serrated slicer and follow the directions carefully. The oval loaf slices somewhat more easily as it exactly fits the feeder tube. The bread must be at least 12 hours old.

The new DLC-7 machine has a slightly different shaped feeder tube that will handle two round loaves (cut in half or thirds) side by side. The slicing blade is also extremely efficient. Making your own melba toast and canape rounds is back to basics with style!

Note: When using the pans, omit glaze. The quick bread recipes that are especially good for the Pain de Mie are indicated. Canape fillings and other fun ideas are also included.

AMOUNT GUIDE FOR EASY REFERENCE

Round Pain de Mie:

Quick Bread or Cakes:	1 cup batter
Yeast Bread:	7/8 cup dough

Oval Pain de Mie:

Quick Bread or Cakes:	1 1/4 cups batter
Yeast Bread:	1 1/3 cups dough

Bake at 350° for 30-35 minutes. Pull out rod and remove bread to cool on a rack.

PREPARATION FOR BAKING

For yeast breads, measure out specified amount of dough . . . don't leave it to chance as even a self cleaning oven will not compensate for the mess. Roll the dough out on a lightly floured surface the length of the pan. Roll up (so it is in a long loaf). Pinch the edges together (at the seam) and place in the pan seam side down. Leave the pan open, cover with a damp cloth and let rise until doubled (30-45 minutes), then close the pan and put in the rod. Bake as directed. If you open the pan and the bread is not done, just close up and bake an additional 5 minutes. Cool on a rack.

For quick breads, measure carefully and pour batter in the side of the pan that has the flat "feet". Close the pan, put in the rod and bake 30-35 minutes. Open and remove cake after it has cooled a few minutes.

HERBED SESAME TOASTS

1 Pain de Mie loaf (whole wheat, white . . . any type)
2 T. sesame seeds
1 stick butter
1/2 tsp. each chervil and salt
1/4 tsp. paprika
1/8 tsp. chili powder

Steel Blade, Serrated Slicing Disk

First slice the bread with the slicing disk according to the directions from Cuisinart. Be sure to use the medium serrated slicing disk. Remove the toasts and using the steel blade process the butter and seasonings together. Butter both sides of the toasts and place on an ungreased baking sheet and bake at 350° until nicely browned (about 10-15 minutes).

Pack in an airtight container and use with soups or with dips or just to munch!

PAIN DE MIE WITH PARMESAN AND HERBS

Basic Dough I or II (p. 294-296)

1	ounce Parmesan or Romano cheese
1	shallot
1-2	T. soft butter

Several sprigs of fresh parsley

Steel Blade

Turn on the machine and drop the cheese and shallot through the feeder tube to mince and grate very fine. Add parsley and mince with a few on/off's.

Roll out the specified amount of dough the length of the pan, spread with softened butter and sprinkle with Parmesan mixture. Roll up and place in the pan, seam side down. Cover with a damp cloth and let rise until almost doubled. Close pan (poking dough in if it squeezes out the edges), put in the rod and bake 30 minutes at 350°.

PAIN DE MIE WITH NUT BUTTER

This is just plain fun . . . the ultimate with peanut butter and jelly.

Basic Dough I or II (p. 294-296)

1	cup roasted peanuts, cashews, mixed cocktail nuts or combination
1-2	T. butter
1	T. honey

Steel Blade

Prepare the nut butter by placing the nuts in the bowl and running the machine until a paste consistency. Add oil and butter with machine running, until the butter is a smooth paste.

Roll out the specified amount of dough the length of the pan, spread with nut butter, roll up and place seam side down in the pan. Cover loaf with a damp cloth and let rise until almost doubled.

Close the pan, put in the rod and bake 30 minutes at 350°.

PAIN DE MIE WITH PATE AND DUXELLES

Delightful . . . fun . . . everyone will want to know what's inside.

2	ounces canned Pate
2	ounces Duxelles (p. 65)
1	T. unsalted butter
1	tsp. lemon juice
1	egg and 1 T. water

Basic Yeast Dough I or II (p. 294-296)

Steel Blade

Mix together (with a fork) the egg and water . . . set aside.

Prepare the Duxelles, leaving 2 ounces (about) in the bowl. Add lemon juice, butter and pate directly to the bowl processing briefly to combine. Remove.

Roll out specified amount of dough, any more and your oven will be a mess . . . into a rectangle the length of the little pan. Spread lightly with the egg wash, then the filling. Spray the pan very well with a vegetable coating spray (hinges too). Roll up the dough tightly and place it in the pan, seam side down and leave the pan open. Cover with a clean cloth and put in a warm place to rise. After it doubles close the pan (gently poke in the dough) put in the rod and bake in a pre-heated 350° oven 30 minutes. Remove rod and open carefully, using a sharp knife to loosen any dough that sticks.

Cool and slice by hand. Butter and serve warm or use as a canape base.

My idea of heaven is eating pate de foie gras to the sound of trumpets.

Sydney Smith

x2 FRESH PINEAPPLE CHEESE WITH SESAME TOASTS

1   fresh pineapple
4   ounces Monterey Jack or Swiss cheese
12   ounces cream cheese
1/3-1/2 of an onion
1   tsp. lemon juice
Jalapeno jelly (medium hot) or chutney

Sesame Toasts

Steel Blade

Cut the pineapple in half and remove the meat. Keep the half shell intact to hold the finished dip. Cut the top in half (vertically), for decoration.

Put the Swiss or Monterey Jack cheese in the processor bowl in chunks and process to a paste consistency by running the machine. Add cream cheese through the feeder tube (machine running) plus lemon juice. Put 4-5 chunks of pineapple and chunks of an onion on top of the cream mixture. Process with on/off's to "chop", then run the machine to incorporate. Adding the onions and pineapple last reduces the bitterness of the onion and leaves both additions in small, diced pieces.

Fill the shell with cream cheese mixture. When ready to serve, top with jalapeno jelly or chutney. Serve with sesame toasts.

The discovery of a new dish does more for the happiness of man than the discovery of a star.

Brillat—Savarin

x2   ARTICHOKE DIP

Serve hot with Parmesan Herb Pain de Mie toasts.

3	fresh artichokes
4	ounces Parmesan cheese
1/2	cup mayonnaise

Several green onions
Lemon juice
Several sprigs fresh parsley
Dash cayenne pepper

1/4	tsp. salt

Steel Blade

Cut the cheese into chunks, put into the bowl and process to a powder.

Cook the artichokes by boiling in lightly salted water about 45 minutes or until tender. Use a grapefruit spoon and scrape the edible meat from the base of the leaves (into the processor bowl). Remove the feathery choke and add the heart to the bowl. Process on/off a few times. Add green onions (in pieces), parsley, juice from half a lemon and seasonings. Process to a puree. Add mayonnaise last, processing just enough to combine. Transfer to a small saucepan over direct heat, stirring until hot. Serve with toasts.

Variation: This is also deliciously rich mounded on the toasts and topped with a small spoonful of Hollandaise Sauce. Or, use Hollandaise instead of the mayonnaise.

x2   SHRIMP PUFFS

Canapes from Pain de Mie loaves (Whole Wheat Cheese
         especially good)

1/2	pound cleaned, deveined shrimp
4	ounces Muenster cheese
2	T. butter
1	T. mayonnaise

Several sprigs fresh cilantro (or 1/4 tsp. dried)
Dash of Tabasco

1/4	of a green pepper
1	egg white

Steel Blade

Saute the shrimp 1-2 minutes in the sizzling butter. Beat the egg
white stiff in another bowl. Put the cheese (in chunks) in the processor bowl and using the steel blade process on/off to grate. Add the
seasonings, pepper, shrimp and mayonnaise processing on/off to
combine and chop. Add the egg white last processing once to incorporate.

Toast the canapes on one side, then spread the shrimp mixture on
the other side. Place 6 inches away from the broiler for about 5
minutes until puffed and browned. Easy, but really very special.

FUN FOOT LONG

1   chunk of round leftover sausage
Muenster cheese
Several leaves of fresh spinach
2   green onions
1   ounce cream cheese
2   T. mayonnaise
1   chunk green pepper
1-2   strips crisp bacon
Butter
Dijon mustard

Thin Serrated Slicing Disk, Steel Blade

Cut the Pain de Mie loaf in half lengthwise, butter and spread mustard on both halves. Slice cheese with the serrated slicer, then slice sausage, and place both on one half. Put the cream cheese, in chunks, in the processor bowl (steel blade) with onions, green pepper and bacon . . . process first with on/off's, then run the machine a few seconds. Add mayonnaise, process in. Spread on the other half.

Place both halves 8" away from the broiler to heat and melt the cheese. Remove, add spinach leaves and put together like a sandwich. Cut the loaf (when serving) on the diagonal.

Jack Sprat will eat no fat,
And Jill doth love no lean,
Yet betwixt them both,
They lick the dishes clean.

John Clarke

These are from one of my creative Canadian cousins, Kaye Lindsay, also a processor fan who sent me this recipe along with a note that powdered milk and margarine work well also. She cuts in the shortening and the end result is nothing less than fantastic which proves there's more than one way to make the processor do what YOU want it to do!

Pre-heat oven to 400°

2	cups sifted all purpose flour
1 1/2	T. sugar
1/2	tsp. salt
1/2	cup butter
1	tsp. sugar
1	package dry active yeast
1/4	cup lukewarm water
1/2	cup milk
1	egg yolk

Pecans or walnuts
Peelings from a lemon

Juice from the lemon
Powdered sugar (about 1 cup)
A few drops hot water

Steel Blade

Put the flour, salt and 1 1/2 T. sugar into the bowl. Add the butter in chunks processing on/off to "cut in" (as in pie crust) . . . or use pulse. Dissolve the yeast in the warm water with 1 tsp. sugar and let it stand to get light and bubbly. Scald milk and cool to lukewarm. Stir egg yolk in yeast mixture, adding all at once to the bowl. Process to blend well. This will be a "soft" consistency and much like a "Brioche". Remove to a buttered bowl and cover with wax paper, then with a cloth and chill at least 2 hours but up to 48 hours. Dump out onto a well floured board (it will be sticky) and roll out about 1/2 inch thick. Square off edges and cut into strips about 8 inches long and 1/2 inch wide. Stretch and twist (like a rope), then place one end on a greased baking sheet winding around and around tucking the end underneath. Cover with a damp cloth and let rise until a dent remains when pressed lightly. Bake in a 400° oven 12-15 minutes or until browned. Cool a few minutes.

Put the peelings and nuts into the bowl (steel blade) processing very fine. Remove. Make a glaze with the lemon juice and powdered sugar, adding hot water if necessary. Use the steel blade if you want to use the processor.

Drizzle with glaze and top with some nut mixture or serve as is.

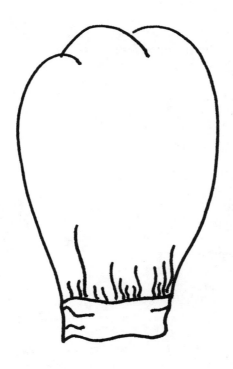

The true essentials of a feast are only fun and food.

Oliver Wendell Holmes

Pre-heat oven to 350°

1	recipe Basic Yeast Dough I (p. 294)
1/2	cup Almond Paste (p. 17)
	(Or grind 1/3 cup almonds, 2 T. butter, and
	2 T. sugar together with the steel blade)
2	T. butter
3	ounces cream cheese

Zest from 1/4 of a lemon and orange

1	T. orange juice concentrate
1	tsp. vanilla extract

Icing:

1	T. lemon juice
1	cup confectioners sugar
1	T. zest of orange and lemon

"Enough" boiling water

Steel Blade

Grate the zest with the sugar using the steel blade. Prepare the almond paste, then add cream cheese, butter, remaining seasonings and process until combined.

Roll out the dough, fold (like a business letter) once and roll out again in a rectangle as you would prepare cinnamon rolls. Spread with the filling generously. Roll up securely and chill. After 30 minutes, cut into slices and place in a buttered pan, leaving space in between for rising. Cover with a clean towel to rise in a warm place. I usually put them in a cold oven with a pan of boiling water on the bottom rack. You can use any shaped pan . . . at Christmas I used a tree shaped mold, at Easter half a bunny mold . . . and sometimes a decorative ring mold. Bake about 20-25 minutes at 350° or until nicely browned. The rolls will pull apart when baked.

Icing:
Process together (steel blade) the zest and half the sugar. Then add lemon juice and the rest of the sugar adding boiling water by the tablespoonful through the feeder tube, with the machine running . . . stop when it's the proper consistency. Ice the warm rolls after removing them from the pan.

315

x2  FLAKY DINNER ROLLS

Pre-heat oven to 375°

Basic Yeast Dough I or II
1/2   stick softened butter (unsalted)

Roll out the dough after it has risen once, spread with softened butter, then fold up like a business letter, folding the top third down and the bottom third up. Pinch the ends to seal in the butter and chill. Repeat the process 2 more times letting the dough chill 30 minutes between each time. Roll out the dough on a floured board 1/4" thick. Cut into rectangles about 2x4 inches. Fold each over and place in a large muffin tin (sprayed with vegetable shortening spray) cut ends up. Let them rise 20 minutes. Brush with egg yolk and milk and bake in a 375° oven about 15-20 minutes or until browned.

x2 CROISSANTS

It seems unusual to consider this a "basic" but it is really quite easy to make with the aid of the processor and is the most marvelous pastry ... wonderful with coffee in the morning ... excellent for rolling up succulent fillings ... a wonderfully flaky light top crust for Beef Wellington.

Pre-heat oven to 400°

1   package active dry yeast
1/4   cup warm water
3/4   cup milk (105-115°)
1   T. sugar
1/2   tsp. salt
2 1/2 cups unbleached flour
2   sticks unsalted butter
Egg yolk and 1 T. cream

316

Steel Blade, Slicing Disk (Fine Serrated)

Dissolve the yeast in the warm water and sugar (you may do this directly in the processor bowl). Let it sit 5-6 minutes until foamy. Add milk and salt. Add 2 cups flour directly into the bowl and process to blend. You'll need to scrape down the sides of the bowl. Now add remaining flour, processing a couple seconds in between, until you have a **soft** dough. Process until smooth and elastic in appearance . . . this will take 15 seconds more or less. Remove and place in a buttered or oiled bowl, turn and cover with buttered wax paper. Let it rise until doubled. Chill several hours for easier handling.

Punch the dough down and roll out on a floured board into a large rectangular shape about 1/4" thick.

Using the slicing disk, push the cold butter (you can fit two sticks at a time) through the feeder tube and "flake". Spread half throughout the middle section of the dough, and fold the top third down, the bottom third up (like a business letter). Use enough flour on your hands to prevent sticking. Use a drop or so of water to seal the edges.

1. Turn the dough around to face the opposite direction, roll it out again, repeat with the remaining butter, fold it up, and wrap in wax paper to chill. (20 minutes to 2 hours)

Note: During the rolling you will incorporate the butter and create the thin layers of pastry with the folding.

2. Remove from the refrigerator, roll out again, fold up the same way, turn, wrap in wax paper and chill.

3. Repeat several more times, letting the dough rest 20 minutes between turns.

To prepare rolls:

Roll dough out on a floured board about 1/8 inch thick. Cut as illustrated (p. 318) and roll up into a crescent. Lay on an ungreased baking sheet . . . be sure the tip of the crescent is against the baking sheet. Cover and let them rise at room temperature about an hour. Brush gently with egg yolk and cream and bake about 25 minutes. You may prepare these the night before, letting the dough rest overnight in the refrigerator. Or prepare, bake until almost done, freeze, and reheat in a 400° oven.

To cut for Croissants ⟶

**Cut cleanly
with a sharp knife...
do not "saw."**

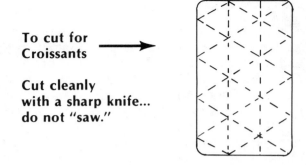

It is very important that the basic dough mixture for Croissants be very **SOFT**. Take care not to add too much flour. After the dough chills, it will be easier to handle. When rolling and folding work quickly and try not to "stretch" dough. A heavy, good quality rolling pin is a worthwhile investment.

Imagine you are a masterchef you most admire ... like James Beard ... you'll never have a failure.

*Honest bread is very well —
it's the butter that makes the temptation.*

Douglas Jerrold

x2 BAGELS

Pre-heat oven to 400°

1	package dry active yeast
1/4	cup warm water
2	tsp. sugar
3	cups flour (about)
1	tsp. salt
1/2	cup warm water
2	eggs
3	T. sugar
3	T. oil

Beaten egg plus 1 T. water

Steel Blade

Dissolve the yeast in 1 tsp. sugar and 1/4 cup warm water. Let it sit until foamy. Put the flour (2 cups) in the bowl with the salt. Add egg, oil and yeast mixture. Process a few seconds. Add additional water and process in. You'll have a smooth batter. Add additional flour, processing in between additions, until a smooth ball of dough forms. Knead by running the machine 5-10 seconds. Cover the bowl with a cloth and let rise in a warm place until doubled.

Remove, place on a floured board and knead a few times by hand. Divide in about 12 portions. Make "ropes" and form a circle, pinching the ends to close. Place on floured baking sheet and put in a hot (400°) oven 3-4 minutes.

Bring about 4 cups water to a boil in a large shallow pan. Add 3 T. sugar. Drop the bagels in, letting the water come back to a boil after adding every other one, and simmer about 10 minutes. Turn over, simmer 5-8 more minutes. They will become light and puffy. Remove and drain on paper towels.

Combine 1 egg and some water. Brush with egg wash and bake in a 400° oven about 20 minutes, or until browned.

x2 PARKER HOUSE ROLLS

Pre-heat oven to 375°

1	package dry active yeast
1/4	cup warm water
2	T. sugar
1	tsp. salt
1/3	cup Crisco
1	T. butter
1	egg
1/2	cup milk
3	cups all purpose flour (about)
3-4	T. melted butter

Steel Blade

Dissolve the yeast in sugar and warm water (110°) and let stand until foamy. Scald the milk and stir in shortening to melt. Cool to 110°.

Put 2 cups of the flour in the processor bowl (steel blade) with the salt and process on/off to combine. Add egg, milk and yeast mixture, processing to combine.

Add additional flour in 1/3 cupfuls, processing in between, until you have a **soft** ball of dough. Run the machine to knead about 30 seconds. If the machine seems to slow down, add additional flour but be careful not to add too much or you will have too stiff a dough. The dough should be smooth, elastic and still soft. Remove and place in a greased bowl (lightly grease the top of the dough) and let rise, covered with a damp towel, until doubled. This takes about 1 1/2 hours.

Punch the dough down and roll out on a floured board about 1/4 inch thick. Cut with a 2 1/2 inch biscuit cutter. Brush with melted butter and fold over to make half circles, ends overlapping. Place on greased cookie sheets to rise until doubled (about 1/2 hour). Brush the tops with melted butter and bake at 375° 10-15 minutes or until lightly browned. Makes about 2 1/2 dozen.

dlc-7 When doubling this recipe with the DLC-7, add 4 cups flour initially and 2 eggs with the milk and yeast mixture.

x2   RUM RAISIN BREAD

Pre-heat oven to 350°

1	large apple or pear
1	cup raisins
1/3	cup hot coffee (or water)
1/2	cup hot rum
2	eggs

Pitted dates and nuts to fill the feeder tube
(alternating dates and nuts)

1	tsp. vanilla
1/3	cup oil
2	T. honey or molasses
1/2	cup each white and brown sugar
2	cups all purpose flour
1/2	tsp. each cinnamon, ground cloves, nutmeg, salt
1	T. baking powder

Steel Blade, Shredding Disk (or Julienne Blade), Plastic Knife

Sift flour with seasonings and baking powder by processing on/off with the steel blade and remove. Heat the coffee and rum and soak the raisins at least an hour. Core the pear (or apple) and process until finely chopped. Add eggs, oil and sugar (honey or molasses also) and process by running the machine 5-10 seconds. Remove the steel blade and use the shredding or julienne blade. Load the feeder tube with dates and nuts starting with the nuts and alternating dates and nuts until the tube is full. Push through using a light pressure, bouncing with the pusher to free up any stubborn dates. Remove the blade and twist on the plastic knife . . . it does not lock into place. Add flour and seasoning mixture on top, then the rum-raisin mixture and vanilla. Process with several on/off's . . . just enough to incorporate flour . . . running the machine can easily over process.

Spoon the mixture into a measuring cup. Use 1 cup for the round Pain de Mie and 1 1/4 cups for the oval. Prepare the pan first by spraying with a non-stick vegetable coating spray. Close the pan and bake 30 minutes at 350°. Remove the bread at once and cool on a cake rack.

Serving Suggestions:

1. Poke holes in the cakes with tines of a fork and coat with a rum or fruit and liqueur syrup (pages 47, 75, 107) or . . . flambe.

2. Cut into little cakes by hand, decorate with a whipped cream rosette and fruit slice.

3. Cut into cakes and frost with sweetened cream cheese and a fruit slice.

Figs are also very good . . . omit raisins and use 1 cup, shredding with the nuts.

x2 AAA BREAD

Pre-heat oven to 350°

1/3	cup each apple juice and water (boiling)
1 1/2	cups loosely packed dried apricots
1	whole, fresh apple
1	cup almonds
"Enough"	buttermilk
3/4	cups sugar
1	egg
2	cups all purpose flour
3	tsp. baking powder
1/2	tsp. salt
1/2	tsp. each allspice, cinnamon, nutmeg
1/2	tsp. almond extract
1	stick butter or margarine (in chunks)

Steel Blade, Medium Slicing Disk

Use the steel blade and combine flour and seasonings with a couple twists of the lid. This sifts the dry ingredients . . . remove and set aside. The nuts may also be chopped at the same time . . . be careful not to run the machine or they will become too fine. Just a couple on/off's will suffice.

Put the apricots in the bowl (steel blade) and run the machine to dice. Add boiling liquid and let stand. After 10 minutes, drain off liquid adding enough buttermilk to make 2/3 cup. Core the apple (do not peel) and add chunks to the bowl, process with on/off's to dice and combine. Add sugar, egg, butter or margarine and almond extract, processing in with on/off's to combine and "cream". Add liquid, process several times to combine, then dry ingredients all at once and process in with on/off's just enough to combine.

Note: If you prefer larger, chunkier nuts, do not chop with the flour. Reserve nuts until you have added margarine and sugar. Change to the slicing disk and slice in the nuts. Then use the plastic knife, with on/off's to mix in the flour.

Spoon mixture into a well greased bread pan and bake at 350° for 1 hour or until done. Cool on rack before slicing.

If you want a glaze, try the following:

1/2	cup apricot preserves
1	cup powdered sugar
1	T. butter

Hot water (or Calvados brandy)

Heat together apricot preserves and butter. Process with 1 cup powdered sugar (steel blade) adding enough hot water or brandy to make glaze consistency. Pour over slightly cooled bread.

All people are made alike.
They are made of bones, flesh and dinners.
Only the dinners are different.

Gertrude Louise Cheney

PUMPKIN BREAD

Pre-heat oven to 350°

1 1/2	cups cooked, pureed pumpkin
1	cup vegetable oil
3	cups sugar
1/4	cup molasses
1/2	cup water
4	eggs
2	tsp. baking soda
1 1/2	cups pecans
3 1/4	cups all purpose flour
1	tsp. each nutmeg and ginger
1 1/2	tsp. salt
1	tsp. each cinnamon and cloves

Steel Blade

Process nuts and flour and seasonings together with a couple on/off's. Remove. (The more on/off's, the finer the nuts.)

Process the pumpkin to puree. Add sugar and eggs, processing together by running the machine. Add oil, machine running, through the feeder tube.

Add half the flour and process in with a couple on/off's. Fold into remaining flour by hand in a large bowl with a spatula. Use a bundt pan or 2 loaf pans.

Bake at 350° 50-60 minutes. Serve as is or as a dessert "cake" with the Sweet Sherry Sauce (p. 47).

You may use applesauce or pureed sweet potatoes to replace some of the pumpkin. If you separate the eggs, beating the whites very stiff separately then folding together by hand, you will have a "lighter" result.

dlc-7 If doubled in the DLC-7, prepare according to instructions instead of using the one bowl method.

Holiday Specials

It's cozy kitchens and fragrance sweet,

It's coming home and trains to meet

Anonymous

STUFFED TURKEY

All appetizing dishes from
sea, earth, and air
Season this high feast day
With especial care

Otis Kidwell Burger

Not only is this stuffing easier on the waistline. . . it's delicious.

1 1/2	pound mushrooms
1	bunch celery
1	green pepper
2	zucchini squash
1	onion
1/4	tsp. parsley, sage, rosemary, thyme
2	dozen oysters
1	T. soy sauce
3-5	T. peanut oil

Salt and pepper to taste
1   cup olives (optional)

The Gravy:

Broth from the simmered neck, giblets and oysters
1   stalk celery
1   carrot
1   fresh tomato
1   T. cornstarch
Salt and pepper

Steel Blade, Slicing Disk

Pre-heat the oven according to the directions on your turkey. . . . you may need to adjust the stuffing according to the size of the turkey.

Using the slicing disk, slice the mushrooms, celery, pepper, squash, and onion, (and olives if using). Saute separately, very briefly, in hot oil and transfer to a large mixing bowl.

Simmer the oysters in their liquid 3-5 minutes. Change to the steel blade and process 5-10 seconds. Save the liquid and transfer the oysters to the stuffing bowl. Add seasonings.

Toss them all together and stuff the bird.

Put the giblets and neck in a saucepan with the carrot and celery. When most of the liquid has boiled away, put the giblets in the processor bowl with the carrot and celery (cut in chunks) and process to a puree. Strain the remaining broth and put in a saucepan with the oyster liquid. Add the tomato and arrowroot to the processor bowl, process a few seconds and add to the sauce. Add enough hot water to make the sauce the proper consistency, stirring to thicken, and set aside.

When you remove the turkey from the oven, separate the drippings from the fat and add to the sauce and adjust the seasonings.

STEAK BALMORAL

8	filets
Scotch whiskey	
French bread	
4	T. Clarified Butter (p. 2)
1	cup beef broth
1	T. demi-glace (p. 63)
1	cup cream
1	T. cornstarch (if needed)
1	pound asparagus

Toast the buttered French bread under the broiler. Place on a serving platter.

Saute the filets in the Clarified Butter, both sides, as you like (rare or medium). Put them on top of the bread . . . they should fit covering the bread entirely. Keep warm. Add the demi-glace to the Clarified Butter in which you sauteed the filets, then the beef broth, and add the cream, slowly. Cook and stir, letting it thicken. (You may need to add a little cornstarch to thicken.)

Cook the asparagus until just tender and arrange it on the platter with the filets and keep warm. When you are ready to serve, heat the whiskey and pour it over the filets and ignite. When the flame dies down, coat with the sauce and serve.

Note: If demi-glace is not "open stock" in your refrigerator, you may purchase it at many gourmet specialty shops or the gourmet section of major department stores . . . well worth acquiring.

HALLOWEEN FUN!

There is an interesting custom in Laos where a fresh pumpkin is seeded, the top cut off, filled with a fresh coconut custard, then baked in the oven. The custard and cooked pumpkin are served from the pumpkin, together, when slightly cooled. Fun!

1	medium size pumpkin
1/2	of a coconut
3	cups milk (scalded)
8	eggs
2	tsp. vanilla
1/4	tsp. cinnamon and salt
1 1/2	cups sugar

Steel Blade, Shredding Disk

Remove the seeds and strings from a pumpkin. Process a coconut (p. 22) and use the liquid and the coconut meat to make coconut milk. Add enough whole milk to make 3 cups total liquid. Beat the eggs by running the machine, adding sugar through the feeder tube. Add gradually, then add seasonings. Combine with scalded milk, then pour into the hollowed out pumpkin, replacing the top.

Bake at 350°, completely covered with foil, on a rack over simmering water, for about an hour. Serve warm, scooping some of the pumpkin meat out with the custard.

Note: See "More Pumpkin Fun" on page 57 for other Halloween Ideas.

It has been believed that Hot Cross Buns have miraculous healing powers. . .whether or not this is true, it's fun to enjoy this Easter tradition with ease. (The processor does most of the work. . .you just watch it rise and shape the rolls.) The recipe makes about 6-8 large rolls. . .make two batches if you wish more as even the processor has its limitations.

1/2	cup milk (115°)
1	envelope dry active yeast
1/4	cup warm water
1/2	of a stick of butter
1/4	cup sugar
1	tsp. salt
1	egg
1/2	cup raisins and currants
1/4	tsp. mace and cinnamon
1	tsp. preserved orange peel
1	T. citron (optional)
2-2 1/2	cups flour
1	egg white, beaten slightly

Glaze:

1	cup confectioners sugar
2	T. boiling water
1	tsp. vanilla

Chopped candied fruit (or)
Chopped, drained cherries and dates

Steel Blade

Scald the milk, add the butter, sugar, salt and let it cool to warm.

Dissolve the yeast in the water. Add to the warm milk in the processor bowl. Add the eggs and spices (not the raisins or currants) and process a few seconds. Add 2 cups flour all at once into the bowl and process until the dough is smooth and elastic. You may need additional flour . . . add in 1 T. amounts. The dough should be soft. Add the raisins and currants and process just to combine.

Remove to a buttered bowl, cover with buttered wax paper and let rise 2 hours, or until doubled.

329

Gather the dough up and turn it out on a floured surface. Shape into round balls (2") and arrange on greased baking sheets. With the tip of a floured knife, mark an "x" on top of each. . .gently. Cover, and let rise until doubled . . . about 1/2 hour. Brush gently with the egg white all over.

Turn the oven on. . .(do not pre-heat) to 400° and put the rolls in the lower middle section. After the first 10 minutes, turn the oven down to 350°, and bake an additional 10—15 minutes. If they appear too brown after the first 15 minutes, cover them.

Cool on a wire rack. Prepare the glaze in the processor (steel blade) adding enough hot water for a spreadable glaze, and pour over the top of the buns . . . or just in the "x"—decorate with candied fruit before the glaze sets.

Note: It is more important that the dough be soft than running the machine to "knead" as in other breads.

330

MOTHER'S DAY BREAKFAST

My first Mother's Day breakfast from the junior gourmet section consisted of bacon fried very, very crisp and eggs scrambled with a lot of love (and salt). I can honestly say there isn't a recipe in this book that I've enjoyed more. However, when my youngest (proudly) displayed his little blistered thumb and told me how "he cooked so hard he had to burn his thumb" it seemed we needed some no-bake ideas. Together, we invented this menu.

1/2	cup cold coffee (from the night before)
1	pint vanilla ice cream, softened
1/2	package vanilla instant breakfast
1/2	cup cold milk
1	tsp. vanilla
1	egg white
2	slices bread
1	cup strawberries
1	T. orange marmalade

Sour cream
Brown sugar

Plastic Knife

(Dad's supervision is helpful.) Put the ice cream, in spoonfuls, in the processor bowl with the egg white, instant breakfast, and vanilla and process until well-combined. Add the milk and coffee, process again. Chill until the toast is ready.

Hull the strawberries and (with a dull knife) cut in half. Toast the bread and spread with the marmalade. Spoon the berries on top, top with a spoonful of sour cream and sprinkle with brown sugar.

Serve on a beautiful tray with a kiss.

My boys insisted chocolate would really improve the coffee shake.

WILL'S SUPERB NACHOS

There's a favorite story in the Southwest about the origin of the "Nacho" . . . it seems a cafe proprietor named Nacho ran out of food but was confronted with a hungry, impatient customer who just wouldn't accept that there wasn't something in the kitchen to eat. This is what he produced after creatively searching around in his kitchen. My son Will learned to make them in school and during Fiesta Week prepared them at one of our parties. While they were baking, he proudly made the 'rounds' announcing that more "superb Nachos" would be out shortly! If your palate has not adjusted to the jalapeno peppers, go very light and remove the seeds.

Pre-heat oven to 475°

Nacho chips or
Corn tortillas, fried crisp
Re-fried beans
Cheddar cheese
Jalapeno peppers
Taco sauce

Avocado spread:

1	ripe avocado
1	tsp. lemon juice
A few drops Tabasco	
2	cherry tomatoes

Out of necessity . . . a new dish is born!

The amounts of cheese and peppers varies with the number of nachos you plan to make. You can make individual ones or spread chips on a serving platter (ovenproof), mounding cheese and peppers on top. If you do not like the hot pepper, use green peppers. Cooked shrimp or sausage are also a nice addition. Two methods of preparation are given, each with a different texture.

1. Cut tortillas into quarters and fry crisp. Cut the cheese into chunks and grate using the steel blade or the shredding disk (using light pressure). Remove cheese and add peppers, dicing (steel blade) with on-offs. Put some beans on the bottom of the chips, then the cheese, peppers and a dash of the taco sauce. Bake at 475° until the cheese melts.
2. This method will have larger chunks of pepper. Put the cheese, in chunks, into the bowl and process on-off to grate. When coarsely grated, add peppers, in chunks (and shrimp or sausage if using) and process on-off again a couple of times. Spread on top of the· beans, add the taco sauce and bake in the same manner.

Avocado spread: Cut avocado in chunks and process smooth with juice and seasonings. Add tomatoes (in chunks) and process on-off to combine. Salt to taste and put on top of the nachos.

Of all the sweet delicious scents
That we smell throughout the year
There's nothing as nice as the
cookies and spice
That comes when the Yuletide is near

Anonymous

This is a real family project which extends all over the neighborhood and to all our little friends. Make lots of dough . . . get out all the cookie cutters. For decorating you'll need:

Food coloring
3-4 egg whites, beaten with a few drops water and 1 tsp. sugar
Paint brushes
Red hots   Crushed peppermint candy
Chocolate chips   Crushed Christmas candy
Little candies   Raisins
Colored sugar   Candied fruit
White sugar

The dough:

1	stick butter (sweet)
1	cup sugar
1	egg
1	T. cream
1	tsp. vanilla
1/2	tsp. salt
1	tsp. baking powder
1 1/2	cups flour

Steel Blade

Put the butter and sugar in the processor bowl and process 5-10 seconds. Add the egg, cream and vanilla, processing 5-10 seconds. Add the baking powder, salt and flour, processing until it forms a ball (just a couple seconds). Wrap in wax paper and chill.

Roll out on a floured board and give everyone some cutters and their own cookie sheet.

Beat 3-4 egg whites with water and divide among 4 or 8 bowls (depending on how many bakers you have) and color with food coloring. Divide the paint brushes and let everyone "paint" their cookies. If you have cookie cutters that leave an imprint design use them for little folks. Put all the decorations out and decorate the cookies before baking. Many of the candies will melt and make interesting designs. . .however, if too many go on one cookie your entire cookie sheet will have an interesting design! Sprinkle lightly with sugar before baking. Bake for 8-12 minutes.

Because of the quick and efficient mixing of the machine, many cookie doughs may be softer than usual. With sugar type cookies I find better results with brief processing after adding the flour, then chilling the dough thoroughly. If it is still too soft (a test cookie will tell you), add additional flour as you roll them out and cut into shapes. There is less risk of a tough cookie because of too much flour.

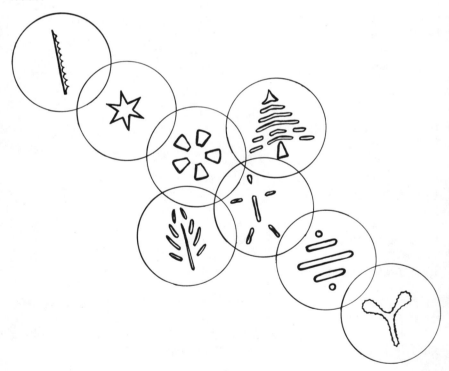

A gift from the home is always a gift from the heart, doubling its value in pleasure

Anonymous

x2 CRANBERRY NUT BREAD

Every year I try a new cranberry bread trying for one everybody likes. This one has been a hit in our family and very popular in my classes and demonstrations.

Pre-heat oven to 350°

The peelings from an orange

1	heaping cup fresh cranberries
1	ripe banana (or apple)
3	eggs
1	cup sugar
2/3	cups oil
1/3	cup buttermilk
1	cup pecans (save several whole for decorations)
2	cups flour
1	T. baking powder
1/2	tsp. salt
1	tsp. vanilla

Steel Blade

Process the peelings and half the sugar until the peelings are minced. Add eggs, oil and banana, processing until light and fluffy. Add the rest of the sugar and buttermilk, processing by running the machine to incorporate. Add vanilla, cranberries and pecans processing with the on/off method to chop the berries and nuts. Add the dry ingredients that are left (stirring in the baking powder) and process with the on/off method to combine . . . takes 2-3 turns.

Bake at 350° about 45-50 minutes . . . time varies with the size of your pan. If you remove 1 cup to do in the Pain de Mie, bake at 350° 30 minutes.

Decorate with whole pecans and an orange glaze . . . process 1 T. orange marmalade, 2 orange sections (membrane removed) until smooth. Add 1 cup powdered sugar, then boiling water by the table-spoonful until spreading consistency. Garnish with frosted berries (p. 59, follow instructions for frosting grapes).

CROQUEMBOUCHE

This is a fantastic pyramid of miniature cream puffs. A lovely and festive dessert.

The puffs may be filled with various custard fillings, and coated with caramelized sugar or chocolate glaze, or filled with whipped cream, fruit, or ice cream.

For a birthday cake no one will ever forget, fill the puffs with assorted ice creams (and this may be done ahead) coat them with icing, and after they are piled high, insert birthday candles in the little spaces.

For Christmas, so you may enjoy a centerpiece as well, fill the puffs with a mixture of diced dates and sugared nuts. . . . . then they will not get soggy or need refrigeration and you can serve with a rich custard cream sauce.

x2 CHRISTMAS CROQUEMBOUCHE

1 1/2   recipes Choux Pastry (p. 12)

Diced dates
Sugared almonds or pecans

Caramelized Sugar:

1	cup sugar
1/4	cup water

Pistachio Custard Cream:

3/4	cups sugar
1/4	cup pistachio nuts
2 1/2	cups half and half
4	eggs
2	T. cornstarch
1/4	tsp. salt
3-4	drops green food coloring

Garnish:

Make some holly leaves using corn flakes coated with melted marshmallows and green food coloring. Use red candies for the berries.

Steel Blade

Use your most beautiful dish or tray.

Prepare the custard by heating the half and half and putting the nuts in the processor bowl and grinding fine using the steel blade. Add the rest of the ingredients to the bowl and 1/2 cup of the liquid through the feeder tube, with the machine running. Transfer to the rest of the liquid and thicken over medium heat . . . do not let it boil. Chill and re-process a few seconds before serving.

Prepare the cream puffs (making about 60 miniature), removing any unbaked dough, and fill them with a small amount of dates and nuts.

Caramelize the sugar by putting the sugar and water in a saucepan, stirring just to dissolve. Let it boil gently, washing crystals down with a brush dipped in cold water. When it turns amber, stir constantly and remove from heat. Set over hot water while dipping puffs.

Put a cone object in the center of the plate. A tall ice cream (quart) container (upside down) works very well . . . then dip the puffs in the caramelized sugar, form the base, and work your way up. The wider the base, the higher the pyramid .

Decorate when you are finished around the base, and if you want, part way up the pyramid.

Serve with Pistachio Custard Cream.

337

Step softly here, respecting royalty,
The queen of cakes is baking now! . . .
. . . But she will rein majestically when
Her court, anticipating her, sits down

Elaine V. Emans

x2 BLACK FOREST FRUITCAKE

3/4	cup pitted dates
1	cup drained, pitted cherries
2	T. of the juice
4	T. cherry brandy
3	eggs
1	cup sugar
1/2	tsp. vanilla
1/2	stick butter
1	cup chocolate chips (miniature)
1 1/2	cups all purpose flour
2	tsp. baking powder
1/4	tsp. salt
2	cups almonds

Slivered almonds
Several whole dark sweet cherries
Heavy cream
Powdered sugar

Kugelhopf mold

Steel Blade

Soak the cherries in juice and brandy overnight. Process (steel blade) the flour, 1 cup nuts, baking powder and salt together. Remove. Add dates and nuts and dice with on/off's until finely chopped. Remove.

Process the butter to cream. Add sugar and vanilla, processing in well. Add eggs processing to "beat" very well. Drain cherries well, combine with dates, nuts and chocolate chips and dredge with a few tablespoons of sifted flour.

Remove the steel blade and use the plastic knife (it does not need to lock into place). Add liquid, process in, then add flour mixture. Process with on/off's just enough so the flour disappears. Add fruits and nuts . . . an on/off or two to combine. Pour into a well buttered Kugelhopf mold and bake at 300° 1 hour and 30 minutes to 1 hour 40 minutes. Cool about 10 minutes, unmold on a cake rack. Dust lightly with powdered sugar and decorate with slivered almonds and dark sweet cherries. Serve with whipped cream, sweetened and flavored with white creme de cacao.

dlc-7 The larger machine will make a double recipe with ease. You can fill 2 molds or a large bundt pan.

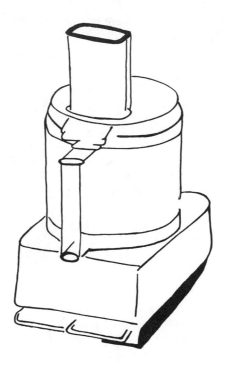

You need all the mechanical help you can get during the holidays.

MACADAMIA CHRISTMAS FRUITCAKE

Someone used to send our family a rich pineapple-almond cake every Christmas. I could never find a recipe that seemed to be anything like it, and in trying many different fruitcakes decided I really didn't like fruitcake. If your sentiments are similar, try this one.

Pre-heat oven to 350°

Almond Cake (p. 19)

6	ounces Macadamia nuts
2/3	cup whole pecans
1	cup drained maraschino cherries
1/2	cup almonds
1	7 ounce can crushed pineapple (undrained)
1	tsp. almond extract

Glaze and Decorations:

3	T. butter
Juice from an orange or	
	2 T. pineapple juice
1/3	cup sugar
2	T. water or fruit liqueur

Whole pecans, almonds or cherries

Steel Blade, Medium Serrated Slicing Disk

Load the feeder tube with nuts and drained cherries . . . slice through (medium serrated slicing disk) and remove.

Prepare the Almond Cake (p. 19) using the steel blade. Remove the dough from the bowl and stir in pineapple, fruits, nuts and almond extract. Spoon into 2 large loaf pans or 3 decorative molds that are slightly smaller. Adjust baking time to the size of the pan, testing after 35 minutes. When baking in 3 pans, at 350°, the time is about 35 minutes. Cool 5 minutes. Remove from pans and cool on a rack.

Melt the butter to sizzling, add juice and sugar and simmer a few minutes. Add water or liqueur and pour over cakes. (Double this amount for 3 cakes.) Just a light coating is sufficient and will allow the decorations to stick.

x2   FROZEN AMARETTO FRUITCAKE

This could easily start a new tradition in your house. When you discover Amaretto, you'll devise many new ways to include it in your cooking.

Coconut Custard (p. 23) or:

Basic Custard:

1	envelope unflavored gelatin
2	cups milk
2	eggs (reserve the whites)
1	egg
1	tsp. vanilla
1/3	cup sugar

Dash salt

3	cups leftover angel food cake or ladyfingers
1 1/2	cups heavy cream
2	egg whites
3	T. sugar
1/2	cup white seedless raisins
1/3	cup Amaretto liqueur
15	maraschino cherries
2	T. candied fruits (red and green)
1	cup pecans
1/2	tsp. vanilla

Optional: Substitute 3/4 cup leftover cranberry sauce, made with whole cranberries, for the candied fruits and cherries

Steel Blade, Medium Serrated Slicing Disk, Shredding Disk

Soak the raisins and diced fruits in the Amaretto liqueur (15 minutes).

Prepare the custard according to the instructions for Coconut Custard on page 23 or prepare a Basic Custard. Combine dry gelatin with 1/2 cup cold milk (steel blade). Heat, stirring to dissolve. Add to remaining milk in a saucepan. Add the liqueur when draining diced fruits and raisins. Process 2 egg yolks (reserving whites) plus 1 whole egg with sugar, salt and vanilla. Add 1 cup hot liquid through the feeder tube, with the machine running, processing to combine, then transfer to the milk in the saucepan. Stir constantly until "scalded" but do not boil or the egg yolks will curdle. Cool completely.

Beat 2 egg whites in a copper bowl until stiff. Add 3 T. sugar and vanilla. Fold into the cooled custard and chill.

Use the steel blade and with the machine running, pour the heavy cream through the feeder tube to "whip". When thick (watch . . . this is very quick), remove the steel blade and use the shredding disk to shred in the cake pieces. Remove and use the slicing disk to slice in cherries and pecans. Use light pressure to chop the nuts coarsely. Remove disk and stir in the drained fruits with a spatula. Fold into custard mixture. Freeze in one large loaf pan or two decorative tin molds. Freeze until firm.

Unmold by dipping briefly in hot water, then turning out onto a serving platter. Freeze again 20-30 minutes. Decorate with marzipan leaves, sugared nuts or freshly grated coconut.

Note: Also good in Macaroon Crust (p. 280).

Let every pudding burst with plums,
And every tree bear dolls and drums,
In the week when Christmas comes.

Anonymous

OLD FASHIONED COCONUT CAKE

You'll be delighted with the new fashioned way of grating coconut and quick binding of egg yolks and sugar with the food processor.

Cake:

2	sticks unsalted butter
2	cups sugar
2	egg yolks
4	egg whites
3	cups cake flour
1	tsp. vanilla
4	tsp. baking powder

Coconut milk and milk to make 3/4 cup

Filling I:

6	egg yolks
1	cup sugar
1	stick butter
1/3	cup sherry, brandy or liqueur
1	cup white raisins
1	cup pecans

Filling II:

Coconut Custard (p. 23)

Icing I:

1	coconut
3	egg whites
1 1/2	cups sugar
3	T. cold water
2	T. corn syrup
1/8	tsp. cream of tartar
1	tsp. vanilla

Icing II:

2	cups whipped cream plus 2 T. powdered sugar and freshly grated coconut

Steel Blade, Julienne Blade

Combine flour and baking powder in the bowl and on/off (or pulse) several times to sift. Remove.

Start the machine (steel blade) and drop the butter through the feeder tube to cream. Add sugar and egg yolks. Scrape the sides of the bowl, then continue running the machine. Add the milk and vanilla, process in well. Add the flour all at once and process with **brief** on/off's (or pulse) just until the flour disappears. Beat egg whites with a dash of salt in a separate bowl until stiff. Add a couple spoonfuls to the processor bowl . . . one on/off (pulse). Gently (but quickly) fold into the remaining whites. Pour into 3 greased cake pans lined with wax paper and bake at 350° 25-30 minutes. The cake should be firm and springy to the touch.

Note: You may use 6 egg whites and omit the yolks in the cake entirely.

Filling I:

Prepare a double boiler by bringing the water to a gentle boil. Process egg yolks and sugar until very light. Melt the butter until it just sizzles and add **slowly** through the feeder tube, with the machine running. Put raisins directly into the bowl and remove steel blade. Use the medium serrated slicer (comes with the machine) and slice in the nuts. Use the plastic mixing blade to mix together, then add sherry and transfer to the double boiler to thicken. (Takes 2-3 minutes rather than the old fashioned 10-15.) Stir while cooking. Cool and spread between layers. Or, try one of the Coconut Custards on page 23.

Icing I:

Use the double boiler again and combine egg whites with sugars, water and cream of tartar and beat with electric beaters 7 minutes or until stiff. Add vanilla. Grate coconut with the julienne or shredding blade and fold into icing. Spread over cake, reserving some of the coconut shreds to pile on the top.

Icing II:

Whip cream by running the machine, pouring cream slowly through the feeder tube. When thick, add powdered sugar and vanilla and fold in freshly grated coconut.

This is really one of the spectacular things you can do with your Pain de Mie pans. You may use either the round or oval.

Pre-heat oven to 350°

3	T. flour
2	cups all purpose flour
1/2	tsp. salt
2	T. sugar
1	package dry active yeast
3	eggs
1/4	cup warm water (110°)
5	T. milk (110°)
5	T. butter
1/4	cup currants or raisins
1/3	cup candied fruit

Marzipan leaves (p. 18)
Halved maraschino cherries

Syrup:

6	T. butter
1/2	cup sugar

Juice from two oranges

1/2	cup rum

Steel Blade

Combine raisins and candied fruit . . . dust with a little flour. Combine 3 T. flour with 2 T. sugar, warm water and yeast and let the mixture stand about 15 minutes or until a thick layer of foam coats the top.

Put the butter in the processor bowl (steel blade) and run the machine to cream. Add eggs and milk, processing together well. Add 1 1/2 cups flour and process to a batter consistency. Add the yeast mixture and remaining flour, processing to mix together. The machine tends to slow down with heavy egg and butter doughs and while you may need to add some additional flour be careful not to add too much. This should be a **very soft** dough . . . it will not form a dough ball on top of the blades as other breads do. Remove the dough, place in an oiled bowl and let it rise (covered with a damp cloth) until doubled . . . about 2 hours. Stir down, stirring in fruits.

Spray the Pain de Mie pans with a non-stick vegetable coating spray or grease and dust with flour. Spoon in the dough (7/8 cup for the round, 1 1/3 cup for the oval), cover with oiled wax paper and let the dough rise in the open pans for about 45 minutes (almost doubled). Close the pans, put in the rod and bake at 350° 30-35 minutes. Remove the baked logs right away and let cool on a rack. Baste with syrup while warm, poking some tiny holes throughout the cakes.

Syrup: Heat the butter to sizzling. Add sugar, stirring in, then orange juice, letting the mixture simmer several minutes over medium heat. Add the rum, heat, return to simmering and spoon over the cakes.

When ready to serve, repeat the process, igniting the rum when pouring over the cakes. Stack them in 3's or 5's like yule logs and decorate with Marzipan leaves and cherries. You may prefer to soak sugar cubes in rum, tucking them in 5 or 6 places and bring the dessert to the table aflame. Whatever you do, do it with style!

May the fire of this log warm the cold;
may the hungry be fed; . . . . .

Anonymous
17th Century

CHRISTMAS SALAD

As a young bride this was one of the first things I had to learn to make. My husband's family served this heavenly salad at Thanksgiving with turkey, Christmas with roasted duck, and New Year's with ham. All the cutting and chopping . . . even the custard, adapt so well to processor methods.

1	cup pineapple juice
2	T. flour
3	T. water
2	egg yolks
1/4	tsp. salt
1	T. butter

Juice from a lemon

1	large can pineapple chunks
12	large marshmallows

Bananas, green seedless grapes, apples, Mandarin oranges

1	cup pecans
1/2	of a coconut
1 1/2	cups heavy cream

Steel Blade

Bring the juice to a boil. Combine flour, egg yolks, salt and water with the steel blade. Pour hot liquid through the feeder tube (machine running), process to combine, then place in a double boiler, stirring to thicken (about 8-10 minutes).

Remove from heat and stir in butter and lemon juice. Cut the marshmallows in fourths with kitchen scissors and stir into custard along with pineapple chunks.

Refrigerate overnight.

When ready to serve, use the medium serrated slicing disk to slice grapes and bananas. Change to the French fryer, cut apples in quarters (removing core) and push through to dice. Combine fruits and custard in a large bowl.

Wipe out the bowl. Use the medium serrated slicing disk to process the nuts (for coarse texture). Use the steel blade, processing with on/off's (for fine texture). Set aside.

Use the julienne or shredding disk to process the coconut. Load the feeder tube horizontally for long shreds. Remove.

Start the machine and pour cream slowly through the feeder tube. Stop processing when thick. Fold into fruit mixture and top with coconut mounded in the center, nuts around the edges.

For the neighbors came in wagons, From half a state away. And the old men brought the banjos, They'd near forgot to play, While the young folk danced a dos-a-dos, And clapped for Christmas Day.

Phyliss McGinley

x2 RUM BALLS

1/4	cup rum (or bourbon)
2	cups Natural Cereal or vanilla wafers plus other leftover cookies
1	cup pecans
1/2	cup dried fruits (dates, raisins or figs)
1	cup powdered sugar
2-3	T. corn syrup
2	T. cocoa

Additional powdered sugar

Steel Blade

If you use dried fruits, dice first with a few of the nuts and soak in heated liqueur. Drain well, reserving liqueur for the batter.

Put cookies (broken up) or cereal in the bowl . . . process to coarse crumbs. Add the rest of the ingredients processing with on/off's to mix and combine. Shape into little balls and roll in additional powdered sugar. Let the cookies sit out on cookie sheets, then refrigerate until firm.

Makes about 20.

DEMONSTRATIONS

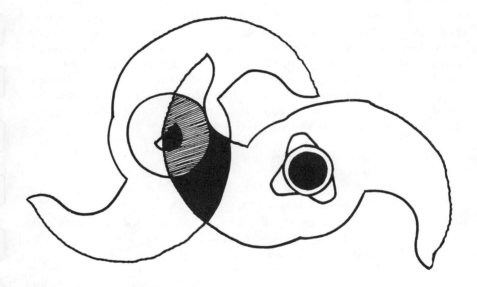

Getting a food processor is like getting your first dishwasher . . . at first you just delight in having a new 'kitchen helper' gadget, but after discovering how to use it to its capacity, you find it impossible to live without.

Chat echaude craint lo 'eau froid

A burned cat fears a cold stove

French Proverb

Many shops and demonstrators have requested recipes, outlines and other ideas to use for classes and demonstrations. I usually find myself planning more than I can possibly do as my enthusiasm to show **everything** the machine can do in two hours seems to take over. In this section I have outlined a guide designed to minimize bowl washing as well as show as many features of the machine and its accessories as possible within a short period of time. Adjust to the speed with which you work, the amount of extra bowls and helpers you have in assistance. I have put together outlines for several occasions; when no kitchen facilities are available, when a full kitchen is available, and when you are presenting a structured class. I usually plan classes to run from two-three hours. Demonstrations are offered on the hour (i.e.: 1:00 p.m., 2:00 p.m., 3:00 p.m.) with 40 minutes of food preparation, leaving 20 minutes to answer questions (and clean up the mess). A successful demonstration need not depend on a hot plate, oven or any array of ancilary equipment . . . easier for you **and** the store.

I. **Without Kitchen Facilities**

　　A. Tips:

　　　　1. You need 1 long table.
　　　　2. Have two bowls of water (large) one for the bowls and blades, one for your hands.
　　　　3. Take lots of paper towels.
　　　　4. Have a small cooler·and ice.
　　　　5. You need a machine, two steel blades, an extra bowl and all the accessory blades.　　．
　　　　6. Take large paper plates for your shredded, sliced, diced results and small paper plates, plastic spoons, napkins and paper cups for your audience.
　　　　7. Have several spatulas, spoons and a pitcher of ice water.

　　B. Order of Presentation:

　　　　1. Grate Parmesan (or Romano) cheese . . . *steel blade.*
　　　　2. Dice onions . . . *French fryer.*
　　　　3. Bread Crumbs (see Process and Bake p. 7) . . . *steel blade.*
　　　　4. Grind meat (the bread crumbs "dry" the bowl) . . . *steel blade.*

350

5. Crush ice (noisy . . . gets everyone's attention and helps clean the bowl) . . . *steel blade.*
6. Slice, dice, shred: (see "Techniques" p. XIII)
   Smooth vegetable slicing disk (mushrooms)
   Medium serrated slicing disk (tomatoes)
   Thin serrated slicing disk (onions)
   Medium serrated slicing disk (green pepper)
   Wavy slicing disk (potatoes . . . "ruffles with ridges")
   Julienne blade (squash, carrots)
   French fry blade (onions, potatoes, celery and apples)
   Shredding disk (soft cheeses)

   You can make a **Waldorf Salad** out of the apple and celery (p. 162). Make a salad out of the sliced tomatoes, mushrooms, peppers and onions . . . cover with your grated Parmesan cheese, add some dressing, croutons and pass around.

7. Wipe out the bowl. Use the steel blade and dice dates, adding 1-2 T. of sugar. Remove. This is a tough sticky job . . . the Cuisinart handles it easily.
8. Whip Cream (p. 373). Bring a cake from home and decorate using a pastry tube: or, fold in diced dates and use to fill an angel food cake, cut in half.
9. Pastry (p. 9-10). Bring pre-measured flour, frozen butter . . . *steel blade.*
10. Bread (p. 15-16). Bring pre-measured flour and salt . . . *steel blade.* There is no need to wash the bowl, just remove pastry and go on.
11. Chocolate Sauce (p. 258) . . . *steel blade.* Fun to do; you can use hot coffee if you don't have a hot plate to boil water and sugar. Drizzle over angel food cake.
12. Other good ideas that travel well:
    Pimento cheese (p. 157)
    Egg Salad (p. 32)
    Chunky Gazpacho (p. 125)
    Pancake Mix (p. 95)
    White Sauce Mix (p. 35)
    Cheesecake (p. 355)
    Tuna fish or ham salad . . . prepare ham salad all in one bowl, everything together (except mayonnaise), with on/off's, (steel blade).

II. **Full Kitchen**

Use the preceeding but replace some things or add the following:

351

1. One-step Brownies (p. 363)
2. One-step Coleslaw (p. 362)
3. Processor Salad (p. 375)
4. Chicken Chalupas (p. 133)
5. Waldorf Salad (p. 162)
6. Pastry to Sauce Series (you'll love this and so will everyone else).

   First, use the French fryer to dice chunks of onion, celery, squash, green pepper and carrots. Remove and saute in several tablespoons butter in a large, deep sided saute pan.

   Next, process equal amounts of cheese, butter and flour to a paste. (**Cheese Pastry**). Add 1 cup scalded milk, slowly through the feeder tube (use the funnel), machine running, and stop to scrape the sides of the bowl a couple times. (**Cheese Sauce**). Transfer to the saute pan and add 1 cup creamed corn, 2 cups chicken broth, salt, pepper, dash of cayenne, a bit of brandy and some freshly minced parsley *(steel blade).* (**Canadian Cheese Soup**).

7. Chef's Salad (p. 180)
8. Artichoke Dip (p. 310)
9. Lemon Crunch Cake (p. 285)

III. Class Ideas

Pineapple Cheese with Hot Jelly (p. 309)
Pizza (p. 354)
Stuffed Mushrooms (p. 372) . . . use the pepperoni ends you cut off to show even slicing for the Pizza.
Orange Amaretto Freeze (p. 361)
Chewy Citrus Bars (p. 291) . . . use the peelings from the orange and remaining juice.

Nachos (p. 332)
Jalapeno Corn Bread (p. 360)
Cucumber-Onion Salad (p. 162)
Fresh Orange Cake with Sliced Strawberries (p. 288)

Artichoke Soup (p. 111)
Chef's Salad with Orange Dressing (p. 180)
Banneton Luncheon Torte (p. 135)
Fresh Fruit Trifle (p. 270)

LEFTOVER SALAD

Bring a few leftovers from your refrigerator, some whole wheat crackers and create something on the spot.

2-3	ounces cheese
1-2	chunks of ham
1	hot dog or piece of salami
1-2	slices luncheon meat

Several pickles
Handful of parsley
Several chunks apple, pineapple or pears

2	stalks celery

Several green onions

2	ounces cream cheese
1-3	T. mayonnaise
1	tsp. mustard

A few walnuts or almonds

Steel Blade

Process cream cheese and parsley first. Add chunks of cheese, meat and vegetables and nuts and process with on/off's to chop. Add mustard, mayonnaise or sour cream, process in. Surprisingly good . . . and fun!

PIZZA

This is not only great for demonstrations, but the perfect recipe for the first night home with the machine. There's lots to slice, dice and chop and the whole family can get in on the fun.

Pizza Dough (p. 14)

1	green pepper
2	T. butter and 1 T. oil
1	onion
1	fresh tomato
1	6 ounce can tomato paste
1-2	cups green or black olives (pitted)

Pepperoni (or)

8-10	chunks of chuck roast

Fresh basil or parsley

1/2	tsp. oregano
1/4	tsp. thyme

Salt and pepper

6	ounces mozzarella cheese
3	ounces Parmesan cheese

All the Blades

Prepare the dough (p. 14).

Use the steel blade (on/off's) and dice the peppers and onions. If you have the French fry blade, cut them in chunks and dice by pushing through the feeder tube. Remove and saute in the butter and oil, adding seasonings. Mince basil and parsley with the steel blade. Dice the tomato by cutting into chunks and using either the steel blade or French fry blade. Add to the vegetables, stir in seasonings, tomato paste and combine. Spread on top of the dough.

Grate the Parmesan (steel blade) beginning with on/off's, then running the machine to grate to a powder. Remove.

Grind the beef by putting chunks in a dry bowl. Process with on/off's, until desired texture. Remove and saute medium rare.

Use the thin slicer for the mushrooms, the medium serrated slicer for the olives, the thin serrated slicer for the pepperoni (load the feeder tube from the bottom) and the thin slicer for the onion.

To Assemble:

Sprinkle the Parmesan cheese over the sauce on the pizza dough. Alternate the assorted vegetables on top.

Use the shredding disk or julienne blade and load the feeder tube with the mozzarella cheese. Push through with light pressure. If the cheese seems to "stick" or is so soft it is difficult to process, release pressure and use a "bounce" with the pusher. Mound cheese on top of the vegetables. Top with meat.

Bake at 400° about 20-25 minutes.

Other Pizza Ideas:

1. Mexican Pizza (p. 188).

2. Use a base sauce of **2 cups cottage cheese, 2 eggs** and **6-8 ounces Parmesan cheese** (instead of tomato) and top with shredded squash, sliced nuts, additional cheese.

3. Use the tomato base, topping with **grated eggplant, thinly sliced onions** and **additional cheese.**

4. Use a **cream cheese (13-16 oz.)** base, adding a **little sugar, butter** and **2 eggs.** Bake 20 minutes and cool. Top with fruit (slice in the processor using the medium serrated slicing disk).

When my children refuse all the nutritious foods I serve, I try to keep the following in mind, abstaining from non-nutritious fillers, until they're really hungry.

Rats are not a dainty dish
to set before a King
But for a really hungry man
they are just the very thing

x2 CRUNCHY CRUST CHEESECAKE

This cheesecake and crust are designed specifically for demonstrations . . . no bake, "sets" quickly, perfect for slicing berries on top, delicious . . . and easy.

Crust:

6-8	coconut or almond cookies
1	cup granola type cereal
3	T. butter

or:

10-12	graham crackers
4	chocolate cookies
1/3	cup almonds
3	T. butter
3	T. sugar

Topping:

Assorted fruits for slicing
        strawberries, kiwifruit, bananas, oranges, grapes

Filling:

Peelings from half a lemon
Juice from half a lemon and orange

1	envelope unflavored gelatin
1	cup whipping cream
1/2	cup sugar
1	8 ounce package cream cheese
1	cup sour cream
1	tsp. vanilla
2	eggs

"Enough" water to make 1/2 cup including fruit juice

Steel Blade, Medium Serrated Slicing Disk

Choose either crust or use any cookie-nut crust you like. Crush cookies (steel blade) running the machine, dropping cookies and nuts through the feeder tube. When completely crushed, add butter, in pieces, and process in with on/off's, then run machine to combine thoroughly. Press into a 9 inch pie plate or white porcelain quiche mold. Wipe out the bowl.

Whip the cream (steel blade) by pouring it through the feeder tube, machine running. It will be thick when you have finished pouring. Remove and wipe out the bowl. Bring juice and water to a boil. Put the peelings plus a few tablespoons of the sugar in the bowl (steel blade) and run the machine to mince. Add gelatin and 1-2 small chunks of the cream cheese. Process smooth. With the machine running, pour boiling liquid through the feeder tube. Add eggs and sugar, processing in. Add the remaining cream cheese directly to the bowl, in chunks, processing first with on/off's, then running machine to cream thoroughly. Add sour cream, process in, then the whipping cream and vanilla. Pour into the prepared shell and (if possible) chill. It will set very quickly. If you prefer a "softer" cheesecake, omit 1 teaspoon gelatin.

Use the medium serrated slicing disk and slice some fruit to arrange decoratively on top of the pie. You may coat fruits with some melted currant jelly or grenadine syrup for a glaze effect.

Variation: Prepare the Instant Chocolate Sauce (p. 258) and drizzle a little over each piece when serving. Flavor with Grand Marnier . . . smashing!

PASTRY POINTERS

Cutting in shortening (butter) very thoroughly gives a tender crust.

Cutting in the shortening (butter) coarsely gives a flaky crust . . . this is why having butter very, very cold helps with the processor which blends shortening in **less** thoroughly when cold.

Do not overwork pastry after you have added ice water . . . when pastry starts to hold together, stop processing and pat together gently by hand.

A mixture of butter and shortening gives the best results with good flavor and tender crust.

The more fat (to the same amount of flour) the "shorter" the pastry (crisper-lighter).

If the pastry is tough, it could be 1) too much flour, 2) over-processing.

If the pastry is soggy, it could be 1) too much liquid.

If the pastry shrinks, it could be 1) inadequate chilling time . . . this is essential to allow the pastry to rest (removes rubberiness), 2) over-processing.

If none of the preceeding rescue less than perfect pastry and you are willing to try another way, combine **4 T. Crisco, 2 sticks butter, 1/2 tsp. salt, 3 cups flour** and **1/2 tsp. baking powder** with the steel blade, using on/off's until a coarse meal. Freeze. When you are ready to prepare, put 2 cups in the processor bowl (steel blade) and add ice water in 1 tablespoon amounts until it begins to hold together. Remove, wrap in wax paper and chill briefly before rolling out. You may use an egg (richer pastry) for some or all of the water or sour cream, or, add **1/4 cup powdered sugar**.

dlc-7 You may double this using the DLC-7. Use the pulse to combine.

Additional Thoughts:

The flour we buy (unbleached or all purpose) has a mysterious group of chemicals and other problems that are often responsible for tough or heavy pastry. Try using half (or all) Wondra flour. If you can buy pastry flour, all the better. If you prefer unbleached or whole wheat flour, add some baking powder and use half Crisco and half butter to produce a more tender crust.

x2   SWEET ALMOND PASTRY

Good for pies and tarts to be eaten cold.

1 1/2	cups flour
1/3	cup almonds
1/3	cup powdered sugar
1/4	tsp. salt
1	egg yolk
2	T. shortening
8	T. butter

Small amount ice water

Steel Blade

Put the almonds in the processor bowl with 1/2 cup flour and run the machine to process to a powder. Add sugar, flour, salt, chilled butter and shortening in small chunks. Process on/off (pulse) several times to combine. Add egg yolk and a couple of tablespoons of ice water . . . process on/off a couple times. If the pastry does not hold together, add a little more ice water, processing on/off until pastry begins to hold together. Remove and chill at least 30 minutes before rolling out.

x2 CHEESECAKE

Pre-heat oven to 375°

Almond Pastry (p. 358)

Peelings from an orange and lemon
2   **8 ounce packages cream cheese**
4   **eggs**
3/4   **cup sugar**
1   **tsp. vanilla**

2   **cups sour cream**
1/4   **cup sugar**
1-2   **sections from an orange**

Strawberries or kiwifruit
Currant jelly

Steel Blade

Process the peelings with several tablespoons of the sugar until well minced. With the machine running add chunks of cream cheese through the feeder tube to cream. When creamed, add eggs, sugar and vanilla, processing in well. Pour into baked crust and bake for 20 minutes. Turn the oven off and leave in an additional 10 minutes. Cool 15 minutes.

Put the orange sections in the processor bowl with the sugar . . . process to mince. Add sour cream and process with on/off's (pulse) just to combine. Spread on top of the cheesecake and bake at 375° an additional 10-12 minutes. Cool.

Slice berries with the medium serrated slicing disk, dip into melted currant jelly and decorate the cheesecake. Serve cold.

dlc-7 When preparing in the DLC-7, use a 9 or 10 inch springform pan. Increase baking time by turning oven down to 350° and bake an additional 15-20 minutes. Do not double the topping.

This is a recipe adapted from a friend. I love to prepare this for demonstrations as it shows the versatility of the processor.

Pre-heat oven to 350°

1	pound pork, including fat
Seasonings:	
1/2	tsp. basil, salt, allspice
1/4	tsp. pepper, chili powder, coriander, nutmeg
Several	sprigs fresh parsley
1	onion
1	jalapeno pepper
1/2	green pepper
1	T. piquant sauce
8	ounces cheddar or Monterey Jack cheese
1	cup corn kernels
1	cup sour cream
1/2	stick unsalted butter
3	eggs
1	cup milk
1 1/4	cups cornmeal
1/2	cup unbleached flour
1	tsp. baking soda
1	tsp. sugar
2	tsp. baking powder

Steel Blade, Shredding Disk

Cut the pork into chunks and place directly into the bowl with the seasonings. Process with the on/off method 5-6 times to grind. Remove and saute in a saucepan. Do half at a time.

Change to the shredding disk and shred the cheese. Remove and set aside. Change to the steel blade and put the onion and peppers directly into the bowl (in chunks), and process to mince. Add butter, corn kernels, sour cream and eggs, processing by running the machine a few seconds. Add the dry ingredients all at once (combining first), then the milk, processing on/off several times to combine and incorporate flour. Do not process too long . . . remove bowl quickly as it is full.

Sprinkle a greased 9x12 pan with a little cornmeal and pour in about 2/3 of the batter. Divide the cooled sausage over the top, then the cheese and finally the rest of the batter.

Bake at 350° for 40-50 minutes or until the center is "set". Let it rest 10 minutes before slicing. Great as an appetizer or makes a meal with soup or salad. Delicious . . .

dlc-7 When preparing this in the DLC-7, mince peppers and onion with the steel blade. Change to the plastic mixing blade to complete the recipe.

ORANGE AMARETTO RE-FREEZE

1/2	gallon vanilla ice cream
1/3	cup Amaretto liqueur
4	almond or coconut macaroons
Peelings from an orange	
1	T. frozen orange juice concentrate
1	T. Triple-Sec

Fresh orange sections, soaked in 1 tsp. sugar and 1/3 cup orange liqueur (4 oranges)

Steel Blade

Process the peelings using about 1 tablespoon sugar to aid mincing. When minced, add the macaroons, processing on/off to chop (or pulse). Add liqueurs and juice and let soak a few minutes. Fold into ice cream and re-freeze several hours. Serve with a few orange sections in beautiful bowls or glasses.

Good also with peach peelings and fresh peaches.

*There is no love sincerer
than the love of food.*

George Bernard Shaw

ONE STEP COLESLAW AND DRESSING

1/2	cup salad oil
1	whole fresh egg
1/4	tsp. dry mustard
2	tsp. lemon juice
1/8	tsp. celery salt and tarragon
Dash of salt and white pepper	
2	tsp. honey
1	tsp. tarragon vinegar

1/3 to 1/2 head of cabbage
1   large carrot
Several chunks of green pepper
Optional: 1/2 tsp. poppy seeds

Steel Blade, Shredding Disk or Slicing Disk (either Medium or Fine Serrated), Plastic Knife

Use the steel blade and put the egg, lemon juice and seasonings in the bowl. Run the machine to beat. With the machine running add vinegar and honey through feeder tube. Then add the oil, slowly, in the same way . . . the dressing will thicken. Taste and adjust seasonings to your preference (additional salt, honey or vinegar). Remove about 1/3 cup and refrigerate.

Use either the shredding disk or the slicing disk for the cabbage:

Shredding Disk: (Makes fine textured coleslaw)

Load the feeder tube with cabbage in chunks, alternating with chunks of pepper and carrot (onion also if you wish to use). Push through with moderate firm pressure. Fill the feeder tube twice or until the bowl is about 3/4 full. Change to the plastic knife, twisting to fit into place, moving the food out of the way but being careful not to spill down the center. Process on/off several times to mix everything together.

Slicing Disk: (Makes longer, larger shreds)

Load the feeder tube with wedges of cabbage, the cut end down. (Load from the bottom . . . less messy than putting through the top and the opening is slightly larger.) Push through, loading the feeder tube several times. Change to the shredding disk to shred in the carrot and peppers and use the plastic knife in the same way to mix everything together.

Creative Options:

Shred in some onion (but use some lemon juice or lime juice to cut the bitterness). Slice in some grapes or apples.

BROWNIES

This is fun to demonstrate for the "instant chocolate" as well as the one-bowl method. Slicing in the nuts allows coarsely chopped nuts without dumping the contents of the bowl.

4	squares semi-sweet chocolate
1 1/2	cups sugar
3	eggs
1 1/2	sticks butter
1	cup flour (all purpose)
1	tsp. baking powder
1/4	tsp. salt
1 1/2	cups nuts (pecans or walnuts)

Steel Blade, Medium Serrated Slicing Disk, Plastic Knife

Use the steel blade to combine flour, 1/2 cup nuts, baking powder and salt. This sifts the flour and chops the nuts medium fine. Remove.

Melt the butter in a saucepan to a sizzle. Put the chocolate pieces in the processor bowl and process (steel blade) with on/off's to break up, then run the machine to grate very fine. With the machine running pour the butter through the feeder tube (instant chocolate sauce is the result).

Add eggs and sugar, processing by running the machine to mix in very well. Change to the slicing disk (remove the steel blade carefully . . . you should not be over the center stem so no liquid will spill down the center) and load the feeder tube with the nuts. Slice in using a "bounce" action with the pusher. Remove the slicing disk and insert the plastic knife. Add flour and process together with on/off's.

Butter a 9 inch square pan. Pour the batter in and bake at 350° 30-35 minutes. The top will be smooth and the inside chewy, rich with chocolate.

SKINNY GOURMET CREPES

Whole Wheat Crepes:

4	eggs
3/4	cup whole wheat flour
3/4	cup all purpose flour
3/4	cup milk
3/4	cup water
2	tsp. oil
1/2	tsp. salt
1/4	tsp. each chervil, cilantro

Skinny Cream:

1/2	cup buttermilk
1 1/2	cups Ricotta or cottage cheese
1	tsp. lemon juice

Filling:
Several sprigs fresh parsley

3-4	chicken breasts
2	squash
1/2	tsp. chili powder
1	T. lemon juice
2	T. chicken broth
1	T. skinny cream

Salt and pepper

Sauce:

1	lemon
6-8	tomatillos (or small green tomatoes)
3-4	tomatoes
1/2	green pepper
1	bunch green onions

Generous sprigs of fresh cilantro or parsley (1/2 tsp. dried)

1	cup chicken broth
8	ounces low-fat Mozzarella cheese

Steel Blade, Slicing Disk, Shredding Disk

To prepare crepes: Put the egg whites and a pinch of salt into the bowl with the steel blade. Run the machine 60-90 seconds until thick and stiff. Add the rest of the ingredients and process smooth. Let the batter rest 30-60 minutes and prepare crepes according to directions on page 25.

Process the Ricotta and lemon juice smooth adding buttermilk through the feeder tube. Remove.

Use the steel blade and mince parsley. Use the slicing disk, pack the chicken in the feeder tube and slice into the bowl. Use the plastic knife and add seasonings, juice, broth and skinny cream. Remove to another bowl.

Use the shredding disk, or the julienne blade, which shreds slightly finer and drier, and cut the squash into chunks to shred. Toss with the chicken.

Shred the cheese using slight pressure . . . remove.

Put the cilantro, onion (in pieces) and green pepper into the bowl with the steel blade and run the machine to mince. Change to the French fryer, push tomatoes (quartered) through the feeder tube. Add the lemon juice and transfer to a saucepan with the chicken broth. Salt and pepper to taste, adding hot piquant sauce if desired.

Fill crepes with chicken filling and roll up . . . place in a buttered dish. Pour sauce over them and top with a dollop of creme and shredded cheese. Bake at 350° 15 minutes.

Variation: If calories are not being counted, omit the skinny cream and stir 1 1/2 cups sour cream or white sauce into the sauce and serve with the crepes.

> *Too often the poet sees but the tears that live in an onion, but not the smiles.*
>
> Anonymous

x2 MEAT LOAF

The problem here is getting the vegetables the right texture without the meat becoming baby food. Both methods work very well with a minimum of changing bowls or washing in between. Substitute your own ingredients freely . . . the important thing here is the order and length of processing.

3/4-1	pound chuck, including fat
1	small squash
1/2	carrot and onion
1	large roll
1/3	of a green pepper
1	small piece celery
Sprig of parsley	
1	T. steak sauce
1/3	cup chili sauce
1	tsp. salt
1	egg

Quick Glaze and Sauce:

1/2	cup chili sauce
2	T. molasses
1/2	cooked carrot
1/2	cup beef broth

Steel Blade, Shredding Disk, Plastic Knife

Tear the bread into several pieces and place directly into the bowl using the steel blade. Process about 5 seconds, until broken up. Add celery, onion and green pepper (in chunks) plus parsley and dry seasonings. Process on/off once. Add meat, in chunks (gristle and sinew removed). Process on/off 3-4 times. Change to the shredding disk and push the carrot and squash through the feeder tube. Change to the plastic knife adding the egg, steak sauce and chili sauce (and any other wet ingredients). Process on/off 2 times . . . just to incorporate without getting the meat too fine. If it seems to need more liquid, add now, processing in the same way. If the celery and onion were processed too long you may have a little too much liquid . . . no problem, as it will leak out when it bakes and you can use it in the sauce.

Shape into a loaf or place in a medium size loaf pan and coat with about half of the chili sauce and molasses. Bake at 350° 35-40 minutes.

Sauce:
Cook the carrot until tender. Heat the beef broth along with any drippings from the loaf pan (remove the meat to a heated platter). Put the carrot, cut in chunks directly into the bowl and process with the steel blade to puree. Add the remaining chili sauce and molasses, process in, then heat with the drippings and broth.

Creative addition:
Process 3 ounces cream cheese and 3 ounces muenster cheese (cut in chunks) until smooth and combined. Put half the meatloaf in the pan, add the cheese mixture down the center, covering with the other half of the meat.

x2 SNAPPY CHEESE SNACKS

1	stick butter
6	ounces cheddar cheese
1	cup flour
1/4	tsp. cayenne pepper

Dash salt
3/4   cup walnuts or pecans
1/2 cup dates

Steel Blade, Shredding Disk

Place the butter, cut into chunks, directly into the bowl using the steel blade. Process 5-10 seconds until cheese and butter are a paste. Put flour and seasonings into the bowl. Process in with on/off's. Use shredding disk, load feeder tube with nuts, then dates. Push through . . . do not force . . . sometimes the machine argues a bit but most will go through . . . just toss the rest into the bowl. Remove shredding disk and fold in dates and nuts by hand while removing. Chill and slice or chill and roll out on a well floured board and cut into fancy shapes. Bake at 375° for 10-15 minutes.

dlc-7 When using the DLC-7, change to the plastic dough mixing blade after creaming cheese and butter.

BAKED OYSTERS WITH SAUSAGE

1	pound pork including fat	1/3	stick unsalted butter
Sausage seasonings (p. 68) plus		2	eggs
1	garlic clove	2	T. butter
4	sprigs fresh parsley	1	tsp. salt
Several celery tops		1/4	tsp. pepper
1	cup walnuts	2	dozen fresh oysters
2	pieces whole wheat bread	Juice of 1 lemon	
1/2	of an onion	1/4	tsp. tarragon and chervil
1	pound raw spinach	1-2	T. cognac
1/4	cup sour cream		

Steel Blade

Prepare the sausage by cutting the pork in chunks and processing with selected seasonings (p. 68, or 1/4 tsp. each nutmeg, chili powder, salt, pepper, allspice, coriander and 1 tsp. parsley and basil). Saute in a saucepan. Tear the bread into pieces and process to make crumbs. Add the parsley, celery tops and butter cut into pieces. Add the nuts last, processing to combine. Remove and toss with the cooled sausage. Using the steel blade, mince the onion and leave in the bowl. Use a little lemon juice as you do this.

Cook the spinach 2-3 minutes and drain. Put it in the processor bowl with sour cream, eggs, 2 T. butter, salt and pepper. Run the machine to puree. Assemble in a buttered dish: spinach, then whole oysters. Sprinkle with tarragon and chervil.

Squeeze the juice from the lemon over the top and then divide the sausage-bread crumb mixture over the top. Sprinkle with cognac.

Bake at 400° 15 minutes or until the top begins to brown.

SOUFFLED TOMATOES WITH HOLLANDAISE

1 Recipe Hollandaise Sauce (p.40)

6	large tomatoes
4	ounces Swiss or Gruyere cheese
4	pieces of bread, any kind

1/2   stick butter
Several sprigs fresh parsley
1/4   tsp. chervil
Salt and pepper
3   T. heavy cream
4   eggs (at room temperature)

Steel Blade, Shredding Disk

Using the shredding disk, push the cheese through the feeder tube. Scoop out the insides of the tomatoes and drain well.

Remove the cheese, and put the bread, torn into pieces, into the bowl with the steel blade. Add parsley and seasonings and process to grate ... run a few seconds, check, run again. Add the butter, in pieces, running the machine on/off to incorporate. Remove. Alternate crumbs and cheese in the tomato ending with the crumbs on top.

Put the eggs and cream into the bowl and process by running the machine until light and well mixed. Pour into the filled tomatoes and let them sit at room temperature about 30 minutes.

Bake in a pre-heated 425° oven, turning the heat down to 350° after 10 minutes. Bake an additional 15-20 minutes or until puffed and browned. Serve with Hollandaise.

CURRANT CALAS

1   cup of currants
1/2   cup Triple-Sec liqueur
1 1/2   cups cooked rice
3   eggs
1/2   cup sugar
1 2/3   cups flour (unbleached)
1/2   tsp. salt
1/2   tsp. nutmeg
1   package dry active yeast plus 1/2 cup warm water
1   cup sugar
1   T. cinnamon
Deep fat fryer and oil

Steel Blade

Soak the currants overnight or at least an hour. Drain. Combine the yeast with the warm water. Process the rice and sugar together with the on/off method (pulse twice) then add the yeast, process on/off once and set aside in a greased bowl, covered, to rise in a warm place. Or put in your refrigerator overnight after the first rising. Using the steel blade process the eggs, salt and spices (keep aside the cup of sugar and cinnamon for topping) to combine well . . . add the yeast-rice mixture and the flour all at once. Process 5 seconds or so then transfer to another bowl and stir in the currants. This will be a fairly loose batter. Let it sit out at room temperature about an hour. Heat the oil to 375°, stir down the batter and fry by generous spoonfuls until well browned on both sides. Drain on paper towels. Sprinkle with the cinnamon sugar which you have combined in the processor bowl using the steel blade, letting the machine run 50-60 seconds. Serve immediately.

x2   STEAK TARTAR

Try with Pain de Mie canapes with Duxelles and Pate. Fabulous.

1	pound lean round steak
1	tsp. capers
1	tsp. lemon juice
2	T. brandy
1	green onion
Several	sprigs fresh parsley
1	tsp. salt
1/4	tsp. pepper
Canapes	
Dijon type mustard	

Steel Blade

Trim the fat from the steak and cut into chunks. Place directly into the bowl with the dry ingredients and process with the on/off method 6-7 times. Add brandy and capers. Spread mustard on the canapes, then meat mixture.

x2   VEGETABLE DIP

1	8 ounce package cream cheese (in chunks)
1	cup sour cream
3	strips crisp bacon
1	clove garlic
Several	sprigs fresh parsley or cilantro
1/2	cup corn kernels
1	zucchini or winter squash

Steel Blade, Shredding Disk, Plastic Knife

Run machine (steel blade) and drop in garlic. Add cream cheese, process smooth. Add parsley, bacon, and corn, process in. Use shredding disk to shred in squash. Use plastic knife to combine with sour cream.

Cortez, the conquistador, offered the Spaniards a drink "xoxo-atl, made of cacao beans and vanilla.

CHOCOLATE-ORANGE MOUSSE

This is very light .

4	squares semi-sweet chocolate
1	T. orange juice concentrate
2	T. grand Marnier
1/4	cup sugar
1/3	cup water
1	cup heavy cream
3	egg whites
1/4	cup sugar
1/2	tsp. vanilla extract

Steel Blade

Bring the orange juice, water, sugar and liqueur to a boil and boil 2 minutes.

Pour cream in the bowl (machine running) and process until very thick . . . remove. Dry the bowl and put the chocolate pieces in. Process on/off to break up then run the machine to crush thoroughly. With the machine running add the hot liquid . . . process smooth (5-10 seconds). Add vanilla, cool slightly, fold into cream.

Whip the whites in a copper bowl until stiff . . . add sugar slowly. Fold in the cream-chocolate mixture and transfer to a melon mold. Freeze. Unmold when frozen (dip in hot water bath a second . . . unmold), and serve sprinkled with praline powder.

x2 CHEESE BALL

This illustrates the principle of working from firm foods to soft foods.

1 1/2   8 ounce package of cream cheese
1/2   bunch of green onions (in pieces)
A few drops of lemon juice
3   ounces Camembert cheese (or Swiss)
6   chunks of pineapple (fresh)
1   cup pecans

Steel Blade

Put the pecans in the bowl and process on/off a couple of times to chop coarsely. Remove. Add the cheeses (in chunks) and process to cream well. Add lemon juice and onions processing in. Add pineapple chunks last, processing just a couple of times to dice and combine. Remove, shape into a mound and cover with the chopped nuts. Chill until firm.

When pomegranates are in season (Christmas), decorate with the colorful red seeds in addition to the nuts.

x2   STUFFED MUSHROOMS

1   pound mushrooms (good size for stuffing)
2/3   stick butter
1/2   of an onion
1/2   cup pepperoni chunks
3   ounces Mozarella cheese (very cold)
1   piece bread
Several sprigs fresh parsley
1/4   tsp. salt

Steel Blade

Brush off the mushrooms and put the stems into the processor bowl. Put the caps in a generously buttered dish. Cut the onion in chunks and add to the bowl, processing on/off several times to mince. Remove and saute in sizzling butter. Put pepperoni and cheese chunks, salt, parsley and bread (in several pieces) directly into the bowl. Process on/off to dice and chop. Remove steel blade and put in plastic knife, twisting to fit down securely. Add mushroom and onion mixture, processing on/off a couple of times to combine. Stuff caps and bake at 350° for 15 minutes.

WHIPPING CREAM

2   cups heavy cream
2   T. powdered sugar
1   tsp. vanilla

Steel Blade

Run the machine and pour cream slowly through the feeder tube. By the time it's all poured in the cream is thick. Add powdered sugar and vanilla . . . process in. Avoid the ultra-pasteurized and you'll have lovely cream to pipe rosettes and fancy decorations.

CARROT CAKE

I find this so much fun to demonstrate both for the cake and the "carrot flowers" I make with the thin vegetable slicing blade. The recipe is very simple.

Pre-heat oven to 350°

1   cup white seedless raisins
1/2   cup heated Triple-Sec,
          orange liqueur or apple
          brandy
1   pound carrots
2   cups flour (all purpose)
1 3/4 cups sugar
2   tsp. baking powder
1   tsp. baking soda
1   small can crushed pineapple
          (including juice)
4   eggs
1   tsp. each salt, cinnamon,
          nutmeg
1 1/2 cups salad oil

Steel Blade

Combine flour, salt, baking powder, baking soda and seasonings with the steel blade and remove. (This sifts as well as combines the dry ingredients.) Heat the liqueur and soak the raisins at least half an hour. Peel carrots, cut into chunks, place directly in the bowl and run the machine to grate with the steel blade. Add drained raisins, and sugar running the machine. Add eggs, processing in to "beat", then add the oil slowly through the feeder tube (machine running).

Remove half this mixture to a large mixing bowl. Add pineapple, processing in, then the combined dry ingredients, processing with on-offs just enough to make the flour disappear. Stir into the rest of the mixture in the large mixing bowl. Bake in two cake pans or one large baking pan 35-40 minutes at 350°.

Icing and Decorations:

1/2	cup nuts
Several	large cooked carrots
1 1/2	8 ounce packages cream cheese
1	stick unsalted butter
2-3	cups confectioners sugar
1	tsp. vanilla
1	T. liqueur

Green food coloring

Cut the cream cheese into chunks and put in the processor bowl with the butter and process to "cream". Add the liquids and run the machine until it is well creamed. Add enough powdered sugar to make a stiff but spreadable frosting. Use all but about 1/2 cup to frost the cake. Add some green food coloring to the remaining frosting and place in a pastry bag with a plain tip. Clean the bowl.

With a vegetable peeler run a groove down the side of the cooked carrots all around. Stack firmly in the feeder tube and slice with the thin vegetable slicer. You'll have "flowers" . . . remove and rinse out the bowl. Use the steel blade and process the nuts to a powder. Now the fun.

First make some green stems and leaves using the pastry bag. Then place your flowers on the top of the cake and around the sides. (Let the artist in you come out.) Then sprinkle decoratively with the nuts and impress your family or guests with a real treat.

Note: Add 1/2 cup finely grated coconut to the batter (about 1/4 of a whole coconut) and bake in Pain de Mie pans. (See p. 22 for directions.)

TING A LING COFFEE CRUNCH CAKE

I have trouble walking through the Tastemaker section of Sakowitz without finding all sorts of things to crunch up in the machine. This was an "inspiration" during a class at Sakowitz. We had some diced dates to use up, some whipping cream and had just sampled the coffee ting a ling mints.

1	prepared angel food cake
8-10	ting a ling coffee mints or coffee candy or peppermint candy
1 1/2	cups whipping cream
5	dates (pitted)
3	T. granulated sugar
1/2	tsp. vanilla

Instant Chocolate Sauce (p. 108)

Steel Blade

Use a sharp serrated knife and divide the cake into 3 layers. Brush the crumbs off the top and sides of the cake.

Use the steel blade and put dates and 3 T. sugar in the bowl. Dice with on/off's. Remove. Put the candies in the bowl and dice with rapid on/off's, then run the machine to crush. Remove and wipe out the bowl.

With the machine running, pour the cream slowly through the feeder tube. When stiff, add candies and dates, combining with a quick on/off. Spread between cake layers.

Prepare the chocolate sauce using 2 T. Kahlua for some of the water. Cool slightly and pour over chilled cake.

PROCESSOR SALAD

1	head iceburg lettuce
1	small jicama, cucumber or 7 ounce can water chestnuts
1/2	pound mushrooms, without bruises
1	package frozen green peas
1	onion
1	lemon

4   ounces fresh Parmesan (in chunks)
1   cup mayonnaise
1   cup sour cream
Generous sprigs of fresh parsley
1   shallot

Cherry tomatoes for garnish

*Medium Serrated Slicing Disk, French Fryer, Steel Blade,
Thin Vegetable Slicing Disk*

Use the steel blade and run the machine to grate the Parmesan. Start with on/off's to break the cheese into smaller pieces, then process. Remove.

Remove core from the head of lettuce and cut in four wedges. Use the medium serrated slicing disk and slice all the lettuce into the processor bowl. Load from the bottom of the feeder tube to fit a large piece in and slice with firm pressure. Remove.

Use the thin vegetable slicing disk and slice all the mushrooms. Remove. Use the same disk for the onion, using a little lemon juice on the onion and the blade to help cut the odor.

Use the French fryer, loading the feeder tube with chunks of peeled, washed jicama or cucumber with seeds removed (not necessary to peel). Or, you may slice water chestnuts (medium serrated slicing disk).

Mince shallot . . . leave in the bottom of the bowl while preparing mayonnaise. Prepare the homemade mayonnaise (p. 39) and remove all but one cup. Add parsley and process to mince. Add sour cream and grated Parmesan, processing with on/off's (pulse) to combine.

Layer the salad alternating vegetables and lettuce, pouring the dressing over the top. May be prepared up to 24 hours ahead.

When melons are in season, I use them (French fryer). Or, zucchini (in place of jicama). When lettuce was $1.00 per head, I used cabbage, sliced with the thin serrated slicing disk.

x2 CHILI CON QUESCO QUICHE

Southwesterners can get the fresh poblano and jalapeno peppers for this piquant cheese and onion quiche, however the bottled peppers of any variety are a marvelous substitute. This is as good for a luncheon, light supper or brunch.

1   recipe Basic Pastry (p. 9) or:
        Cream Cheese Pastry (p. 10)
2   T. cornmeal

Roll out chilled, prepared pastry and line an 8 inch pie pan. Sprinkle with cornmeal, prick holes with a fork along the bottom and prebake 15 minutes at 375°.

8   ounces cheddar cheese
4   ounces Monterey Jack or another soft yellow cheese
6   ounces cream cheese or cottage cheese
4   eggs
1/2   tsp. salt
Coarse ground pepper
1/4   tsp. chili powder
Several sprigs fresh parsley
1   large or 2 small tomatoes
1/2   a large green pepper
1   small onion
1   poblano pepper or
        1 can small green chilies
1   small, mild banana pepper
1   small jalapeno pepper
1   small strip pimento

1/2   stick very cold unsalted butter

Steel Blade, Shredding Disk, French Fryer, Medium or Thin Slicing Disk

Use the shredding disk and shred the cheddar cheese with light pressure. Remove. Use the French fryer and load the tomato (in chunks) in the feeder tube. Process to dice. Remove.

Put the Monterey Jack cheese in the bowl (steel blade) and process to grate with on/off's ... it should be pasty in consistency. Add cream cheese (or cottage cheese) processing to combine. Add eggs, parsley, chunks of onion, all peppers and pimento. Process with a couple on/off's, then run the machine to combine well. (The peppers and onions will be coarsely chopped ... stop processing before they get too fine.) Add the rest of the seasonings.

Put half of the cheese in the pre-baked crust. Put diced tomato on top (if extremely juicy, drain off some of the juice) and cover with the rest of the cheese. Pour the mixture from the processor bowl over the top. Use the slicing disk to slice the butter thinly and dot all over the top.

Bake at 350° 35-45 minutes or until nicely browned and "set". Let the quiche cool slightly before serving. **Super** served with a little hot pepper jelly.

HAVARTI SHRIMP SOUFFLE

This may be served for brunch, lunch or a light supper. For a luncheon, try filling a zucchini or large tomato (removing the inside meat) and bake in the tomato.

Pre-heat oven to 375°

Use the stuffing for Stuffed Artichokes (p. 134) adding 4 ounces Havarti cheese or:

2	medium size French rolls
1	onion
1/2	of a green pepper
1 1/2	pounds cooked, cleaned shrimp
4	ounces fresh Parmesan or Romano cheese
1	stick butter

Several sprigs fresh basil or 1/2 tsp. dried
Generous sprigs of fresh parsley

1	clove garlic
1/2	tsp. chervil
1/2	tsp. salt
4	ounces Havarti cheese
4	eggs
2	cups milk or half and half

Steel Blade, Shredding Disk

Use the steel blade, put garlic and chunks of Parmesan in the bowl, processing first with on/off's to break up the cheese, then running the machine to grate to a powder. Remove.

Put chunks of the roll, pepper, onion, parsley and basil in the bowl and process with on/off's to prepare a coarse dressing. Add butter, in chunks, and process in with on/off's. Change to the medium serrated slicing disk, load the feeder tube with shrimp and "slice in". Insert the plastic mixing blade, twisting in place and process together with a couple on/off's. Mix with Parmesan in a separate bowl (or omit mixing with the plastic blade and just combine everything in a separate bowl). Butter a large gratin dish or souffle dish and spread with half this mixture.

Use the shredding disk, with light pressure and shred the cheese. Put on top of the crumb mixture, then add the rest of the shrimp mixture.

Use the steel blade to combine eggs and milk (or half and half) and pour over the entire dish. If you do not have enough liquid to completely soak the mixture, process an additional egg and 1/2 cup milk and add to it.

Let this rest in the refrigerator overnight or at room temperature at least an hour.

Bake at 375° 35-40 minutes, or until "set" and nicely browned. Serve with sliced tomatoes or a fruit salad.

The more absolute the rulers in the Renaissance and ancient times, the more elegant their tables.

UNIVERSAL PICANTE SAUCE

This is a piquant sauce of Southwest origin which adds zest to an egg dish (quiche, omelette, crepes), seafood cocktails, fish, corned beef hash, or a vegetable souffle. Use whenever a chili style or spicy tomato sauce is called for. In many places it is served fresh, with chips (as a dip). Try serving with whole wheat crackers or raw vegetables. Very fresh taste and a good way to process bits of parsley, celery, radishes, tomatoes or peppers leftover from demonstrations. You might even come up with a few original vegetable sauces of your own with your leftovers.

1-2	garlic cloves
1/2	bunch green onions
1/2	cup each fresh parsley and cilantro
2	stalks celery

Juice from a lemon

2	bell peppers (green or red)
6-8	radishes
4-6	tomatoes (in chunks)
2	hot peppers (serrano, jalapeno)
3-4	assorted fresh, mild peppers (poblano, Anaheim, banana) or: Additional bell peppers and canned green chilies or bottled peppers
6	ounces tomato paste
2	T. vinegar

Salt and pepper to taste

Steel Blade, Shredding Disk, French Fryer, Plastic Knife

Use the steel blade to mince the garlic, parsley, cilantro, green onions, hot peppers (canned green chilies) and celery. Add lemon juice to cut some of the odor.

Change to the shredding disk and load the feeder tube with chunks of radishes, fresh peppers and process through. Use the French fryer to dice in the tomatoes (for chunky texture). Insert the plastic knife last, twisting into place (it does not lock in), and add tomato paste, vinegar, salt and pepper. Process with on/off's to combine and adjust seasonings to taste.

Use fresh or simmer 20-30 minutes (or microwave on high 4-5 minutes, stirring several times).

Kitchen
Equipment

*. . . . .a good cook is more essential to the
community than a good poet.*

Boswell

and
Notes

A word about Kitchen Equipment . . .

If you can answer "yes" to half of the following questions then your kitchen should be the most cheerful, most efficient, best equipped, brightest room in the house. Not because you're a great cook, or have a birthday coming up . . . but because you prepare the "staff of life" and provide for the health and good nutrition of your family.

1. Do you spend more than two hours a day in the kitchen?
2. Do your children enter the kitchen during the first 5 minutes they come home from school?
3. Does your husband ever use the kitchen with you, or in a little gourmet project of his own?
4. Does anyone in your house ever ask you "what's to eat?"
5. Do you ever work "overtime" in your kitchen?
6. Do you prepare more than one meal a day?
7. Do your guests ever come into your kitchen?
8. Do you eat in your kitchen more than twice a week?
9. Do you ever utilize food to help celebrate special occasions?
10. Do you ever have to entertain unexpected guests. . . . .on short notice?
11. How about cub scouts, boy scouts or girl scouts or picnics?
12. Do you ever bake or prepare gifts for others in the kitchen?
13. Do you spend additional time at holidays preparing everyones favorite food?
14. Do you wash your clothes by hand or use a machine?
15. Do you use a dishwasher or wash dishes by hand?
16. Does your husband use a power lawn mower or grass clippers?
17. Do you ever reject preparing a certain dish or vegetable because it's too much trouble?

Following are some of the gadgets and equipment I've found helpful, time saving, and useful in creating that "final touch" that makes everything look so great. Also some food items you may find in your local stores, some grocery stores, or you can order them easily through one of the many catalogs you receive in the mail.

Cooking Equipment And Gadgets:

Food Processor
Copper bowl (for beating egg whites—no more cream of tartar)
Crepe pans in varying sizes
Fruit corers, (for pears, apples, pineapples)
Large meat forks to lift a roast or turkey
Beautiful, efficient pots and pans

Flambe Equipment (ask your husband to do this at your next dinner
    party and you'll have the equipment tomorrow)
Cannoli forms
Meat Ball maker
Cookie gun (what a great little time saver)
Spring form pan
Fluted edge quiche pans
Flan pans
Rosette iron
Fancy tart shell forms
Fat Separater (great gadget. . . don't know how I managed without
    one)
Candy molds (for Marzipan)

Food items to look for:

Birds Custard Powder. . . . .smooth—marvelous flavor.
Romanoff's or Knorr's bouillon powders (superior)
Vanilla beans
Currant and other jellies
Freeze dried shallots
Pate de foie gras
Candied violets (for your spectacular desserts)
Chalet Suzanne soups and sauces (fantastic soups and sauces—add
    a little fresh this or that)

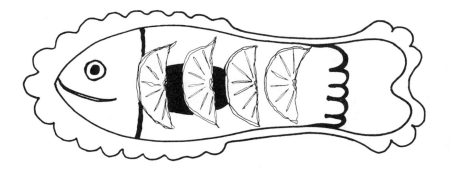

As the kitchen goes, so goes
the rest of the house

IDEAS — NOTES — RECIPES

from

Food Processor Demonstrations

---

x2

Peel 1 lemon and remove the seeds and membrane. Put it in the processor bowl with 1 1/2 sticks butter, 1/2 cup honey, 1/4 tsp. each cinnamon and nutmeg; process with the steel blade until smooth. Use on nut breads, rolls or French toast. Refreshing!

IDEAS — NOTES — RECIPES

from

Food Processor Demonstrations

_____

_____

_____

_____

_____

_____

_____

_____

_____

_____

_____

_____

x2

For BLUEBERRY MUFFINS a quick way, start with the mix putting the peelings from a lemon and 2 T. sugar in the bowl with the steel blade, processing to mince. Add 2 eggs, 3/4 cup buttermilk, 1/3 cup coconut, 2 tsp. lemon juice and 2 T. butter. Process 10 seconds to make very light. Add the dry ingredients from the mix plus 1/3 cup sifted all purpose flour and 1/2 tsp. baking powder. Process on/off once mixing in the blueberries (drained) gently by hand. Bake according to the package . . . sprinkle the tops with a little cinnamon sugar.

IDEAS — NOTES — RECIPES

from

Food Processor Demonstrations

_____

_____

_____

_____

_____

_____

_____

_____

_____

_____

_____

_____

FRIED MUSHROOMS . . . prepare a stale beer batter by processing (steel blade) 3 egg whites until very stiff. Add 2 egg yolks, 1/2 tsp. salt, 2 T. butter, 1 cup stale beer and 1 cup flour. Let the batter sit at room temperature about an hour. Coat mushrooms (or cauliflower, zucchini, broccoli flowers) and deep fat fry until golden. Try rolling in cornmeal after dipping in the batter for crunchier texture.

386

IDEAS — NOTES — RECIPES

from

Food Processor Demonstrations

---

x2

To make CHOCOLATE CHIP COOKIES try two methods: 1) Measure flour and baking soda and "cut in" nuts (steel blade) with the on-off method. Set aside. Cream butter and sugars with the steel blade, add egg and flavoring. Change to the plastic knife, add flour and nuts processing on-off several times to combine. Add chips, on-off several times . . . or stir in by hand. 2) Steel blade only . . . cream butter, sugar and vanilla. Add egg and process smooth. Add nuts, flour, baking soda (or oatmeal also) processing on-off about 3 times. Stir in chips by hand.

IDEAS — NOTES — RECIPES

from

Food Processor Demonstrations

For a quick OYSTER STEW drain the liquid from 1 dozen oysters and scald with 2 cups half and half and 1 cup cream. Using the steel blade process together several sprigs parsley, 1/2 tsp. chervil, 1/2 tsp. salt, 3 T. flour, 1/2 stick butter, and 6 oysters. Add 1 cup of the hot liquid through the feeder tube, process briefly, then return to the rest of the liquid in the saucepan, adding 6 oysters, 2 T. brandy, several drops of Tabasco, and heat 5 minutes.

IDEAS — NOTES — RECIPES

from

Food Processor Demonstrations

_____

_____

_____

_____

_____

_____

_____

_____

_____

_____

_____

_____

_____

_____

Slice leftover or stale bread thinly (chill first for easier slicing). Process (steel blade) 3 ounces blue cheese, 1 stick butter, 1 T. lemon juice, 1/4 tsp. salt, and several sprigs parsley. Spread on both sides of the bread and toast at 350° until browned. Serve with dips, soups or spreads.

IDEAS — NOTES — RECIPES

from

Food Processor Demonstrations

_____

_____

_____

_____

_____

_____

_____

_____

_____

_____

If you are fortunate enough to have the juicer for the Cuisinart try this combination: first tie a plastic bag over the ejecting spout . . . then juice 4 apples by cutting into pieces and pushing with the pusher. Change to the steel blade and add 3 egg yolks, 1 tsp. lemon juice, 1/2 cup sugar (or 1/3 cup honey) and process about 30 seconds. Add 1/2 cup heavy cream and process an additional 30 seconds . . . enjoy . . . there are not many recipes that call for much processing! In a separate bowl beat the whites very stiff and add to the bowl with 1 tsp. vanilla, a dash of nutmeg and 1 cup milk. (Omit lemon juice and add 1/2 cup Calvados brandy and 1/4 cup rum for a delightful "nog.")

A word in closing . . . .

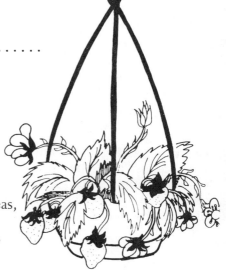

Plant some peas along your fence
and some carrots in the ground,
Put some parsley in your window
and some cabbage in a mound
Plant mint around your spigets
and tomatoes on your porch.

Then use the steel blade with the peas,
the shredding disk with cabbage,
use the French fry blade for onions,
the slicing disk for carrots -
Create a Soup, a Stew, a Salad!

A special word of gratitude . . . .

. . . to all the marvelously creative chefs and gourmets whose talents
are an inspiration to everyone preparing food and who helped return
the kitchen to its rightful place as the center of conviviality in the
home.

. . . to my family who have assumed most of my domestic duties over
the past few months, tolerated an enormous typewriter and a moun-
tain of papers on the kitchen table for months . . . and who have
consumed, with a smile, the failures as well as the successes.

. . . to my very special sons, Don and Will, who contributed original
recipe ideas, nutritious thoughts, adventuresome appetites and heap-
ing amounts of support.

Creative cooking and painting go hand in hand . . . first one studies the masters; then the media and the technical knowledge necessary to master the materials; then a generous input of your personal imagination . . . the preparation, presentation and sheer enjoyment of fresh, seasonal food is the perfect combination of form and function.

To achieve true creative brilliance, scientific, artistic or culinary, one must walk on the very edge of disaster.

INDEX

AAA Bread 322
ABC Coffee Cake 83
Adapting Recipes XI
Almonds, about 17
Almond Bread 299
Almond (Broccoli) Soup 116
Almond Cookie Dough 20
Almond French Toast 75
Almond Macaroons 18
Almond Paste 17
Almond Pastry 358
Almond Pastry Cream 20, 21
Almond, processing of 17
Almond Rolls, Tangy 315
Almond Tea Cakes 19
Amaretto Freeze 51
Appetizers 143-158
Apple-Almond Pie 282
Applejack Bundt Bake 284
Apple Nog 390
Apple Potato Bake 246
Artichoke Dip 310
Artichoke Puffs 157
Artichoke Soup 111
Artichoke, stuffed 134
Avocado, see also Guacamole
Avocado Cream Sauce 101
Avocado Soups
    Champagne 124
    Quick 118
Bagels 319
Baked Alaska 254
Baked Oysters with Sausage 368
Baklava 255
Banneton Luncheon Torte 135
Bars, see Cookies
Basic Bread 15-16, 294-296
Basic Bread Crumb Topping 7
Basic Custard 341
Basic Muffins 8
Basic Pasta 10
Basic Pastry 9
Basic Yeast Dough, see Basic Bread
Batters, crepe 25-30
Bearnaise Butter 67
Bearnaise Sauce 40
Beef Canapes 154
Beef and Pasta 182

Beef Wellington 200-201
Beverages
    Amaretto Freeze 51
    Chocolate-Banana Milkshake 51
    Fresh Apple Nog 390
    Frog Nogger 53
    Mint Chocolate Freeze 52
    Orange Julius 53
    Super Coconut Freeze 52
Biscuits, Old Fashioned 85
Black Forest Fruitcake 338
Beef, see Main Dish, Roasts
Beef Stock 63
Blades VII
Blueberry Muffins 95,385
Blue Cheese Butter 389
Breads
    AAA (Almond-Apricot) 322
    Almond 299
    Basic 15-16, 294-296
    Brioche 301
    Cranberry-Nut 335
    Date Nut Yeast (Whole Wheat) 298
    Granola Raisin 297
    Jalapeno Corn Bread 360
    Kugelhopf 303
    Lemon-Coconut 297
    Pain de Mie 305-306
    Pumpkin 324
    Rum Raisin 321
    Tips and Techniques 293-295
    Whole Wheat Cheese 300
Breakfast 69-92
Breakfast in a Glass 81
Breakfast Puffs 13
Breakfast Sausage 81
Breakfast Souffle 76
Brioche 301
Broccoli Soup Almondine 116
Broiled Streusel Topping 46
Brown Butter Sauce 41
Brownies 363
Bouillabaise 215
Bunuelos 28
Butters
    Almond (Paste) 17
    Bernaise 67
    Blue Cheese 389

INDEX

Butters (continued)
Brown Butter (Sauce) 41
Cheese 135
Clarified 2
Horseradish 67
Lemon-Honey 384
Mint 67
Olive 135, 154
Peanut 307
Strawberry 269
Butterhorns 313
Butterscotch Date Bars 290
Cakes, see also Coffee Cakes
Almond Tea 19
Applejack Bundt 284
Black Forest Fruitcake 338
Carrot 373
Cheesecake 356, 359
Chocolate Sundae Cake 265
Coconut 343
Darth Vadar (Chocolate) 289
Dutch Almond 90
Flaming Babas 345
Fresh Lemon Crunch 285
Fresh Orange 288
Frozen Amaretto 341
Orange Candy 286
Pineapple 340
Pumpkin (Bread) 324
Ting-a-Ling Coffee Crunch 375
Canadian Cheese Soup 128
Cannoli Batter 30
Cannoli Filling 104
Carrot Cake 373
Carrot Pie 279
Carrot Salad 165
Cedar Key Salad 168
Cereal, Natural (Granola) 3
Champagne Avocado Soup 124
Cheese Ball, (Cheddar) 146
Cheese Ball, (Pineapple) 309, 372
Cheesecake, no bake 356
Cheesecake 359
Cheese Sauce 37, 352
Cheese Pastry 148
Cheese Puffs 149
Cheese Puffs with Olive Butter 154

Cheesy Chicken Crunch 226
Chef's Salad 180
Cherry Orange Coffee Cake 71
Chewy Citrus Bars 291
Chicken, see Poultry
Chicken Breasts in Brandy 224
Chicken Chalupas 133
Chicken and Chilies 233
Chicken Chili Casserole 234
Chicken in Creole Sauce 226
Chicken-Endive Bake 229
Chicken in Pastry 230
Chicken Salad 33, 135
Chili Con Queso Quiche 377
Chilled Cauliflower and Beans 242
Chilled Melon Soup 123
Chilled October Soup 110
Chocolate Banana Milkshake 51
Chocolate Chicken 225
Chocolate Chip Cookies 387
Chocolate Coconut Flan 261
Chocolate Mandarin Crepes 260
Chocolate-Orange Mousse 371
Chocolate Sauce 108, 258, 292, 375
Chocolate Sundae Cake 265
Chorizo Sausage 184
Choux Pastry 12-13
Choux Pastry Crepes 13
Choux Pastry Popovers 13
Choux Pastry White Sauce 13
Christmas Cookies 333
Christmas Salad 347
Chunky Chicken Salad 33
Chunky Gazpacho 125
Chunky Guacamole 158
Clam and Chutney Cheese Round 147
Clarified Butter 2
Coconut, about 22
Coconut Cake 343
Coconut Cream Crepes 105
Coconut Crust 5
Coconut Custards 23
Coconut Filling 23
Coconut Freeze (Super) 52
Coconut Frosting 24
Coconut Macaroons 24
Coconut Milk 22

INDEX

Coconut, processing of 22
Coffee Cakes
  ABC 83
  Cherry-Orange 71
  Dutch Almond 90
  Fruits, Dates, Nuts 84
  Kugelhopf 303
  Sour Cream 91
Coffee Crunch Custard 267
Coleslaw 362
Continental Dessert 262
Cookies (and Bars)
  Almond 20
  Almond Macaroons 18
  Brownies 363
  Butterscotch Date Bars 290
  Chewy Citrus 291
  Chocolate Chip 387
  Christmas 333
  Granola Bars 4
  Nutrition 262
  Pumpkin 56
  Rum Balls 348
Cool and Creamy Mushrooms 240
Corned Beef Hash 70
Corned Beef Hash (Creative) 70
Crab Alaska 178
Crab Mold 150
Cranberry Nut Bread 335
Cream Crowdie 276
Cream Cheese Pastry 10, 136
Creamed Eggs 79
Creamy Calvados Filets 210
Cream Soup with Chives 123
Creamy Marinated Mushrooms 153
Creamy Vegetable Casserole 241
Creating Hash with Leftovers 71
Creole Quiche 136
Creole Sauce 38
Crepe Batters 25-30
Crepes, International
  (and Pancakes) 93-108
Crisp Vegetable Salad 173
Croissants 316
Croquembouche 336
Crumb Crusts 5-6
Crumb Toppings 7, 46
Crunchy Crust Cheesecake 356

Cucumber-Onion Salad 162
Currant Calas 369
Curry 232
Custard and Pastry Creams
  Basic 258, 271, 292, 341
  Coconut 23
  Coffee 267
  Pumpkin 328
Darth Vadar Chocolate Cake 289
Date Nut Yeast Bread 298
Date Rum Ice Cream Pie 278
Demi-Glace 63
Demonstrations 349
Demonstration Outlines 350-352
Demonstration Recipes 353-380
Desserts 253-292
DLC-7 IX
Don's Sandwich Spread 31
Doughnuts, Quick 89
Dressings, see Salad Dressings
Dutch Almond Cake 90
Duxelles 65
Egg Roll Batter 27
Egg Roll Fillings and Sauces 99-100
Egg Salad 32
Eggplant Creole 252
Endives with Ham 137
Family Fun 49-50
Fantastically Rich Chocolate Pie 280
Fettucine Squash 240
Fiesta Egg Scramble 77
Filet of Sole in Beer 216
Fish, see Seafood
Flaky Dinner Rolls 316
Flambeing, about 259
Flaming Mandarin Chocolate Crepes 260
Flaming Yule Logs 345
Flavorings 61
Flounder 217
Flour Tortilla 29
French Fried Pumpkin Rings 56
French Toast, Almond 75
French Toast Batter 27
French Toast with Fruit Soup Sauce 73
Fresh Fruit Trifle 270
Fresh Garden Salad 174
Fresh Leek Salad 167
Fresh Pear Salad 169

INDEX

Fresh Lemon-Coconut
  Crunch Cake 285
Fresh Orange Cake 288
Fresh Pineapple Breakfast Parfait 82
Fried Crepe Appetizers 98
Fried Mushrooms 386
Fried Pastry Appetizers 156
Fritter Batter 28
Frog Nogger 53
Frosting, see Icing
Frosting Grapes 59
Frosty Orange Crepes 108
Frozen Amaretto Fruitcake 341
Frozen Strawberry Jam 269
Fruits, Dates and Nuts Coffee Cake 84
Fruitcakes 338-341
Fruit Quiche 74
Fruit Pancakes 96
Fun Foot Long 312
Ginger-Spice Crust 6
Glaze, Topping 47
Glaze, see Icings
Glaze, meat 203, 206
Glazed Miniature Cream Puffs 263
Good Morning America Crepes 94
Grand Marnier Torte 257
Granola Bars 4
Granola Raisin Bread 297
Grapefruit Appetizer 166
Greek Style Cheese Pie 142
Green Beans with Blue Cheese 161
Green Rice 244
Guacamole (Chunky) 158
Halloween Fun 328
Ham 203, 228
Ham Asparagus Roll-ups 145
Happy Easter Breakfast 78
Harvest Quiche 238
Havarti Shrimp Souffle 378
Herbed Mayonnaise 39
Herbed Sesame Toasts 306
Holiday Specials 325-348
Horseradish Butter 67
Hot Cross Buns 329
Hot Hearty Low Calorie Soup 115
Hot Mustard Sauce 100
Icing
  Coconut 24, 286

Icing (continued)
  Glaze, plain powdered sugar 47
  Orange 107, 286, 346
International Crepes and Pancakes 93-108
Italian Creme Crepes 107
Jalapeno Corn Bread 360
Jambalaya Crepes 103
Jicama Salad 172
Jicama-Melon Salad 160
Julienne of Vegetable Garden
  Casserole 251
King's Cabbage 237
Kitchen Equipment 381
Kugelhopf 303
Lamb or Beef with Oyster Sauce 190
Lamb, stuffed 205
Late Summer Layered Salad 179
Layered Salad 171
Leftover Salad 353
Lemon-Coconut Bread 297
Lemon-Crunch Cake 285
Lemon-Honey Butter 384
Light Supper 131-142
Lobster and Scallops in
  Cream Sauce 219
Lorraine Soup 112
Low Calorie
  Crepes 26, 106
  Savory Sauces 42-46
  Sweet Sauces 46-48
Luncheon 131-142
Louisiana Remoulade 41
Macadamia Pineapple Fruitcake 340
Macaroon Crust 6, 280
Macaroon Pie 281
Main Dish 181-196
Marinade for Beef 63
Marinade Brown Sauce 64
Marzipan 18
Mayonnaise 39
Meat Extract (Flavoring) 64
Meat Loaf, 366
Mexican Corn Chowder 129
Mexican Pizza 188
Mint Butter 67
Mint-Chocolate Freeze 52
Mock Puff Pastry 11
Mother's Day Breakfast 331

INDEX

Muffins
  Basic 8
  Blueberry 95, 385
  Choux Pastry 13
  Mix 95
  Peanut Butter and Jelly 88
Muffin Mix (also Pancake) 95
Mushroom Tart 177
Mystery Mashed Potatoes 249
Nachos 332
Natural Cereal 3
Nut Butter Pain de Mie 307
Nutrition Cookies 262
Nutrition Crust 5
Old Fashioned Biscuits 85
Olive Butter 135, 154
One-Step Brownies 363
One-Step Coleslaw 362
Onion Soup 114
Orange Amaretto Re-freeze 361
Orange Cake 288
Orange Candy Cake 286
Orange Julius 53
Outlines for Demonstrations 349-352
Oysters, Baked in Sausage 368
Oyster Creation 176
Oysters Rockefeller 152
Oyster Stew 388
Pain de Mie
  About 305-306
  Artichoke 310
  Canapes 309-311
  Foot Long 312
  Herbed Sesame Toasts 306
  Nut Butter 307
  Quick Breads
    AAA 322
    Cranberry-Nut 335
    Orange Cake 288
    Pumpkin 324
    Rum Raisin 321
  Parmesan-Herb 307
  Pate-Duxelle 308
  Pineapple Cheese 309
  Sesame Toasts 306
Pancakes, Fruit 95, 96
Pancake Mix 95
Parker House Rolls 320

Parmesan-Herb Bread 307
Pasties 195
Patriotic Peanut Appetizer 148
Pastry
  Almond 9, 358
  Basic 9
  Choux 12-13
  Cream Cheese 10, 136
  Mock Puff 11
  Pointers 357-358
  Sour Cream 9
Pastry Cream
  Italian (Almond) 21
  Quick Almond 20
Pastry Pointers 357-358
Pate 65
Pate and Duxelle Pain de Mie 308
Peaches and Cream 277
Peanut Butter 307
Peanut Butter and Jelly Muffins 88
Peppers and Cheese
  (Appetizer Crepes) 98
Picante Sauce, Universal 380
Pies
  Apple-Almond 282
  Carrot 279
  Date Rum Ice Cream 278
  Fantastically Rich Chocolate 280
  Macaroon 281
  Shoo-Fly Pecan 283
  Strawberry Ice Cream Tortoni 273
  Very Berry Ice Cream 275
Pimento Cheese 158
Pimento Grilled Cheese 158
Pineapple Breakfast Parfait 82
Pineapple Cheese 309
Pineapple-Nut Salad 163
Piquant Sauce 151, 380
Pizza Dough 14
Pizza
  Ideas 355
  Italian 354
  Mexican 188
Play Clay 60
Ponnukokur 97
Popcorn Trees 59
Popovers 86
  Choux Pastry 13

INDEX

Pork Roast 206
Potato Plus Pancakes 250
Potato Puffs 243
Poultry 223-234
   see also Chicken, Turkey
Prime Rib, boned 204
Process and Bake 7
Processing of:
   Almond 17
   Coconut 22
   Pumpkin 54
Processing, Joy of 1-400
Processing Techniques XIII
Processor Beef Ranchero 196
Processor Salad 375-376
Processor Tuna Fish Casserole 191
Pumpkin, processing of 54
Pumpkin Bars 58
Pumpkin Bread 324
Pumpkin Cookies 56
Pumpkin Fun 57, 328
Pumpkin Ice Cream 55
Pumpkin Rings, French Fried 56
Pumpkin Seeds 55
Pumpkin Soup 56
Quiche
   Chili Con Queso 377
   Fruit 74
   Harvest 238
   Spinach and Blue Cheese 132
Quick Almond Pastry Cream 20
Quick Avocado Soup 118
Quick Breakfast Rolls 92
Quick Doughnuts 89
Quick Napoleons 292
Quick Vegetable 127
Renaissance Soup 121
Red Snapper in Brown Sauce 211
Red Snapper Soup 121
Roasts, about 197-198
Rocky Road Pumpkin Ice Cream 55
Rolls
   Bagels 319
   Butterhorns 313
   Croissants 316
   Flaky Dinner 316
   Hot Cross Buns 329
   Parker House 320

Rolls (continued)
   Tangy Almond 315
Round, Stuffed Eye 208
Romaine Soup 120
Rueben Fondue 192
Rump Roast 202
Rum Babas 345
Rum Balls 348
Rum Raisin Bread 321
Salads 159-180
Salad Dressings
   Beef Vinaigrette 175
   Blue Cheese 161
   Cheese 173
   Cheese-Parsley 173
   Cole Slaw 362
   Lemon-Parsley 167
   Low-Calorie 171
   Orange French 180
   Tomato 165
   Sour Cream 162
   Vinaigrette 174
Salmon Stuffed Avocados 138
Sandwich Spreads
   Cheese 135
   Chicken 33, 135
   Don's 31
   Egg 32
   (Ham) 353
   Leftover 353
   Olive 135, 154
   Pimento Cheese 158
   Shrimp 32
   Turkey 34
Sauces, savory
   Avocado Cream 101, 133
   Brown Butter 41
   Cheese 37
   Creole 38
   Eggplant-Tomato 103
   Hot Mustard 100
   Mayonnaise 38-39
   Orange 199
   Oyster 38
   Picante 380
   Red Sauce (Sugarless) 45
   Remoulade 41
   Sweet Sour 100

INDEX

Sauces, savory (continued)
  White (chicken) 36
  White (Choux Pastry) 13
  White (fish) 37
  White (mix) 35
  Vegetable 102
Sauces, sweet
  Chocolate 108, 258
  Ice Cream 265
  Mint 265
  Orange Brandy 107
  Pineapple 105
  Sherry 47
  Sweet Orange 75, 335
  Sweet-Sour 100
Saucy Shrimp Cocktail 144
Sausage
  Breakfast 80
  Chorizo 184
Sausage Popovers 86
Sausage Seasoning 68
Scallops in Cucumber Sauce 140
Sculpture Dough 60
Seafood Bisque 113
Seafood Crepes 102
Seasoning Salt 68
Seafood Wild Rice Casserole 221
Senegalese 126
Sesame Toast Rounds 145, 306
Sherry Sauce 47
Shoo Fly Pecan Pie 283
Shortcake 14
Shrimp Balls 151
Shrimp de Jonghe 170
Shrimp in Brown Butter Sauce 214
Shrimp Puffs 311
Shrimp Salad 32
Shrimp and Tomatoes in Cognac 213
Shredded Squash Salad 163
Skinny Bearnaise 44
Skinny Hollandaise 44
Skinny Lemon Sauce 45
Skinny Pancake Sauce 48
Skinny Sweet Sauce 48
Skinny White Sauce 43
Skinnier Crepe Batter 26
Skinnier Crepes 106
Snappy Cheese Snacks 367

Soups 109-130
Sour Cream Coffee Cake 91
Spinach and Blue Cheese Quiche 132
Steak Balmoral 327
Steak Butter 67
Steak and Kidney Pie 185
Steak Tartar 370
Stir-Fry Chicken with Nuts 227
Stocks 62-63
Stovies 190
Strawberry Butter 269
Strawberries and Cream 272
Strawberry Desserts 268-276
Strawberry Jam 269
Strawberry Ice Cream Tortoni Pie 273
Streusel Topping 46
  Broiled 47
Stuffed Artichokes 134
Stuffed Eye of Round 208
Stuffed Leg of Lamb 205
Stuffed Mushrooms 155, 372
Stuffed Onions 242
Stuffed Pears Alaska 266
Stuffed Tomatoes 247
Stuffed Turkey 326
Stuffed Veal 199
Sugarless Red Sauce 45
Summer Appetizer 147
Sunday Supper 187
Super Coconut Freeze 52
Supermarket Vegetable Soup 118
Supremes Veronique 139
Sweet Sherry Sauce 47
Sweet Sour Sauce 100
Tangy Almond Rolls 315
Three Cheese Soup 117
Ting-a-Ling Coffee Crunch Cake 375
Tips and Techniques XIII–XVI
Tomatoes with Hollandaise 87, 368
Tomato Salad Soup 175
Tomato Tom Gratin 245
Toppings, Savory 7
Toppings, Sweet 46-48
Trim Tomato Soup 128
Tuna Casserole 191
Turkey and Ham Bake 228
Turkey Salad 34
Turkey, stuffed 326

INDEX

Veal
  Roast 199
  with Seafood Sauce 186
Vegetable Garden Casserole 239
Very Berry Ice Cream Pie 275
Vegetables 235-252
Vegetable Dip 370, 380
Vegetable Shrimp Loaf 212
Waldorf Salad 162
White Sauce (Basic) 35-37
  Mix 35
  Cheese 37
  Chicken 36
  Choux Pastry 13
  Fish 37
Whipping Cream 373
Whole Fresh Ham 203
Whole Wheat Cheese Bread 300
Whole Wheat Crepes with
  Chicken and Salsa 365
Will's Superb Nachos 332
Yorkshire Pudding 26
Zesty Chicken Crepes 101